Neither Man nor Woman

The Wadsworth Modern Anthropology Library

Richard de Mille: The Don Juan Papers: Further Castaneda Controversies

Philip R. DeVita: The Humbled Anthropologist: Tales from the Pacific

Conrad Phillip Kottak: Prime-Time Society: An Anthropological Analysis of Television and Culture

Mac Marshall and Leslie B. Marshall: Silent Voices Speak: Women and Prohibition in Truk

R. Jon McGee: Life, Ritual, and Religion Among the Lacandon Maya

Serena Nanda: Neither Man nor Woman: The Hijras of India

Neither Man nor Woman
The Hijras of India

Serena Nanda
John Jay College of Criminal Justice
City University of New York

Wadsworth Publishing Company
Belmont, California
A Division of Wadsworth, Inc.

Anthropology Editor: *Peggy Adams*
Editorial Assistant: *Karen Moore*
Production Editor: *Jerilyn Emori*
Designer: *Donna Davis*
Print Buyer: *Randy Hurst*
Copy Editor: *Margaret Moore*
Cover: *Donna Davis*

Printed in the United States of America

3 4 5 6 7 8 9 10—94 93   49

Library of Congress Cataloging-in-Publication Data

Nanda, Serena.
    Neither man nor woman : the Hijras of India / Serena Nanda.
        p.   cm. — (Wadsworth modern anthropology library)
    Includes bibliographical references.
    ISBN 0-534-12204-3
    1. Eunuchs—India.   I. Title.   II. Series.
HQ449.N36   1989   89-36901
305.3—dc20   CIP

For Ruth
in whose classes it all began

If we want to discover what man amounts to, we can only find it in what men are—and what men are, above all other things, is various. It is in understanding that variousness . . . that we shall come to construct a concept of human nature that, more than a statistical shadow and less than a primitivist dream, has both substance and truth.

Becoming human is becoming individual, and we become individual under the guidance of cultural patterns . . . which give form, order, point, and direction to our lives. . . . [But] we must . . . descend into detail, past the misleading tags, past the metaphysical types, past the empty similarities to grasp firmly the essential character of not only the various cultures but the various sorts of individuals within each culture, if we wish to encounter humanity face to face.

Clifford Geertz
The Interpretation of Culture

# Contents

❦ Foreword to the Series

Modern cultural anthropology encompasses the full diversity of all humankind with a mix of methods, styles, ideas, and approaches. No longer is the subject matter of this field confined to exotic cultures, the "primitive," or small rural folk communities. Today, students are as likely to find an anthropologist at work in an urban school setting or a corporate boardroom as among a band of African hunters and gatherers. To a large degree, the currents in modern anthropology reflect changes in the world over the past century. Today there are no isolated archaic societies available for study. All the world's peoples have become enveloped in widespread regional social, political, and economic systems. The daughters and sons of yesterday's yam gardeners and reindeer hunters are operating computers, organizing marketing cooperatives, serving as delegates to parliaments, and watching television news. The lesson of cultural anthropology, and this series, is that such peoples, when transformed, are no less interesting and no less culturally different because of such dramatic changes.

Cultural anthropology's scope has grown to encompass more than simply the changes in the primitive or peasant world, its original subject matter. The methods and ideas developed for the study of small-scale societies are now creatively applied to the most complex of social and cultural systems, giving us a new and stronger understanding of the full diversity of human living. Increasingly, cultural anthropologists also work toward solving practical problems of the cultures they study, in addition to pursuing more traditional basic research endeavors.

Yet cultural anthropology's enlarged agenda has not meant abandonment of its own heritage. The ethnographic case study remains the bedrock of the cultural anthropologist's methods for gathering knowledge of the peoples of the world, although today's case study may focus on a British urban neighborhood or a new American cult as often as on efforts of a formerly isolated Pacific island people to cope with bureaucracy. Similarly, systematic comparison of the experiences and adaptations of different societies is an old approach that is increasingly applied to new issues.

The books in the Wadsworth Modern Anthropology Library reflect cultural anthropology's greater breadth of interests. They include introductory texts and supporting anthologies of readings, as well as advanced texts dealing with more specialized fields and methods of cultural anthropology.

However, the hub of the series consists of topical studies that concentrate on either a single community or a number of communities. Each of these topical studies is strongly issue-focused. As anthropology has always done, these topical studies raise far-reaching questions about the problems people confront and the variety of human experience. They do so through close face-to-face study of people in many places and settings. In these studies, the core idiom of cultural anthropology lies exposed. Cultural anthropologists still, as always, go forth among the cultures of the world and return to inform. Only where they go and what they report has changed.

James A. Clifton
Series Editor

❧ Foreword to the Book

Search the unabridged first edition of the Oxford English Dictionary for the term *hijra,* and you will not find it there. It is not one of those words that the British in India added to their own vocabulary, even though they had no exact equivalent for a correct translation. Consequently, through errors of translation, the definition of the term *hijra* has itself been defective. This book remedies that defect.

In early records, it was impossible for a writer to refer to hijras as homosexuals, for the terms *homosexual* and *heterosexual* were not coined until 1869 (Herzer, 1985). They were not adopted into general usage until after the original publication by K. M. Kertbeny was republished in 1905 by the Berlin sexologist Magnus Hirschfeld, in Vol. 7 of the *Yearbook for Sexual Intermediacy* (see review by Money, 1989).

In the 19th century and earlier, the most commonly used terminological predecessor of homosexuality was sodomy. Sodomy, however, referred to a range of "vile and unnatural vices." Sexual practices other than copulation exclusively for procreation, and in the male-superior position, were regarded as immoral or criminal. A hijra might have been said to commit sodomy, but hijra and sodomite could not be equated.

One of the two early mistranslations of hijra was hermaphrodite. In classical Greek and Roman art, Hermaphroditos was portrayed as a youth with penis and breasts. In 16th century legal and medical usage, a hermaphrodite was a person of indeterminate sex, with genitalia that were congenitally deformed. In fetal life they had differentiated as neither completely male nor completely female. In the late 19th century, hermaphroditism was subclassified on the basis of the gonads as true hermaphroditism, if both ovarian and testicular tissue were present; and as male or female pseudohermaphroditism if only testicular or ovarian tissue, respectively, was present. All three forms of hermaphroditism are genuine. They are also sufficiently rare in occurrence that it would be impossible for all the hijras of India to be genuine hermaphrodites.

The early misconception of the hijra as hermaphrodite has persisted. It is no doubt reinforced by the hijra claim, "I was born this way," which is prevalent not only among hijras but among their counterparts in other regions and cultures. Dr. Nanda does not fall into the error of equating hijra with hermaphrodite. That pitfall was avoided when, in 1983, Dr. Patrick Suraci, her colleague in psychology at John Jay College, put her in touch with me, in view of my expertise on hermaphroditism and gender identity (Money, 1986; Money & Ehrhardt, 1972).

The second early mistranslation of hijra was eunuch. It is correct, of course, that the hijra legacy includes the surgical art of castration, as performed on conquered slaves since time immemorial, by removal of penis, testicles, and scrotum. The surgical creation of a eunuch does not itself entail living as a woman, however. Thus, a hijra may be a eunuch, but the two terms are not synonymous.

Serena Nanda, in this book, has surmounted the problem of mistranslation by adopting the Indian term *hijra* into English and naming hijras by the same name with which they name themselves. That is a very wise thing to have done. It allows the author to present an accurate descriptive and phenomenological record of the ways of hijra society and of the biographies of individual hijras. All good science begins with good recording of data. It proceeds next to good classification, which is contingent on having a good defining criterion of classification, and categories of classification that are complete in their coverage but not overlapping.

The defining criterion that applies to hijras must apply to corresponding groups of people in other places and times. Dr. Nanda mentions in particular the xanith of Oman; the mahu of Tahiti; the French-named berdache among native North American Indians (superbly well updated in prize-winning research by Walter Williams, 1986); and the hormonally and surgically sex-reassigned transsexuals of occidental culture. Ethnically and culturally, there are many other similar groups in different regions of the world.

It is feasible to compare all of these groups with one another insofar as they all share one defining characteristic. That characteristic is that, whereas they are not born as females and declared to be girls, they grow up so that, at some stage of life and to some degree, they act like women. That is to say, they manifest themselves as women-mimetics (Money & Lamacz, 1984). The Greek-derived term for woman-miming is gynemimesis (*gyne,* woman + *mimos,* mime).

Gynemimesis is the characteristic that different gynemimetic communities have in common. There are other characteristics that are not shared, chief of which is that each group has a different cultural heritage. For example, the cultural heritage of India's hijras differs from that of occidental transsexuals. In the Indian heritage, gynemimetics have a long history of being defined and more or less tolerated in society as partly a religious sect and partly a caste, and a long history of genital surgery, which only recently has begun to be legally defined as criminal mutilation and, when performed on those not yet 21, as sexual assault and child abuse (*India Today,* September 15, 1982, p. 84). By contrast, gynemimetics in the occident have a long history of intolerant persecution as social and criminal deviants and a brief history of genital sex-reassignment surgery, which is still in the process of being defined as legal. On the criterion of surgery, hijras and transsexuals may gradually have more in common if ever the hijra communities incorporate modern plastic surgery for vaginoplasty as well as castration into their customs, and at the same time add feminization of the body by hormones to the demasculinization effects of castration.

Despite the differences, there is a remarkable similarity between Indian hijras and occidental transsexuals, even though their two traditions have developed independently without influencing one another. Moreover, what they share appears also in other gynemimetic traditions around the world. This worldwide similarity points to the conclusion that gyne-mimesis is of similar origin, no matter where it appears, and that the differences in its outcome are a secondary overlay, shaped by local traditions.

The search for origins will be doomed to failure if secondary determinants are misidentified as primary ones. That would be putting the cart before the horse—like saying that the sex difference in the division of labor is the cause of the sex difference in procreation.

The final answer as to what are the primary determinants of gyne-mimesis is not yet in. It is unlikely that gynemimesis develops under the direct control of DNA and the genome. Whereas it is certainly pro-grammed in the brain, the details of how it gets in there, and what fixes it there, are only beginning to be deciphered (reviewed in Money, 1988, 1989). Neurochemically, the steroidal sex hormones have an organizing influence on the male/female dimorphism of the brain in prenatal life. At puberty, their influence is activational only. Loci of male/female dimor-phism have been discovered in the preoptic area of the brain's hypothala-mus (Allen et al., 1989; Swaab & Hofman, 1988) but not yet in the cerebral cortex, which is where gynemimesis will definitely be eventually found to have some neurosexological representation. Presumably, this representa-tion will be shown to be programmed into the cortex postnatally, chiefly by means of social learning and assimilation, the port of entry being the five senses. There is some evidence to suggest that malprogramming is related to neglect, abuse, and wrong timing of sexual learning and the sexual rehearsal play of early childhood.

New discoveries concerning the origins of gynemimesis will not qualify as authentic unless they prove to be substantiated cross culturally. In sexological science, it is of utmost importance to have information such as Dr. Nanda provides in this book on the hijras, and of equal importance to maintain an open channel of continued updating and advancement of information.

Dr. Nanda raises the question of whether, in India, there are three genders: male, female, and hijra. The question is a rhetorical one, for its answer is dependent on the definition of gender. In American social science, it is still extremely popular to split biology from social science and to assign sex to biology ("sex is what you're born with") and gender to social science ("gender is your identity and social role"). This is another version of the nature/nurture dichotomy, and it doesn't hold water. What you are born with includes the precursors of your identity and role, no matter whether it be male, female, or hijra; and what you become under the influence of social learning and remembering becomes part of the biology of your brain.

The concept of a third gender has a history that dates back to Karl Ulrichs (Kennedy, 1988), who in an 1864 sexual-reform tract entitled *Inclusa* (Ulrichs, 1864) promulgated the maxim, *anima muliebris corpore virili inclusa* (the mind of a woman entrapped in the body of a man). This maxim, eventually adopted by transsexuals as their own, earlier led to the idea of an intermediate sex. After gender entered the sexological literature (Money, 1955; 1986, Ch. 19), it led also to the idea of a third gender. In feminist and gay literature, the concept of a third gender had the appeal of apparently breaking down the rigidity of the stereotypes of the masculine and the feminine roles in society. The appeal was cosmetic only, for the degree of tolerance or intolerance of the so-called third gender in a society bears no preordained relationship to male/female stereotyping. Thus, whereas there is a high tolerance of the blurring of occupational male and female roles in American society, there is low tolerance of the gynemimetic who has or has not undergone formal sex-reassignment. By contrast, in India, whereas there is tolerance of the role of hijra, tolerance of role overlap between men and women, husbands and wives, is low, even among the highly educated.

The long and short of all the foregoing is that Serena Nanda has written a conceptually challenging book. It provides ready access to an important body of knowledge and to data, hitherto unavailable, on the hijras of India. As a harbinger of the newly evolving specialty of ethnographic sexology, it is an excellent piece of work.

John Money
Johns Hopkins University and Hospital

 Preface

This ethnography is about a unique and extraordinarily interesting group, the hijras (HIJ-ras) of India. The hijras are a religious community of men who dress and act like women and whose culture centers on the worship of Bahuchara Mata, one of the many versions of the Mother Goddess worshiped throughout India. In connection with the worship of this goddess, the hijras undergo an operation in which their genitals are removed. The hijra emasculation operation consists of a combined penectomy and orchiectomy (surgical removal of the penis and testicles) but no construction of a vagina. This operation defines them as hijras— eunuchs—neither men nor women. It is through their identification with the Mother Goddess, and the female creative power that she embodies, that the hijras are given a special place in Indian culture and society. Hijras, as neither men nor women, function as an institutionalized third gender role: Their ambiguous sexual nature accounts for their traditional occupation, that of performing after the birth of a child, at weddings, and at temple festivals. As an institutionalized third gender role, the hijras are of interest not only in themselves, but also for their significance to the study of gender categories and human sexual variation.

I have long had an interest in the relation between gender roles and culture, particularly in the relation of both to sexual variation. Within the last 20 years there has been an increase in social science literature on these issues. This has led to the reexamination of anthropological data from new perspectives and the accumulation of new data from a great variety of cultures. I hope that this ethnography, on one of the few functioning third gender roles in a contemporary society, will make its contribution to this field.

I begin, in Chapter 1, by describing the hijras as culturally significant ritual performers, because that is where hijras begin in legitimating themselves to themselves and to the larger society. In this chapter I also introduce the hijras in their other important social role, that of homosexual prostitutes. In Chapter 2, I explore the role of the hijras as an alternative gender category and examine what it means to be neither men nor women in the context of Indian culture—a culture in which third gender roles and gender transformations are important mythological themes and real-life possibilities.

In Chapter 3 I continue to explore the theme of the ritual significance of the hijra role in India in relation to the major ritual of hijra culture, the emasculation operation. In this chapter I also focus on two kinds of identifications that give religious meaning to the hijra role: their identification with Shiva, a major Hindu deity, and their identification with the Mother Goddess. Here I also explore some possible links between hijra emasculation in the service of the Mother Goddess and some aspects of Indian family life that may increase the tendency of some men to adopt certain kinds of feminine identifications.

Chapter 4 shifts focus from the cultural meanings of the hijra role to the way in which their community is organized. I describe the social structure and economic organization of the hijras and indicate how these are both reflective of and adapted to the social and economic organization of Indian society as a whole. Thus, whereas Chapter 3, which considers hijras as a religious cult, emphasizes a symbolic and psychoanalytic interpretation, Chapter 4 uses a more materialistic perspective, showing how hijra self-definition, rituals, and social organization help them adapt economically in society.

Beginning with Chapter 5, I introduce the personal narratives of four hijras. Each chapter highlights the various roles available to hijras and the similarities and differences among hijras in gender identity, life experiences, and pathways to and through their "deviant" careers. I make no claims that these four informants represent any random or statistically valid sample. From my substantial knowledge of more than 20 hijras and informal, open-ended interviews and observations of scores of hijras from many parts of India, I feel assured that these four informants are in no particular way unrepresentative in their behavior, motivations, or life experiences, except where I have specifically noted this.

Kamladevi, who speaks to us in Chapter 5, is a prostitute, a role which, although stigmatized, nevertheless is an important source of income for many hijras. Chapter 6 is the personal narrative of Meera, who is both a hijra leader and a wife. Her narrative particularly illustrates the opportunities for social mobility within the hijra community and gives some indication of how complex the social interaction of a hijra may be. In Chapter 7 we meet Sushila, a former prostitute who has become a wife, mother, mother-in-law, and grandmother, thus fulfilling the goals of nearly all women in India. Last, in Chapter 8, I introduce Salima, a "real" hijra, born intersexed, who joined the hijras as a child but was cast out of the community 7 years earlier for breaking some important community rules. Salima is a performer and also a wife, and her narrative gives a different perspective on these roles.

These personal narrative chapters not only give individual hijras a voice of their own, but also illustrate a larger point. They show how individuals, each in a slightly different way, draw together threads from the larger culture to create a viable subculture which, while stigmatized, nevertheless provides their lives with significant meaning. Through these personal narratives we see how different individuals gradually commit themselves to a transformed identity, creatively fashioning their lives from a variety of cultural and individual resources. Here we also see more clearly a point emphasized in Chapter 2: the ability of the hijra role to serve as a magnet for individuals with different needs and gender identities.

As is the case of marginal and oppressed peoples in many cultures, very little of what has been written on the hijras gives them a voice of their own at any length or on a wide range of topics. This both distorts data and, more importantly, dehumanizes the subjects. It is for these two reasons that I have included such extended personal narrative chapters and leave my interpretations for Chapter 9, where I provide some contexts for interpreting the narrative material. For the reader who prefers to have a framework for reading and interpreting the narrative material beyond that which is given in Chapters 1 through 4, Chapter 9 may be read before the personal narrative chapters.

Finally, in Chapter 10, I expand the context in which to view the hijras by looking at alternative gender roles cross culturally. The anthropological significance of the hijra role is that it is one of the very few alternative gender roles currently functioning in any society. Many of the institutionalized cross-gender and third gender roles in non-Western societies have fallen into disuse with the cultural imperialism associated with colonialism, modernization, and Westernization. Thus, the hijra role is not only of great interest in and of itself, but also for the light it sheds on broader issues related to gender.

The hijra role in India and some cross-cultural parallels provoke reflection on our Western belief that there are only two sexes and two genders, each naturally and permanently biologically determined, and each exclusive of the meanings and characteristics of the other. The data in this chapter testify to the possibilities of alternative genders, demonstrating the culturally constructed nature of both gender categories and gender identities. These data reinforce the need to understand gender systems in relation to their cultural and social contexts. A cross-cultural perspective raises questions about our own gender system and the logic that underlies its construction. In concluding in this manner, I follow the traditional path of anthropology, which in beginning with the examination of the "other," leads us back to an examination of ourselves.

NOTE ON SPELLING, PRONUNCIATION, USE OF GENDER PRONOUNS, AND TRANSLATION OF FOREIGN WORDS

Indian words in this book have been anglicized for easier reading. Where a spelling variation of an unfamiliar word more accurately conveys its pronunciation, I have included that spelling in parentheses next to the word. I have pluralized Indian words by adding "s." There are many different spellings of the word *hijra* used in English language publications. None of them exactly captures the middle consonant sound of Hindi. The spelling *hidjra* would come closest, but I have decided to use *hijra* because it is the form most commonly used in English language publications both in India and abroad. Where I am quoting verbatim, I have retained the author's spelling.

All foreign words are italicized and given a brief translation when they are first used. Most italicized words, both foreign and English, are found in the glossary.

Indian languages have three kinds of gender pronouns: masculine, feminine, and a formal, gender-neutral form. Hijras, in their conversations, use these forms randomly and indiscriminately to refer to individual hijras. They insist, however, that people outside their community refer to hijras in the feminine gender. When I am quoting a hijra verbatim, I use the gender pronoun used by that speaker if it is masculine or feminine. If it is the gender-neutral pronoun, I have translated it as a feminine gender pronoun. When I am referring to a hijra, I use the feminine gender pronoun to conform to hijra norms, unless I am referring to the hijra in the past, when he considered himself a male.

ACKNOWLEDGMENTS

My own work in India on the hijras, begun in 1981 and extending through 1986, has substantially benefited from the work of others, as I have been fortunate in being able to draw on the data and insights of scholars from many disciplines. It gives me great pleasure to acknowledge the many people—colleagues and friends—who have encouraged me in this project and who have in so many ways helped bring it to realization. First, I want to express my deep gratitude to John Money, of the Johns Hopkins School of Medicine. His encouragement of my work, his correspondence with me while I was in India, his generosity in taking the time to read and comment on my work, and the importance of his insights as a pioneer in the field of sex, gender, and gender transpositions have all been invaluable.

Numerous other colleagues have encouraged me, discussed this research project with me, reviewed parts of the manuscript, and made many valuable suggestions. I have tried to take into account the many insights offered me, but am, of course, entirely responsible for all of the conclusions drawn here. Among the colleagues to whom I would like to express my gratitude are: Barbara Aziz, David Brandt, Charles Brooks, Joseph Carrier, S. M. Channabasavanna, William Coleman, Douglas Feldman, Abraham Fenster, (the late) J. Scott Francher, Ruth Freed, Eva Friedlander, Marty Fromm, Gillian Gillison, Nathan Gould, David Greenberg, Judith Hanna, Gilbert Herdt, Miriam Lee Kaprow, Billie Kotlowitz, William Lewis, Mark Lubovsky, Charles Lindholm, Owen Lynch, Jill Norgren, Veena Oldenburg, S. N. Ranade, Alan Roland, G. R. Salunkhe, Tobias

Schneebaum, A. M. Shah, Satish K. Sharma, H. S. Subrahmanyan, Pat Suraci, Anita Volland, Indu Vyas, Tina Wheeler, and Unni Wikan. I particularly want to acknowledge the encouragement and help of my sister and very dear friend, Joan Young Gregg, and of my husband, Ravinder Nanda.

Over the course of the several years I have been engaged in this research, I have had the opportunity to participate in a number of seminars and symposia on the relation between the individual and culture and the presentation of this relationship in the form of personal narratives. In this connection, I would like to thank the participants in the faculty seminar at John Jay College and its director, Robert J. Lifton; the Columbia University seminar on the Indian self, coordinated by Leonard Gordon and Alan Roland; the workshop on personal narrative and life history, at the May, 1988, first annual meeting of the Society for Cultural Anthropology; the symposia on anthropology and deviance, at the American Anthropological Association meetings, chaired by Morris Freilich; and the Mellon Foundation Community Colleges Project on "Inner and Outer Voyages: Language, Autobiography, and Personal History," directed by Vincent Crapanzano. This research was supported in part by a grant from The City University of New York PSC-CUNY Research Award Program, to which I am very grateful.

The staff of various departments at John Jay College were critical to the timely completion of this book: My many thanks to Marvelous Brooks and Antony Simpson of the library, Richard Duprey for his assistance in library research, Alice Gentile and Dorothy Manning of technical services, and to Mary Koonmen and her staff—Jaime Aguilar, Esther Preiser, Michael Yip, and Peter Olsen of the microcomputer labs. I most particularly want to thank Linda John, of the department of anthropology, whose enthusiastic willingness to go the extra mile contributed in so many different ways to this project. I am grateful to President Gerald Lynch and Provost Jay Sexter at John Jay College for providing me the opportunity for a sabbatical fellowship to work on the manuscript in its final stages.

In addition, I would like to express my appreciation for the encouragement and assistance of Leo Wiegman, formerly of Dorsey Press; James Clifton, advisory editor of this series; and Jerilyn Emori and Peggy Adams of Wadsworth. I am very appreciative of the helpful comments made by the reviewers: Charles Brooks, Memorial Sloan–Kettering Cancer Center; Ellen Gruenbaum, California State University, San Bernardino; and Shirley Lindenbaum, City University of New York.

I am indebted to my many friends in India who contributed to this research in countless ways: Shiv Ram Apte, Rajni Chopra, Raksha Chopra, Toral Dalal, Kalyani Gandhi, Bharati Gowda, Arundhati (Kaura) Kapoor, Malveka Kaura, Happy Kaushal, Purnima Kishandas, Prema Sarathy, Amar Singh, Mayura Sreenath, Divyang Trivedi, and Hemang Trivedi. I particularly want to thank Bhanu Vasudevan, my research assistant in Bastipore.

My deepest gratitude goes to my friends among the hijras, without whom this work would not be possible. I have used pseudonyms for all of the individuals mentioned in the book, as well as for all place names, with the exception of the major cities in India. I have also rearranged details of description of both people and places so that the anonymity of all of the individuals in the book may be preserved. I wish I could thank my hijra friends more publicly and hope that their trust and confidence in me will be partly repaid by their view that I have represented their lives and their culture faithfully. The hijras I met were eager to tell their stories to the public so that "people everywhere will know we are full human beings." I hope that in some measure this book serves to help the public, both in India and abroad, to experience the deep human connections between themselves and the other people like the hijras, who live on the margins of society but who are in every sense part of the human community.

❦ Introduction

My first encounter with the hijras was in 1971, in Bombay. While walking down a main street with an Indian friend one day, we were confronted by two persons in female clothing, who stood before us, blocking our passage. They clapped their hands in a peculiar manner and then put out their upturned palms in the traditional Indian gesture of a request for alms. My friend hurriedly dropped a few pennies into the outstretched palms in front of us, and only as she pulled me along at a quick pace did I realize that these persons were not females at all, but men, dressed in women's clothing. When I asked my friend who these people were and why she had reacted so strongly to their presence, she just shook her head without answering and changed the subject. Sensing her discomfort, I let the subject go but raised it again with other friends at a later time. In this way I found out a little about the hijras, whose lives appeared shrouded in great secrecy and around whom there appeared to be a conspiracy of silence.

For the next 10 years my professional interests centered on gender roles, and during this time I did research on homosexual couples in the United States. As part of my interest in sexual variation I sought to read the little that was published on the hijras and also asked my Indian friends and relations about them. None of these sources of information was very helpful; with few exceptions, writing on the hijras is contradictory, superficial, and sensationalist. This is partly due to hijras' reluctance to talk about themselves to outsiders.

Most of the people I knew through my previous visits to India were middle class and only acquainted with the hijras through their most public function—that of performing on auspicious occasions such as births and marriages. Some male acquaintances told me that hijras serve as male prostitutes, and this had been briefly reported in the literature, but beyond this suggestion, all doors on the subject seemed closed. Hijras were referred to as "eunuchs" and simultaneously said to be born intersexed, a contradiction that I could not untangle. I realized that without meeting hijras themselves, I could not distinguish fact from fiction, myth from reality.

FIELDWORK

In 1981 I had a sabbatical leave from my college and for family reasons decided to spend the year in India, writing, and visiting relatives and old friends. During most of this time, I lived in the city I here call Bastipore, which was located in south central India, and in Bombay. I was surprised to find that Bastipore contained several hijra households and a fairly large number of hijras—about 200. Hijras mainly live in North India, and Basti-pore's location put it at the periphery of hijra culture. This turned out to be a unique opportunity to learn about the hijras: Living at the periphery of hijra culture, the hijras of Bastipore were less under the control of the senior members of their community and were therefore much freer and much more willing to talk to outsiders than were those who live in the centers of hijra culture in Bombay, Ahmedabad, or Delhi. During the 8 months I lived in Bastipore, I spent most of my time among the three largest hijra households in that city. From time to time I also visited other hijras in the city, some of whom lived with three or four other hijras, some by themselves, and some with men whom they called their husbands. I came to know about 20 hijras relatively well, most of them members of one of these three major households in Bastipore.

Many hijras in Bastipore have social connections in Bombay, which is the major point of their cultural orientation. Thus, when I came to Bombay, which I did twice during 1981–1982, I arrived with introductions to the hijras there rather than as a stranger. During this year I also visited the major hijra temple, which is near Ahmedabad, in Gujarat, and spoke with some hijras there who earn their living by greeting and blessing visitors to the temple in the name of the goddess, Bahuchara Mata. During this time, I also made some initial contacts with hijras in Delhi and Chandigarh, in North India. On a 3-month return visit to India in 1985, and again in 1986, I revisited the hijra temple in Gujarat and spent most of my time in Bombay, Delhi, and Chandigarh, revisiting hijras I had met previously in those cities.

A major disadvantage of meeting hijras in such a wide variety of areas was the constant need for translators. In Bastipore alone, the hijras spoke three different languages: the language of the state in which Bastipore is located, the language of the neighboring state from which many of Basti-pore's hijras originate, and a form of Urdu influenced by those Indian languages spoken by Muslims. Several of the hijras in Bastipore spoke some English; one, whose personal narrative appears in this book, was fluent in that language. In Ahmedabad, Delhi, and Chandigarh, my conversations with the hijras were mediated by translators in Gujarati, Hindi, and Panjabi. All of these conversations were translated and tape recorded as they occurred. In addition, I worked with a different translator to transcribe the taped conversations and interviews into verbatim English. This double translation process was extraordinarily time consuming, but I felt it was necessary to make sure that I had correctly understood the subtleties and complexities in such conversations and to increase the reliability of my data.

The hijra emasculation operation is both illegal and life threatening, and I was not permitted to observe it. Many hijras who had had the operation told me about it in great detail, as did one hijra who had performed many operations. I did see the physical results of the operation many times, and the occurrence of this operation as part of hijra culture is documented both historically (Preston, 1987) and in the present (Bobb & Patel, 1982; Ranade, 1983; Rao, 1955).

The material in this book is heavily dependent on lengthy personal narratives and conversations. Such conversations and narratives are the richest source of information for many subjects I was interested in, which concern the inner life: how individuals incorporate cultural meaning in constructing and presenting their "selves" in and to society; how culture is perceived and experienced by those at the margins; how culturally specific gender-role ideologies influence human development, especially sexuality; and how different individuals perceive and play similar roles. Furthermore, as I have mentioned, hijras are secretive about their culture and often hostile to outsiders from whom they frequently receive abuse, ridicule, or prurient curiosity. Getting to know such people is a difficult process, and so I began to spend more time with those who not only had more time to spend with me, but who were more articulate and with whom I developed a closer personal relationship. It is these individuals whose words and lives are more prominently presented in this book.

DEFINING HIJRAS

One of the difficulties in writing in a clear and accurate way about the hijras is the disjunctions that exist between the cultural definition of the hijra role and the variety of individually experienced social roles, gender identities, sexual orientations, and life histories of the people who become hijras. These disjunctions appear in several ways. One important disjunction has to do with the fact that although hijras are culturally defined in terms of their traditional occupation as performers on auspicious occasions, many, if not most, hijras do not earn their living solely in this manner; indeed, many hijras do not perform at all.

A second disjunction has to do with the cultural definition of hijras as neither men nor women and the experienced gender identity of many hijras as women. Thus, whereas many hijras did indeed tell me that they were neither men nor women, other hijras answered my questions by saying, "We hijras are like women," and proceeded to enumerate the ways in which they felt and behaved like women. A third disjunction has to do with the definition of the hijra role as based on sexual impotence due to an ascribed physical condition of intersexuality, and the reality that most hijras are not *hermaphrodites*.[1] There is a widespread belief in India that hijras are born hermaphrodites and are taken away by the hijra community at birth or in childhood, but I found no evidence to support this belief among the hijras I met, all of whom joined the community voluntarily, most often in their teens.

The hijra role and identity appear to be adopted by persons whose impotence has a psychological rather than an organic basis, but this, of course, does not make it less real. The concept of a psychologically compelling desire that motivates a man to live as a woman is not well understood in India generally and certainly not among the lower-middle and lower classes from which hijras are generally recruited. This may be part of the reason that hijras say they are "born that way."

Still another disjunction comes from the contrast between the cultural definition of hijras as emasculated men and the fact that not all hijras do undergo the emasculation operation. The question of whether most hijras are born hermaphrodites or "made" (through emasculation) is exacerbated by the collapsing of the categories of eunuch and hermaphrodite in the Indian folk gender classification so that both people "born that way" and those who have been emasculated, either in childhood or adulthood, are called hijras. In the absence of medical examinations, there is no way to make an accurate judgment on this point. Given the small number of people born with a physical condition that would be called hermaphroditic, it would probably be well to assume that most hijras are "made" rather than "born that way."

And finally, although the core of the cultural meaning of the hijra role and the basis of the hijras' claim to power rest on their renunciation of male sexuality and their identification with "other-worldly" religious ascetics, in fact, many hijras have sexual relations with men and earn their living through prostitution.

What all of this goes to emphasize is that, as anthropologist Clifford Geertz suggests, "we must descend into detail . . . to grasp firmly . . . the various sorts of individuals within each culture." We must do this not only because individuals are different by virtue of psychology, biology, and social role, but also because each individual always has a different version of the common culture. Some variation, however slight, of subjective meaning is always attached to behavior and norms. A major problem in a person-centered ethnography is that of creating a balance between the authenticity that comes from an individual's perceptions expressed in his or her own words, and the need for the anthropologist to communicate the cultural meanings and norms through which individual lives can be contextualized and made accessible to those outside the culture. This task is even more problematic in a nation of such extreme social and cultural complexity as India, with its differences of regional culture, language, class, caste, religion, and rural and urban settings.[2] These differences affect both hijra culture, which varies throughout India, and the lives and personalities of the individuals who participate in it. I have tried to indicate some of this sociocultural and individual variability, while providing the reader with a sufficient description of the norms of hijra culture so that the individual variability can be contextualized.

Margaret Laurence, in praising the work of the Nigerian writer Chinua Achebe, says that "it seeks to send human voices through the thickets of our separateness." This, to me, has always been the aim of a humanistic anthropology. In this book, I hope to send "through the thickets of our separateness" the very human voices of individuals who seem, at first glance, very different from most people, exotic, perhaps even bizarre, but who share in our common humanity. Like human beings everywhere, hijras experience and organize their lives within a framework of cultural meanings; it is only through these meanings that we can understand their emotions, motivations, world view, and behavior. Also, like all humans, hijras engage in the essentially and characteristically human activity of interpreting and constructing culture, so that their lives are not merely lived, but are given meaning, even as they exist on the fringes of society.

At a cultural level, hijras share much with other Indians, and hijra culture mirrors, perhaps in some oblique way, much in Indian society and culture. At an individual level there is as much diversity among hijras as among any group of people. I have tried, in this ethnography, not only to convey the specifically Indian cultural context in which the hijras must be understood, but also to be faithful to their individuality and diversity and thus to their humanity as well.

CHAPTER ONE

🌀 Hijra Roles in Indian Society

HIJRAS AS CULTURAL PERFORMERS

The most important and well-known traditional role for the hijras in Indian society is that of performing at homes where a male child has been born. The birth of a son is the most significant event for an Indian family and a cause for great celebration. It is on this happy and auspicious occasion that the hijras bless the child and the family and provide entertainment for friends, relatives, and neighbors. The following is a description of one of the several performances I observed. It is typical in its major details, though somewhat more elaborate than usual because the family celebrating the birth was from the upper-middle class. The hijras call these performances *badhai,* which refers to the traditional gifts of cash and goods that they receive as payment on such occasions.

> The burning Panjab sun beat down on the crowd that was gathered that afternoon to celebrate the birth of the 6-week-old infant, Ram. At 2:30 the sound of clapping, drumming, and ankle bells announced that the hijras were arriving. Tossing their spangled scarves, flashing their heavy jewelry, and carrying with them the *dholak,* the two-sided drum that accompanies all of their performances, the group stood in the small courtyard in front of the house where Ram had been born.
>
> The drummer and the harmonium (accordian) player settled themselves on the ground and began to play in a rousing rhythm. The dancers clapped their hands wildly in the special manner of hijras—with hollow palms—and began to sing and shout and dance, making comic gestures to the audience. Tamasha, the leader of the group, twirled in a grotesque, sexually suggestive parody of feminine behavior, which caused all of the older ladies to laugh loudly and all of the younger women to giggle with embarrassment behind their hands.
>
> With boundless energy the performers danced and sang songs from popular films and from the folk music of the region. Then Tamasha took the infant Ram from his mother's arms and held him in her own. As she danced with him, she closely inspected his genitals. "Give money to

bless this baby," she demanded of the baby's grandmother. Taking the proffered two-rupee note, Tamasha passed it over the baby's head in a ritualized gesture that is a blessing and that wards off evil spirits. The other hijras in the group, Kokila, Manjula, and Shakuntala, continued their dancing, while the accompanists played loudly on the drum and harmonium. The hijras called on the Indian Mother Goddess, Parvati, and their own special goddess, Bahuchara Mata, to confer fertility, prosperity, and long life on the baby, as the ladies in the audience threw them one- and two-rupee notes.

Then Tamasha returned baby Ram to his mother. While the audience was watching the other hijras, Tamasha retired to a corner of the courtyard unobserved, where she stuffed a large pillow under her *sari* [women's dress]. She then returned to the group, clowning and imitating the slow, ungainly walk of a pregnant woman. Now with exaggerated gestures, which made the audience rock with laughter, she sang a traditional hijra song describing the time of a woman's pregnancy from beginning to childbirth:

> Little kid, may you be healthy and live long
> Someone has brought you a ring
> In the house of your friends, the dholak is being played.
> And your *bhabi* [sister-in-law] makes a lot of noise.
> Little kid, may you be healthy and live long
> Mother of the child, yes, yes,
> Grandmother of the child, yes, yes.
> What will this first male child be when he grows up?
> Headache, yes, yes,
> Heartburn, yes,
> I cannot stand up,
> I cannot sit down.
> How will the pregnancy be?
> I'll throw up, yes, yes.
> You'll have the desire to eat these sour things.
> Bring me a lemon, bring me tamarindo [a sour fruit].
> The kid says in the stomach, *dadi, dadi* [paternal grandmother].
> Little kid, may you be healthy and live long.
> What will the fourth month be like?
> What will the fifth month be like?
> In the fifth month you won't be able to walk.
> You'll have a pain in the side.
> Sixth month, yes, yes,
> Seventh month, yes, yes.
> How will it be?
> I have difficulty walking, I cannot walk.
> I have difficulty sitting.
> And now the eighth month, what will it be?

Go to the hospital
Have some tests done.
How will it be, how will it be.
Hot water, cold water.
The little kid in the stomach says *nani, nani* [maternal
    grandmother].
Little kid, may you be healthy and live long.
Ninth month, how will it be?
Pain in the waist, yes, yes.
Almost delivery time.
Heavy in the front, heavy in the back.
And how will it be?
Get the taxi.
Go to the hospital.
In the final month, how will it be?
In the jungle there's a tiger.
The tiger shouts "the birth has taken place."
And the kid in the stomach says "the birth has taken place."
Little kid, may you be healthy and live long.

Exhausted by her performance, Tamasha then leaned back against the courtyard wall to rest, while the other hijras took turns dancing with each other and making advances to those in the audience, few of whom had the courage to move to the center. Then Kokila, who is so beautiful one cannot believe she was born a man, moved toward a group of small boys shyly hiding behind their mothers' saris as they peeked out to watch the fun. She danced before them in an outrageously inviting and sexual way, and winking salaciously at five-year-old Kishan, she bent down to touch his genitals. Embarrassed and a little panicky, he quickly retreated again behind his mother's sari, bringing the audience into gales of laughter.

After another few dances and songs, the hijras stopped their performance and demanded their traditional badhai: wheat flour, cane sugar, sweets, and cloth or a sari and a sum of money (which is relatively fixed for different social classes in different regions of the country; in 1981 it was between 101 and 151 rupees) from the elders of the household. As the elder of the group, Tamasha was given the badhai and the hijras departed happily, tired but content that there are still people who respect their powers and call them to perform their traditional ritual of blessing male infants.

In a final gesture, Tamasha passed her hands over the head of the infant Ram to bless him, giving to him what she herself does not possess: the power of creating new life, of having many sons, and of carrying on the continuity of his family line. It is for this role that the hijras are given the greatest respect, and it is this role that defines their identity in relation to the world around them.

HIJRA PERFORMANCES AT MARRIAGES

Another aspect of the ritual role of the hijras is their performance at marriages. When the hijras find out that a marriage is going to take place, they come to the groom's family and arrange for a performance one or two days after the ceremony. The performance is planned for a time when the bride and groom are at the groom's house and when a number of neighbors, friends, and relatives can gather. The more people that form the audience, the greater will be the payment for the hijras. The hijras' function at this performance is to bless the married couple for fertility: The birth of a son to the couple is not only the desire of the family, but also means more work for the hijras who, upon the son's birth, will have another opportunity to perform. In many of the songs that the hijras sing at this time, they insert lines directed at various members of the family, such as "you will have a grandson, you will have a son."

Like the performance at a birth, the typical performing group at a marriage in a middle-class family consists of five to nine hijras; most of them dance, one plays the drums, and one plays the harmonium. The group is accompanied by their *guru,* or leader, who normally does not perform herself but rather supervises the proceedings in a dignified manner. The size of the group varies with the social class of the groom's family. The more elaborate performances described here occur in upper-middle–class families, and the money and gifts (similar to those given at a birth) demanded by the hijras correspond to that status. It is expected that elder members of the audience will bless the groom by circling his head with rupee notes and this money is also collected by the hijras.

The houses in North India typically have open courtyards and it is here that the hijras perform. They call for the bride and the bridegroom and different members of the family to dance with them in the center of the audience, causing great hilarity. Some more orthodox families do not allow the bride to be present in the courtyard with the hijras, however, believing that the hijras' infertility will contaminate the girl and keep her from having a son. In this case, the bride watches the festivities from a window in the house. This belief does not affect the groom, however, and he participates in all of the entertainment. This prohibition on the bride is one of the many that reflects the ambivalence that Indian society has about the hijras. Even these orthodox families, nevertheless, take great care not to offend the hijras by refusing overtly to allow their new daughter-in-law to dance with them; some excuse for the girl's absence is made in a placating way.

Currently, much of the hijras' performance at marriages consists of film songs and well-known folk songs sung only for entertainment, along with verses giving blessings for a happy marriage, a long life, and many sons. But the performances at marriages also include improvised verses making fun of the groom and his family, suggesting perhaps that the groom was born out of wedlock or casting aspersions on the family's social rank and pretentions to high status. The verses may criticize the groom's looks, saying that he is as thin as a scarecrow or that his skin is dark because his mother was so poor that she had to give birth to him outdoors, exposed to the sun. These verses are all received in fun although there is a more serious undercurrent. In India the groom's family has a higher status than that of the bride's family, a relationship that lasts as long as the marriage and can be the occasion for resentment and conflict. Thus, the hijras' verbal play functions as a kind of "ritual of reversal," a phenomenon in many cultures in which those who are in high and mighty positions are brought lower and humbled.[1]

Some of these verbal "short takes" also comment on the tensions and conflicts that arise within marriage. Because a woman in North India moves into her husband's home after marriage, one of the greatest difficulties for a new bride is the process of adjusting to her husband's relatives. Thus, the songs the hijras sing at marriages deal not only with the tensions between husband and wife, but also those between a wife and her husband's relatives.

Although there is some variation in hijra performances, depending on the region of India, the talent of the group, the size and preferences of the audience, and the economic status of the family celebrating the event, there are also some core elements obligatory in all but the most perfunctory performance. The performers must be "real" hijras, that is, they must be emasculated or intersexed, and the hijra dancers must be dressed in women's clothing. The dances always involve an aggressively displayed female sexuality. In all cases the hijras bestow blessings in the name of the Mata, the Mother Goddess. In a badhai for a birth, the hijras always examine the genitals of the infant, reinforcing the belief that hijras have a legitimate claim on infants whom they observed to be intersexed; they say that "these children belong to us because they are like us, neither man nor woman."

It would seem to be a paradox that the hijras, impotent and emasculated men, have this traditional ritual role of conferring blessings of fertility on newborn males and on newlyweds. But the hijras are not merely ordinary, impotent men. As ritual performers, they are viewed as vehicles of the divine power of the Mother Goddess, which transforms their impotence into the power of generativity.[2] It is this power, which is displayed in the shameless, aggressive feminine sexuality of the hijras' performances, that legitimates, even demands, their presence on such occasions. The faith in the powers of the hijras rests on the Hindu belief in *shakti*—the potency of the dynamic female forces of creation that the hijras, as vehicles of the Mother Goddess, represent. As we shall see later, the hijras are also identified with the creative power of ascetics, particularly with Shiva, who simultaneously, and paradoxically, contains the power of both the erotic and the ascetic.

Wherever a child has been born or a wedding has taken place, the hijras demand their right to perform as they have from time immemorial. These performances are the sanctioned cultural function of the hijras and the major legitimization of their existence. When I asked hijras, "What work do hijras do?" I invariably received the answer "we perform at a house where a baby is born," even when it turned out, as was often the case, that the hijra I was speaking with did not earn her living in that way. Most Indians also define hijras as people who perform on these auspicious occasions. These performances are the most respectable and prestigious way to earn a living within the hijra community and the major source of the hijras' claim to respect from the larger society.

HIJRAS AND THEIR AUDIENCES

Hindu society, as we have seen, accords the hijras, as sexually ambiguous figures, a measure of power and requires (or at least accepts) their presence on auspicious occasions. But Hindu society's attitude toward the hijras is ambivalent. Although hijras have an auspicious presence, they also have an inauspicious potential. The sexual ambiguity of the hijras as impotent men—eunuchs—represents a loss of virility, and this undoubtedly is the major cause of the fear that they inspire. Thus, the stout, middle-class matrons who are so amused by the hijras' performances, and who may even pity them as tragic, hermaphroditic figures, also have an underlying anxiety about them. As mentioned earlier, this is translated into a taboo of orthodox Hindus that the hijras should not touch, or even see, a new bride, so that their infertility will not contaminate her reproductive potential.

The belief in the hijras' abilities to confer blessings in the name of the Mother Goddess is a double-edged sword for their audiences. The hijras can praise the good qualities of families, but they also can insult them; they can bless one's house with prosperity and fertility, but they also can curse it with infertility and other kinds of misfortunes. Hijras are infamous for insulting and cursing families who do not meet their demands of money and gifts. They may start with mild verbal abuse in the form of ridicule: "Hey, when you got married and enjoyed yourself with your bride, didn't you think then that there would be expenses connected with this later on?" They gradually move on to stronger insults: "OK, then, we will perform for free since you are so poor and such lowlife and will not give us our due." The act that is most feared is the threat that the hijras will expose their mutilated genitals to public gaze. If at the end of a performance, the hijras' demands are not met, one hijra, more aggressive than the others, will lift up her skirt and shout: "See, if you don't give us any cloth, or money to buy cloth, then we must go naked. Here, take this dress. As you are too poor to give us anything, then we will have nothing to wear." At this gesture all the women present cover their eyes to prevent themselves from seeing this shameless, shocking, and threatening exposure, which in itself is a curse for causing impotence. This hijra behavior is usually enough for someone in the audience to persuade the family to give the hijras what they want just to get rid of them.

When hijras insult a family for not giving in to their demands, they do not limit themselves to insults for the family's ears only, but shout their abuse up and down the lanes for all to hear. In one case, for example, when a hijra group came to a house to perform for a wedding, the woman of the house told them to go away, as another hijra group had already performed there. The hijra troupe claimed that this house was in their exclusive territory and proceeded to perform anyway. When they finished, the woman adamantly refused to pay, threatening to call the police. The hijras invited her to do so and remained on her doorstep, shouting obscenities and curses. At this point the police arrived and the woman complained to them, with the hijras shouting their side of the story. The police refused to do anything, and the woman finally had to meet the hijras' demands in order to get them to leave. Several hijras I spoke with expressed full confidence that the police would always back them up on such occasions. As one hijra told me:

> There are always those people who try to send us away; they tell us, "We don't want this singing and dancing, we will call the police." We tell them, "Call the police, the police also love us, they also have children and we have good relations with them." The police understand that this is our profession. We also give blessings to them, we ask God to give them a promotion, to give them a male child, to give them 10 children. This is how we get our business, we get our happiness only from our work. We go to the house of the newborn or the wedding couple and dance and sing and feel happy. By making others happy, we also feel happy. So why should we be afraid of the police?

All of the hijras I met professed to take their powers to curse very seriously; all insisted such powers were never carelessly used and many had never used them at all. Prema, a hijra performer in Delhi who considered herself generally a gentle soul, once used these powers with such disastrous results, she vowed she would never curse anyone again:

> See, whatever we say, Serena, for good or for bad, will come true. Just as we bless with such intensity so also we curse with such power that if we curse any person the food in their house will get spoiled. I know this is so because I have done it myself. After that I felt so bad that I made a vow never to curse anyone again, even if he shows me his shoe [showing someone a shoe, or touching someone with a shoe, is a grave insult to Hindus].

What happened was that in this one locality where we had gone dancing there was an important man who never permitted the hijras to entertain in front of him. When his daughter-in-law gave birth to a son and we came to know of this, we went to his house to give the blessing, but he insulted us so badly, I could not stand it. He practically threw us down the stairs. So I made this wish to the *Mata* [Mother Goddess], "The way you have sent us down, so your son's child's bier will go the same way."

This curse just slipped from my tongue, I was so angry. The day after this that small boy fell sick. They treated him with many medicines, but the child never got better and then he died.

A year later, when we were again roaming in that vicinity, this same man was sitting in his house. He said to me, "Mataji, mataji [literally, mother; used here as a respectful form of address], you people came to my house and I did not give you permission to dance. I should have let you go away happily. Instead I sent you away with kicks and today my daughter-in-law's lap is empty, she is childless. I had a gift from heaven and now God has taken that gift away."

He asked us to listen to him, but we told him we would not listen because he had sent us away like that. We told him, "We are not going to listen to anything you say; you insulted us so badly. You thought we were nothing. You did not have to insult us, you could have given us five rupees or even two—any small sum of money—and said, 'Mataji, we don't allow this dancing to take place, you take these two rupees and enjoy some tea with them, just bless my grandson before you go.' "

"Our hearts would have swelled up so much and we would have said, 'Never mind, he never let us dance but at least he gave us money for our tea, 10 rupees or 2 rupees. God keep him happy and instead of one son give him two sons.' But you pushed us away with insults."

See, Serena, what we felt in our minds at this time was that our respect was at stake. After all, we are neither men nor women. If we were men we would have a good job, be working in some factory. We would also get married and bring a daughter-in-law into the home and our parents would have some satisfaction and some hope.

But God has made us this way, neither man nor woman, and all we are left with is to go wherever a child is born or a wedding is performed and sing a couple of songs so that we can sell our art or talent and make a little money and fill our stomachs. We don't rob or steal from anyone's house, we don't go to burgle anyone's house—this man should have at least thought this much. If I had been on my own, I could have calmed myself down, but I had my troupe of hijras with me. If I had not said anything to him, these hijras would have said, "See how he has insulted us and you have not said anything to him."

Like many sexually ambivalent figures in Indian mythology, the hijras are treated with a combination of mockery and fear. When they move about in public, they are always vulnerable to teasing; sometimes they are called *kaurika* (literally refers to an old penny coin with a hole in the middle that is no longer used; now connotes an "empty shell", or some-thing that is absolutely useless). This teasing is usually done by small or adolescent boys. Some hijras have trained themselves to ignore it; other hijras respond indignantly with the kind of abuse they are famous for. Madhu, a hijra whose somewhat dirty and disreputable appearance often brings her insults, combines her abuse with an attempt to educate the public:

> If someone insults me, or teases me as I pass, I feel so small in my mind, I say to God, why did you make us in this way, you should have made us in such a way that no one would have the guts or the opportunity to tease us in passing. In this manner I try to placate myself. Then I abuse those who insult me; I say: "Go away, may your mother or your daughter or your wife or your sister give birth to a hijra like me, let a hijra be born in your house as well. Then God will tell you, this is the result of your teasing a hijra, that is why you have a hijra born in your house. You can finish him off, or bury him as soon as he is born, or smother him. . . . Will you try that or will you try to make him grow up? And when he grows up he will wear a sari like us, and one day he will be standing on the road and your friend who is with you, not knowing, will tease him and call him hijra, what will you say then? What will you feel? This is how we feel, this is what our minds are saying, this is how we have suffered. So now, before you tease us, just think how we suffer from this."

Part of the teasing of hijras derives from their often blatant and bawdy flirting with men and their aggressive caricatures of feminine sexuality. Because many hijras are homosexuals, this decreases their respect in society and leaves them vulnerable to public mockery.

HIJRAS AND INSTITUTIONALIZED HOMOSEXUALITY

The dominant cultural role of the hijras, as we have seen, is that of ritual performers. It is also true, however, that hijras often engage in homosex-ual prostitution, a subject about which I will have more to say later. The importance of the social role of the hijras as institutionalized homosexuals is a controversy that has been the focus of the scant anthropological literature which discusses them. In a psychoanalytical study of high castes in a village in Rajasthan, G. Morris Carstairs (1957) asserted that the hijra role is primarily a form of institutionalized homosexuality developing in response to tendencies toward latent homosexuality in the Indian national character. This view was challenged by anthropologist Morris Opler (1960), who claimed that hijras were not thought of as homosexuals, and further, denied that they engaged in any sexual activity, saying they were "dancers only." Opler traced the use of hijras as dancers at life-cycle rituals to the Indian disinclination to allow women of good name to dance publicly. In an attempt to mediate between these opposing views, A. M. Shah, an Indian sociologist, agreed that the main business of the hijras was to dance at births and marriages, but he also noted that some hijras, who lived alone outside the organized hijra communes, might well earn a living through homosexual prostitution (1961).

There is absolutely no question that at least some hijras—perhaps even the majority—are homosexual prostitutes (see Ranade, 1983). Sinha's (1967) study of hijras in Lucknow, in North India, acknowledges the hijra role as performers, but views the major motivation for recruitment to the hijra community as the satisfaction of the individual's homosexual urges, a satisfaction related to their engaging in prostitution.

More recently, Freeman (1979) describes a group of transvestite prostitutes in the state of Orissa, in eastern India, who are men who dress as women, who have a specialized feminized vocabulary, who live singly or in small groups, and who seek out and are sought out by men in the surrounding area for sexual relations. Freeman does not use the term *hijra* for these people nor does he describe the organized or religious aspect of their community, but it seems fairly clear that he is indeed writing of hijras. So in Orissa, too, hijras are both performers and prostitutes. Historical sources also support the view that homosexual prostitution is important, if not central, to the maintenance of the hijra community, at the very least, economically. Nineteenth- and early twentieth-century ethnographic accounts of hijras in the Indian census claim that hijras kidnap small boys for the purposes of sodomy or prostitution (Bhimbhai, 1901; Faridi, 1899; Ibbetson, MacLagen, & Rose, 1911). A historical account of Poona, in western India, also notes that a particular section of the city was known for hijra prostitution (Preston, 1987).

In drawing a composite portrait of hijras in Hyderabad, one of the major traditional centers of their culture, Lynton and Rajan (1974) indicate that whereas recruitment to the hijra role may grow out of a period of homosexual activity by young men with effeminate characteristics who are harassed in public, once they join the hijra community, they cease these sexual activities in order to conform to community rules, which, as Lynton's informants told her, specifically forbid them. The hijra leaders told Lynton that this restriction is necessary if the hijras are to maintain the respect for themselves as *sannyasis*—"other-worldly" people—ascetics and religious mendicants. This illustrates the thesis, central in this book, that it is the conception of hijras as ascetics and neither man nor woman that gives the role its institutionalized character. That hijras, at least in modern historical times, engage in widespread homosexual activity, undermines their respect in society but does not negate their ritual function.

Hijras are well aware that they have only a tenuous hold on legitimacy in Indian society and that this hold is compromised by even covertly engaging in sexual relations and practicing prostitution. The idea of hijras as "wives" (of ordinary men) and prostitutes obviously runs counter to their claims to be ascetics or other-worldly religious mendicants, that is, people who have renounced sexual activity. In an early 20th century account of the hijras, they speak tauntingly of those men called *zenana*, who "are given to sodomy. . . . They are prostitutes; if we acted like them how could our [patrons] allow us to come near them? They have deprived prostitutes of their living—we are not such" (Ibettson et al., 1911:332).

In this conflict between the respect due ascetics and the reality of lust and sexual relations occurring among ascetics, the hijras are not alone. Ascetics have always been regarded with skepticism in Indian society, and the notion of the "false ascetic"—those who pretend to be ascetics in order to satisfy their lust—abounds in Hindu mythology. This explains the behavior of some members of the audience at hijra performances who challenge the hijras' authenticity by lifting their skirts to see whether they are emasculated and real hijras or "fake hijras," men who are only impersonating women. There are other female impersonators who do not have the religious powers ascribed to hijras but who sometimes try to perform on the occasions where it is the hijras' right to do so. Emasculation distinguishes real hijras from the fakes, and if a challenge reveals that a performer's genitals have not been removed, the whole group will be reviled and driven away without payment as imposters. Hijras themselves constantly deride those "men who are men and can have children" who join their community only to earn a living or out of the desire to have sexual relations with men. As one hijra vehemently protested to me:

There are other people who imitate us, who dress up in women's clothing and go where a baby is born, but only we have the power of giving it the blessing. This is because we are neither men nor women and have been separated from God, so that God grants our special prayers in every place, to us only. A hijra is born from the stomach of a woman, but can be counted neither among the men nor the women. This is why we are called hijras and why we have a right to nothing except singing and dancing.

These other people, who imitate us, they are real men, with wives and children. They come to join us only for the purpose of making a living. How do we know what a person is when he comes to join us? Just recently there was a case in our group. This man's name was Hari. He was the father of four children and he dressed up as a woman and put on a woman's hairstyle. He behaved like a hijra and danced at people's houses, disguised as a hijra. One day we caught him red handed. We beat him up bodily and handed him over to the police. It cannot be allowed for someone to take our place as it deprives us of our right and our income.

One time, when I myself left my group after a quarrel, out of desperation I also joined a group of these zenana and went to dance and sing with them. One day we went to dance for a family where a man had a son after having five daughters. We came to the house and one of these imposters said, "I will dance today, give me the ankle bells." So she started dancing, and while she was dancing, her skirt flew up and all the people said, "This is not a hijra, this is a man." They chased us away and we lost all respect. I also lost respect. So I thought to myself, I am so different from them, like the earth and the sky; these people are men whereas I am neither a man nor a woman. From that day on I stopped dancing with them and went back to my troupe.

The special powers that the hijras derive from their alternative gender role legitimate their function as ritual performers, and it is this role that forms the core of their self-definition and the basis of their positive, collective self-image. Only the hijras—those who are "neither man nor woman"—are given the power by God to make their words—whether blessings or curses—come true.

Hijras who act as homosexual prostitutes cloud the clear-cut distinction described above: They may be "real" hijras (in that they are emasculated), but they are also engaging in an activity that is contrary to the hijra ideal as ritual performers who have renounced sexual desire and activity. Many Indians are not aware, or at least do not acknowledge publicly, that many hijras are homosexual prostitutes. Even some social science research has overlooked this role (e.g., Opler, 1960; Sharma, 1983) though the sexual activities of hijras are often emphasized in the popular press (Raghuvanshi & Navalkar, 1980). In spite of the undeniable fact that many hijras earn a living from homosexual prostitution, to view their social place as one of institutionalized homosexuality is to overlook the important cultural role the hijras play as ritual performers, a position linked to their definition as an ambiguous gender category—neither man nor woman.

CHAPTER TWO

🦚 Hijras as Neither Man Nor Woman

In the time of the Ramayana, Ram fought with the demon Ravenna and went to Sri Lanka to bring his wife, Sita, back to India. Before this, his father commanded Ram to leave Ayodhya [his native city] and go into the forest for 14 years. As he went, the whole city followed him because they loved him so. As Ram came to the banks of the river at the edge of the forest, he turned to the people and said, "Ladies and gents, please wipe your tears and go away." But those people who were not men and not women did not know what to do. So they stayed there because Ram did not ask them to go. They remained there 14 years and when Ram returned from Lanka he found those people there, all meditating. And so they were blessed by Ram.

"And that is why we hijras are so respected in that part of India," added Gopi, the hijra who told me this story. Gopi was about 40 years old, a Hindu from South India who had just returned to the hijra household I was visiting in Bastipore. She had recently spent several years telling fortunes outside a Hindu temple in another city and was well versed in Hindu religious lore. The story she told me, in response to my question, "What is a hijra?" expresses the most common view, held by both hijras and people in the larger society, that the hijras are an alternative gender, neither men or women. This story, and others like it, makes explicit both the cultural definition of this role in India, and for many (though not all) hijras, it defines a personally experienced gender identity as well.

The story is thus an origin myth, similar to those told by many Indian castes. Such myths "explain" the caste's origin by linking the caste to Hindu deities, providing religious sanction for its claimed place in Indian society. The many myths, such as the one that opens this chapter, validate a positive identity for hijras by identifying their alternative gender role with deities and mythic figures of the Great Tradition of Hinduism.

The view of hijras as an alternative gender category is supported by linguistic evidence. The most widely used English translations of the word *hijra,* which is of Urdu origin, is either "eunuch" or "hermaphrodite" (intersexed). Both terms, as used in India, connote impotence—an inability to function in the male sexual role—and the word *hijra* primarily implies a physical defect impairing the male sexual function (Opler, 1960:507). In both cases the irregularity of the male genitalia is central to the definition: *Eunuch* refers to an emasculated male and *intersexed* to a person whose genitals are ambiguously male-like at birth. When this is discovered, the child, previously assigned to the male sex, would be recategorized as intersexed—as a hijra. Although historically in North India a linguistic distinction was made between "born hijras" (hermaphrodites) and "made hijras" (eunuchs) (Ibbetson et al., 1911:331), the term *hijra* as it is currently used collapses both of these categories.

Impotence is the force behind both the words *eunuch* and *hermaphrodite* as they are used in India, and impotence is central to the definition of the hijra as not man. Some 19th century accounts report that impotence was an essential qualification for admission into the hijra community and that a newcomer initiated into the community was on probation for as long as a year. During this time his impotence was carefully tested, sometimes by making the person sleep four nights with a prostitute.[1] Only after impotence was established would the newcomer be permitted to undergo the emasculation operation and become a full member of the community (Bhimbhai, 1901:506). Another 19th century account of the hijras also reports that "all state that they were incapable of copulation and that becoming [hijras] was on that account only." (Preston, 1987: 375).

While in South India, where hijras do not have the cultural role that they do in North India, the terms used for hijra, such as *kojja* in Telegu (Anderson, 1977) or *pottai* in Tamil, are epithets that connote a derogatory meaning of a cowardly or feminine male, the term *hijra* itself is rarely used this way. Nor does hijra mean homosexual; I have never heard it given that English translation. Because it is widely believed in India that a man may become impotent through engaging in homosexual relations in the receiver role in anal intercourse, passive homosexuals who become impotent may identify themselves as hijras, not because they have sexual relations with men, but because they are impotent.

In parts of North India, effeminate males who are assumed to play the passive role in homosexual relationships are referred to as zenana (Ibbetson et al., 1911:332), literally meaning woman: By becoming a hijra, one removes oneself from this category (see Lynton & Rajan, 1974). Zenana are said to think of themselves in the male gender, generally wear male clothing, and sometimes may be married and have children. Some zenana may live with hijras (Ranade, 1983) and perform with them, but they are not "real" hijras (Sinha, 1967). Although hijras assert that such men are "fake" hijras, merely "men who impersonate hijras," some zenana do go through the formal initiation into the hijra community. Whereas hijras are sometimes cited in the literature as transvestites (Kakar, 1981:35) or transvestite prostitutes (Freeman, 1979), it is clear, as we will see, that the role refers to much more than a man who dresses in women's clothing.

HIJRAS AS "NOT MEN"

> We go into the house of all, and never has a eunuch looked upon a woman with a bad eye; we are like bullocks [castrated male cattle].

As indicated by this quote (Ibbetson et al., 1911:331), the view of hijras as an "in-between" gender begins with their being men who are impotent, therefore not men, or as Wendy O'Flaherty aptly puts it, "As eunuchs, hijras are man minus man" (1980:297). But being impotent is only a necessary and not sufficient condition for being a hijra. Hijras are men who are impotent for one reason or another and only become hijras by having their genitals cut off. Emasculation is the *dharm* (religious obligation) of the hijras, and it is this renunciation of male sexuality through the surgical removal of the organ of male sexuality that is at the heart of the definition of the hijra social identity. This understanding is true for both hijras and their audiences.

That the core meaning of the hijra role centers on the aberrant male genitals was brought home to me many times by hijras, who in response to my question, "What is a hijra?" would offer to show me their ambiguous or mutilated genitals. In some cases, a hijra I was talking with would jump to her feet, lift up her skirt, and, displaying her altered genitals, would say, "See, we are neither men nor women!"

Hijras' expressions of what they are often take the form of stating that they are in-between, neither men nor women, but the term *hijra* itself is a masculine noun suggesting, as does the word *eunuch,* a man that is less than a perfect man. In fact, however, several hijras I met were raised from birth as females; only as they failed to develop secondary female sexual characteristics (breast development and menarche) at puberty, did they change their gender role to hijra (see also Anderson, 1977; Mehta, 1947).[2] Indeed, hijras claim that one of their founders was "a woman, but not a normal woman, she did not menstruate," a point about which I shall have more to say later.

The primary cultural definition of hijras, however, is that they begin life as men, albeit incomplete men; this is consistent with my observations that those hijras who exclaim that they are neither man nor woman always begin with an explanation of how they are *not men.*

The hijra view of themselves as "not men" as it occurred in my conversations with them focused primarily on their anatomy—the imperfection or absence of a penis—but also implicated their physiology and their sexual capacities, feelings, and preferences. These definitions incorporated both the ascribed status of "being born this way" and the achieved status of renouncing sexual desire and sexual activity.

Lakshmi, a beautiful young hijra dancer, who had undergone the emasculation operation a year before I met her, said, "I was born a man, but not a perfect man." Neelam, a transvestite homosexual who had not yet had the emasculation operation, told me, "I was born a man, but my male organ did not work properly so I became a hijra." Shabnam, a hijra elder who now only wears women's clothing, showed me some photographs of her youth. Pointing to one in which she appears dressed as a man, with a mustache, she said, most casually, "See, that is when I was a boy. In those days I lived and worked for a Christian family." Sonya, a middle-aged hijra who had not had the emasculation operation and who looked very masculine, but who otherwise had adopted all of the clothing and gestures of a woman, explained, "We are not like men, we do not have the sexual desires men have." Krishna, a slim young man who mainly dressed in men's clothes, except for important hijra social occasions, when he put on female attire, said, "We are not men with the ordinary desires of men to get married and have families. Otherwise, why would we choose to live this life?" Bellama, a hijra elder, told me, "We hijra are like sannyasis (ascetics), we have renounced all sexual desire and family life."

But Kamladevi, a hijra prostitute, is skeptical: "Of course we have the sexual desires," she said. "Older hijras like Bellama and Gopi, now they say they don't have the sexual desires and all, they have become very religious minded and don't do all that. But when they were young, I can tell you, they were just like me. We hijras are born as boys, but then we 'get spoiled' and have sexual desires only for men."

Lalitha, a hijra whose sexual relationships with her "man" dominated her life, told me:

> See, we are all men, born as men, but when we look at women, we don't have any desire for them. When we see men, we like them, we feel shy, we feel some excitement. We want to live and die as women. We have the same feelings you have, Serena, just as you women fall in love and are ready to sacrifice your life for a man, so we are also like that. Just like you, whenever a man touches us, we get an excitement out of it.

Shakuntala is a hijra who had once been a dancer and a prostitute, but who now has a husband and only does domestic chores for a hijra household. She had the emasculation operation in 1978, 3 years prior to my meeting her. One day, as we were talking about what a hijra is, she burst out in anger:

> In many places men who are perfect men have joined this community only for the sake of earning a living. This is not good. Only men who have not spoiled any lady or got any children should come into the hijra company. You should not have had any affairs with ladies, not have loved ladies, or done any sexual thing with them or have married a lady. We true hijras are like this from childhood. From a small age we like to dance and dress as women. Even when we go away from this world, in our death, we must wear the sari. That is our desire.

If hijras, as eunuchs, are man minus maleness, they are also, in their outward appearance and behavior, man plus woman.[3] The most obvious expression of hijras as women is in their dress. Although some hijras do wear male clothing—sometimes because they work outside their traditional occupations or for other reasons—wearing female attire is an essential and defining characteristic of the hijra. It is absolutely required for their performances, when asking for alms, and when they visit the temple of their goddess Bahuchara. Hijra prostitutes also invariably wear women's clothes. This clothing may follow the custom of the region: In South India, hijras wear saris, whereas in North India they may wear *salwar-kameez* (the loose shirt and pants worn by women in North India) or even Western fashions. All hijras who dress in women's clothes wear a bra, which may be padded or, more likely, stuffed, as padded bras are expensive; sometimes it just is there, empty, on the flat male chest.

Hijras enjoy dressing in women's clothing, and their female dress is typically accompanied by traditionally feminine jewelry, such as wrist bangles, nose rings, and toe rings, as well as *bindi*—the colored dot applied to the forehead of all Hindu women who are not widows. Long hair is a must for a hijra. One of the punishments meted out by the elders to a hijra who has misbehaved is to cut her hair. This is considered a disgrace and an insult; even hijras who normally dress in men's clothing keep their hair long. Some wear it merely pulled back in a ponytail or tied up and covered with a male head covering; others wear it openly in a woman's hairstyle. Arjun, the hero of one of the two great Hindu epics, the Mahabharata, is required to live for 1 year as a eunuch, and he specifically refers to how he shall wear his hair like a woman and adorn himself with bangles. Hijras are forbidden to shave but rather must pluck out their facial hair so that their skin remains smooth like a woman's.[4]

Hijras also adopt female behavior: They imitate, even exaggerate, a woman's "swaying walk," sit and stand like women, and carry pots on their hips, which men do not. But hijras may engage in male occupations: One hijra I knew delivered milk on a bicycle and another was an electrician; some work on construction, which in India is a woman's as well as a man's job. Nevertheless, most hijras who work outside traditional hijra occupations take jobs that are generally held by both men and women, for example, as household servants and cooks.

Hijras also take female names when they join the community, and they use female kinship terms for each other, such as "sister," "aunty," and "grandmother" (mother's mother).[5] In some parts of India they also have a special, feminized language, which consists of the use of feminine expressions and intonations (Freeman, 1979:295). In public transport or other public accommodations, hijras request "ladies only" seating, and they periodically demand to be counted as females in the census.

HIJRAS AS "NOT WOMEN"

If hijras are clearly not men by virtue of anatomy, appearance, and psychology, they are also not women, though they are "like" women. Their female dress and mannerisms are often exaggerations, almost to the point of caricature, and they act in sexually suggestive ways that would be considered inappropriate, and even outrageous, for ordinary women in their significant and traditional female roles as daughters, wives, and mothers. Hijra performances are most often burlesques of female behavior, and much of the fun of the performance derives from the incongruities between their behavior and that of women of the larger society whom they pretend to imitate. Their very act of dancing in public is contrary to what ordinary women would do. They also use coarse and abusive speech and gestures, again in opposition to the Hindu ideal of demure and restrained femininity. The act of a hijra who lifts up her skirt and exposes her mutilated genitals is considered shameless and thoroughly unfeminine. In Gujarat, an important center of hijra culture, hijras smoke the *hookah* (water pipe), which is normally done only by men; and in Panjab, hijras are noted for smoking cigarettes, which is ordinarily done only by men. Although some emasculated hijras do experience bodily feminization, for example, in the rounding of the hips, hijras who have not been emasculated may retain a heavy male facial structure and body muscularity and facial hair (Rao, 1955).

The "not woman" aspect of the hijra role is attested to by 18th century reports which note that hijras were required by native governments to distinguish themselves by wearing a man's turban with their female clothing. A century later hijras were also noted to wear "a medley of male and female clothing", in this case wearing the female sari under the male coatlike outer garment (Preston, 1987:373). However, today, this mixture of clothing is not required, and hijras who wear any female clothing at all wear completely female attire.

As I suggested, it is the absence of menstruation that is the most important signal that a person who has been assigned to the female sex at birth and raised as a female, is a hijra. This sign—the absence of the onset of a female's reproductive ability—points to the essential criterion of the feminine gender that hijras themselves make explicit: They do not have female reproductive organs, and because they cannot have children they cannot be considered real women.

To help me understand this, a hijra told me this story:

See, two people got into a fight, a man and a hijra. The hijra said, "I am a lady," and the man said, "No, you are not." The fight went so long that they went to the magistrate. The magistrate said, "I agree, you look like a woman, you act like a woman, but I'll ask you a simple question—can you give birth to a baby? If that is not possible, then you don't win." The hijra answered, no, she could not give birth to a baby, so the magistrate said, "You are only a hijra, you are not a woman."

The hijras I was sitting with nodded vigorously in assent to the tale's conclusion. This story was immediately followed by another, which is further testimony to the hijra view of themselves as "not women," at least not real women:

> In Ajmer, in North India, there is a holy place that belongs to the hijras. It is called Baba Darga, and it is on top of a hill. One time, during Urs [a Muslim festival], many people were going up the hill to pay respects to Baba. One hijra was also there. She saw a lady with four children and offered to carry one or two of them. The lady became very angry and told the hijra, "You are a hijra, so don't touch my children."
>
> This made the hijra feel very sad, so she asked Baba for his blessings for a child of her own. But she only asked for a child and didn't ask Baba to bring the child out. The pregnancy went on for ten months, and her stomach became very bloated. She went to the doctors but they didn't want to perform an operation [Caesarean section] on her. Eventually she couldn't stand the weight any longer so she prayed to the Baba to redeem her from this situation. But Baba could only grant her the boon, he could not reverse it.
>
> When the hijra felt she could stand it no more, she found a sword at the *darga* [Muslim shrine] and slit herself open. She removed the child and placed in on the ground. The child died and the hijra also died. Now at this darga prayers are performed to this hijra and the child and then to the Baba.

This story reveals an ambivalence: On the one hand, it expresses the wish of some hijras to have a child, yet on the other hand acknowledges its impossibility. The death of the hijra and the child suggests that hijras cannot become women—in the most fundamental sense of being able to bear a child—and that they are courting disaster to attempt something so contrary to their nature. Meera, the hijra who told me this story, was convinced it was true. She had many times expressed to me her wish for a child and said that she had read in a magazine that in America doctors would help people like her have babies. The other hijras sitting with us laughed at this suggestion.[6]

ALTERNATIVE GENDERS IN INDIAN CULTURE AND SOCIETY

The hijra role is a magnet that attracts people with many different kinds of cross-gender identities, attributes, and behaviors—people whom we in the West would differentiate as eunuchs, homosexuals, transsexuals, hermaphrodites, and transvestites. Such individuals, of course, exist in our own and perhaps all societies. What is noteworthy about the hijras is that the role is so deeply rooted in Indian culture that it can accommodate a wide variety of temperaments, personalities, sexual needs, gender identities, cross-gender behaviors, and levels of commitment without losing its cultural meaning. The ability of the hijra role to succeed as a symbolic reference point giving significant meaning to the lives of the many different kinds of people who make up the hijra community, is undoubtedly related to the variety and significance of alternative gender roles and gender transformations in Indian mythology and traditional culture.

Whereas Westerners feel uncomfortable with the ambiguities and contradictions inherent in such in-between categories as transvestism, homosexuality, hermaphroditism, and transgenderism, and make strenuous attempts to resolve them, Hinduism not only accommodates such ambiguities, but also views them as meaningful and even powerful.

In Hindu mythology, ritual, and art—important vehicles for transmitting the Hindu world view—the power of the combined man/woman is a frequent and significant theme. Indian mythology contains numerous examples of androgynes, impersonators of the opposite sex, and individuals who undergo sex changes, both among deities and humans. These mythical figures are well known as part of Indian popular culture, which helps explain the ability of the hijras to maintain a meaningful place for themselves within Indian society in an institutionalized third gender role.

One of the most important sexually ambivalent figures in Hinduism with whom hijras identify is Shiva, a deity who incorporates both male and female characteristics.[7] Shiva is an ascetic—one who renounces sex—and yet he appears in many erotic and procreative roles. His most powerful symbol and object of worship is the phallus—but the phallus is almost always set in the *yoni,* the symbol of the female genitals. One of the most popular forms of Shiva is that of *Ardhanarisvara,* or half-man/half-woman, which represents Shiva united with his shakti (female creative power). Hijras say that worshipers of Shiva give them special respect because of this close identification, and hijras often worship at Shiva temples. In the next chapter, I look more closely at the identification of the hijras with Shiva, particularly in connection with the ritual of emasculation.

Other deities also take on sexually ambiguous or dual gender manifestations. Vishnu and Krishna (an *avatar,* or incarnation, of Vishnu) are sometimes pictured in androgynous ways. In one myth, Vishnu transforms himself into Mohini, the most beautiful woman in the world, in order to take back the sacred nectar from the demons who have stolen it. In another well-known myth, Krishna takes on the form of a female to destroy a demon called Araka. Araka's strength came from his chasteness. He had never set eyes on a woman, so Krishna took on the form of a beautiful woman and married him. After 3 days of the marriage, there was a battle and Krishna killed the demon. He then revealed himself to the other gods in his true form. Hijras, when they tell this story, say that when Krishna revealed himself he told the other gods that "there will be more like me, neither man nor woman, and whatever words come from the mouths of these people, whether good [blessings] or bad [curses], will come true."

In Tamil Nadu, in South India, an important festival takes place in which hijras, identifying with Krishna, become wives, and then widows, of the male deity Koothandavar. The story behind this festival is that there were once two warring kingdoms. To avert defeat, one of the kings agreed to sacrifice his eldest son to the gods, asking only that he first be allowed to arrange his son's marriage. Because no woman could be found who would marry a man about to be sacrificed, Krishna came to earth as a woman to marry the king's son, and the king won the battle as the gods promised.

For this festival, men who have made vows to Koothandavar dress as women and go through a marriage ceremony with him. The priest performs the marriage, tying on the traditional wedding necklace. After 1 day, the deity is carried to a burial ground. There, all of those who have "married" him remove their wedding necklaces, cry and beat their breasts, and remove the flowers from their hair, as a widow does in mourning for her husband. Hijras participate by the thousands in this festival, coming from all over India. They dress in their best clothes and jewelry and ritually reaffirm their identification with Krishna, who changes his form from male to female.

Several esoteric Hindu ritual practices involve male transvestism as a form of devotion. Among the Sakhibhava (a sect that worhips Vishnu) Krishna may not be worshiped directly. The devotees in this sect worship Radha, Krishna's beloved, with the aim of becoming her attendant: It is through her, as Krishna's consort, that Krishna is indirectly worshiped. The male devotees imitate feminine behavior, including simulated menstruation; they also may engage in sexual acts with men as acts of devotion, and some devotees even castrate themselves in order to more nearly approximate a female identification with Radha (Bullough, 1976:267–268; Kakar, 1981; Spratt, 1966:315).

Hinduism in general holds that all persons contain within themselves both male and female principles. In the Tantric school of Hinduism, the Supreme Being is conceptualized as one complete sex containing male and female sexual organs. Hermaphroditism is the ideal. In some of these sects, male (never female) transvestism is used as a way of transcending one's own sex, a prerequisite to achieving salvation. In other Tantric sects, religious exercises involve the male devotee imitating a woman in order to realize the woman in himself: Only in this way do they believe that true love can be realized (Bullough, 1976:260).

Traditional Hinduism makes many specific references to alternative sexes and sexual ambiguity among humans as well as among gods. Ancient Hinduism, for example, taught that there was a third sex, which itself was divided into four categories: the male eunuch, called the "waterless" because he had desiccated testes; the "testicle voided," so called because he had been castrated; the hermaphrodite; and the "not woman," or female eunuch (which usually refers to a woman who does not menstruate). Those who were more feminine (whether males or females) wore false breasts and imitated the voice, gestures, dress, delicacy, and timidity of women (Bullough, 1976:268). All of these categories of persons had the function of providing alternative techniques of sexual gratification, some of which are mentioned in the classical Hindu sex manual, the Kamasutra.

Another ancient reference to a third sex, one that sounds similar to the hijras, is a prostitute named Sukumarika ("good little girl"), who appears in a Sanskrit play. Sukumarika is accused of being sexually insatiable. As a third sex, she has some characteristics advantageous in her profession: "She has no breasts to get in the way of a tight embrace, no monthly period to interrupt the enjoyment of passion, and no pregnancy to mar her beauty" (O'Flaherty, 1980:299).

As just suggested, ancient Hindus, like contemporary ones, appeared to be ambivalent about such third gender roles and the associated alternative sexual practices. The figure of Sukumarika, for example, was considered inauspicious to look upon and, not coincidentally, similar to the hijras today, inspired both fear and mockery. Historically, both eunuchism and castration were looked down on in ancient India, and armed women and old men were preferred to eunuchs for guarding court ladies (Basham, 1954:172). Whereas homosexuality was generally not highly regarded in ancient India, such classic texts as the Kamasutra, however, did describe, even prescribe, sexual practices for eunuchs, for example, "mouth congress."[8]

Homosexuality was condemned in the ancient lawbooks. The Laws of Manu, the first formulation of the Hindu moral code, held that men who engaged in anal sex lost their caste. Other medieval writers held that men who engaged in oral sex with other men were reborn impotent. But homosexuals were apparently tolerated in reality. Consistent with the generally "sex positive" attitude of Hinduism, Vatsyayana, author of the Kamasutra, responded to critics of oral and anal sex by saying that "in all things connected with love, everybody should act according to the custom of his country, and his own inclination," asking a man to consider only whether the act "is agreeable to his nature and himself" (Burton, 1964:127).

Even the gods were implicated in such activities: Krishna's son Samba was notorious for his homosexuality and dressed as female, often a pregnant woman. As Sambali, Samba's name became a synonym for eunuch (Bullough, 1976:267). An important ritual at the Jagannatha temple in Orissa involves a sequence in which Balabhadra, the ascetic elder brother of the deity Jagannatha, who is identified with Shiva, is homosexually seduced by a transvestite (a young man dressed as a female temple dancer) (Marglin, 1985:53). In some Hindu myths a male deity takes on a female form specifically to experience sexual relations with another male deity.

Islam also provides a model of an in-between gender—not a mythological one, but a true historical figure—in the traditional role of the eunuch who guarded the ladies of the harem, under Moghul rule. Hijras often mention this role as the source of their prestige in Indian society. In spite of the clear connection of hijras with Hinduism, Islam not only provides a powerful positive model of an alternative gender, but also contributes many elements to the social organization of the hijra community. Hijras today make many references to the glorious, preindependence Indian past when the Muslim rulers of princely states were exceedingly generous and renowned for their patronage of the hijras (see Lynton & Rajan, 1974).

Today the religious role of the hijras, derived from Hinduism, and the historical role of the eunuchs in the Muslim courts have become inextricably entwined in spite of the differences between them. Hijras are distinguished from the eunuchs in Muslim courts by their transvestism and their association with men. Muslim eunuchs dressed as males and associated with women and, unlike the hijras, were sexually inactive. More importantly, the role of hijras as ritual performers is linked to their sexual ambiguity as this incorporates the elements of the erotic and the ascetic; Muslim eunuchs had no such powers or roles. Today, the collapsing of the role of the hijra and that of the Muslim eunuchs leads to certain contradictions, but these seem easily incorporated into the hijra culture by hijras themselves; only the Western observer seems to feel the need to separate them conceptually.

The hijras, as human beings who are neither man nor woman, call into question the basic social categories of gender on which Indian society is built. This makes the hijras objects of fear, abuse, ridicule, and sometimes pity. But hijras are not merely ordinary human beings: As we shall see more clearly in the next chapter, they are also conceptualized as special, sacred beings, through a ritual transformation. The many examples that I have cited above indicate that both Indian society and Hindu mythology provide some positive, or at least accommodating, roles for such sexually ambiguous figures. Within the context of Indian social roles, sexually ambiguous figures are associated with sexual specializations; in myth and through ritual, such figures become powerful symbols of the divine and of generativity.

Thus, where Western culture strenuously attempts to resolve sexual contradictions and ambiguities, by denial or segregation, Hinduism appears content to allow opposites to confront each other without resolution, "celebrating the idea that the universe is boundlessly various, and . . . that all possibilities may exist without excluding each other" (O'Flaherty, 1973:318). It is this characteristically Indian ability to tolerate, even embrace, contradictions and variation at the social, cultural, and personality levels that provides the context in which the hijras cannot only be accommodated, but even granted a measure of power.

CHAPTER THREE

🐚 Emasculation Ritual Among the Hijras

"Why must you have this operation?" I asked Kamladevi. She answered by saying that the hijras have many powers, but only if they have the operation. She then told me this story:

> There once was a king who asked a hijra to show him her power. The hijra clapped her hands three times and immediately the door of the king's palace opened automatically, without anyone touching it. Then the king said, "Show me your power in some other way." By the side of the road there was a thorny cactus. The hijra just took the thorn of the cactus and emasculated himself. He showed the king that he had the power. The hijra just stood there with the blood oozing out and raised his hand with his penis in it. Then the king realized the power of the hijras.

As this tale so graphically illustrates, emasculation is the major source of the ritual power of the hijras. It is the source of their uniqueness and the most authentic way of identifying oneself as a hijra and of being so identified by the larger society. It is the emasculation operation that links the hijras to two of the most powerful figures in the Hindu religion, Shiva and the Mother Goddess, and it is emasculation that sanctions the hijras' ritual role as performers at marriages and births. If we accept the view (Hiltelbeitel, 1980) that the various kinds of eunuch priests who serve the Mother Goddess in India are ultimately impersonating Shiva, or Shiva in union with the Mother Goddess, this accounts for the third aspect of the hijra role, that is, their presence at temple festivals.

While hijras may worship at all Mother Goddess temples, as well as at Shiva temples, their major object of devotion is Bahuchara Mata, a version of the Indian Mother Goddess whose main temple is near Ahmedabad, in the state of Gujarat. Every hijra household has a small shrine dedicated to Bahuchara Mata, and ideally, every hijra should visit her temple. It is in the name of this goddess that hijras shower blessings of fertility and prosperity on a newborn child or a married couple. In Bahuchara's temple, hijras act as temple servants of the Mother Goddess, blessing worshipers who approach the deity and explaining the stories of Bahuchara to them. But it is only after the emasculation operation that hijras become vehicles of the Mother Goddess's power.

Bahuchara is one of the most important goddesses in the Gujarat region and is worshiped by a large part of the population, but she is particularly associated with male transvestism and transgenderism and thus has a special relation to the hijras. The origin of her worship is told in a legend well known throughout this area. Bahuchara was a pretty, young maiden in a party of travelers passing through the forest in Gujarat. The party was attacked by thieves, and, fearing that they would outrage her modesty, Bahuchara drew her dagger and cut off her breast, offering it to the outlaws in place of her virtue. This act, and her ensuing death, led to Bahuchara's deification and the practice of self-mutilation and sexual abstinence by her devotees to secure her favor. Bahuchara is also specifically worshiped by childless women in the hope of bearing a child, particularly a son (Mehta, 1947).

Many myths attest to Bahuchara's special connection to the hijras as impotent men who must undergo emasculation. In one story, a king prayed to Bahuchara for a son. She granted him his wish, but his son, named Jetho, was impotent. One night Bahuchara appeared in a dream and commanded Jetho to cut off his genitals, dress in female clothing, and become her servant. Jetho obeyed the goddess and from that time on, it is said, impotent men get a call from the goddess in their dreams to be emasculated. Indeed, there is a belief in Gujarat that impotent men who resist the call of Bahuchara to get emasculated will be born impotent for seven future births. Such is the price one pays for disobeying the goddess.

Another story that is an important part of hijra folklore illustrates even more dramatically the connections of Bahuchara to the hijras as impotent men who must undergo emasculation:

> Once there was a prince whose parents wanted to get him married. The boy did not want to get married, but his parents insisted. They selected this goddess as his wife, and the marriage took place. He was a very handsome boy, but the Mata was also a very beautiful lady. But after the marriage the husband and wife never joined together. On the first night, leaving the goddess alone in the nuptial room, the prince rode away into the forest. The goddess waited till dawn and felt very angry that her husband had left her. This went on for some months.
>
> The goddess felt very hurt and decided to investigate. So one night she followed him on a path to the forest clearing where the prince had been acting like the hijras. She was puzzled by what she had seen and returned home. When her husband returned, she said to him, "I want to ask you something, do not get angry at me. Don't you feel that you must have your wife by you?" Then the prince fell at her feet and told her, "Mother, if I had the urge for a wife and children I wouldn't have left you and gone away. I am neither a man nor a woman, and that is the truth."

The goddess got very angry and said, "They have spoiled my life by hiding the facts, and therefore your life will also be spoiled. Hereafter, people like you should be *nirvan* [undergo emasculation in order to be reborn]." So saying, she cut off his genitals. After cutting off his genitals she said, "People like you, who are going to have this nirvan, should call me at that time." After this the prince took on the form of a woman.

"So that is why," the storyteller continued, "whenever there is an (emasculation) operation to be performed, we call the Mata. During the operation she is with us and afterwards we live in her power."

THE OPERATION

The hijras call the emasculation operation nirvan. Nirvan is a condition of calm and absence of desire; it is liberation from the finite human consciousness and the dawn of a higher consciousness. The Hindu scriptures call the beginning of this experience the second birth, or the opening of the eye of wisdom. The hijras, too, translate nirvan as rebirth.

Emasculation is explicitly a rite of passage, moving the "nirvan" (the one who is operated on) from the status of an ordinary, impotent male to that of a hijra. Through the operation, the former, impotent male person dies, and a new person, endowed with sacred power (shakti), is reborn. Like other rites of passage described in the anthropological literature (van Gennep, 1960), this passage consists of three stages: In the first, a preparatory period, the person is separated from his former, male status. In the second, the liminal period, which corresponds to the recovery period after the operation, the person is in a liminal state, betwixt and between, no longer a male but not yet invested with the Mata's powers. In the third stage, in an elaborate ceremony, the individual becomes nirvan, a "real" hijra: The curse of impotence is removed and she is reborn as a vehicle of the Mata's powers.

Traditionally, the emasculation operation was performed as part of the initiation into the hijra cult, at the site of the Mata's temple. In 1888, however, this rite was outlawed by the Raja of the area, in spite of strong hijra protests against its prohibition (Bhimbhai, 1901). Today, the operation may be performed wherever hijras are in India. Although the operation was always performed in secret, today this is also necessary because emasculation is a criminal act under the Indian penal code (1981:1068–1069). In spite of its criminalization and strong government pronouncements against it, however, the operation does not seem to be dying out; indeed, it may even be increasing in frequency (Ranade, 1983).[1]

Ideally, the emasculation operation is performed by a hijra called a *dai ma* (midwife), a clear and strong symbolic statement of emasculation as rebirth. Meera, the dai ma whom I knew well, and whose personal narrative appears later, had a dream in which the Mata gave her the call to perform the operation. She, like other dai mas, has no medical training; she believes that she operates with the power of the Mata so that the result is not in her hands.

Prior to the operation there is a preparatory stage, in which the dai ma and the client seek the Mata's blessing in a *puja* (ritual of worship). A lamp made of rice flour mixed with milk is covered with *ghee* (clarified butter) and then burned. This is an offering to the Mata and is placed beside a picture of the deity. The same flour used in making the lamp is then mixed with brown sugar, cardamon, cashew nuts, and raisins—traditional offerings in Hindu pujas—and this becomes the *prasad* (sanctified food).[2]

The dai ma asks the prospective nirvan to look at the Mata's picture. If the Mata appears to be smiling and laughing, that is a sign that the operation will succeed. It is not necessary for the dai ma to see the Mata smiling her approval; it is sufficient for the client to do so. The dai ma then breaks a coconut; if it breaks evenly in half, the operation can take place. If it breaks unevenly, the operation will be postponed. Clients who do not receive these positive omens translate this into their own lack of courage, and some of the hijras I met had gone two and three times for this puja before the signs were propitious. Given the irreversible and life-threatening nature of the operation, it seems reasonable to interpret the puja as a way of attempting to resolve the ambivalence that anticipation of the operation generates.

If it is decided that the operation will take place, the client is isolated for a period of several days to a month. During this time she is not permitted to leave the house and all of her personal needs are taken care of by hijras. She is surrounded by a number of prohibitions, such as not looking in a mirror, not having sex, and not eating spicy food, which suggest the creation of a psychological state of mind of peace and passivity.[3]

The operation takes place at about 3:00 or 4:00 in the morning, a usual time in India for auspicious ceremonies, such as marriages. Only the dai ma and her assistant are present, along with the client. A photograph of the Mata is also placed in the room. While the client is still sleeping, the dai ma and her assistant perform a puja in front of the Mata's picture, to ask Bahuchara's blessing to make the knife effective. After this puja, the dai ma puts the knife out of sight in the hipfold of her sari. Then the sleeping client is awakened and given a drink of water.

The client's clothes and jewelry are removed; "they must be as naked as the day they were born." After being given a bath the client is ready for the operation. She is seated on a small stool and held from the back by the dai ma's assistant, who also crosses the client's hair over her face for her to bite on. The client's penis and scrotum are tightly tied with a string, so that a clean cut can be made. The client looks at the picture of Bahuchara and constantly repeats her name, Mata, Mata, Mata. This apparently produces a trancelike state during which the dai ma takes the knife from her sari and makes two quick opposite diagonal cuts. The organs—both penis and testicles—are completely separated from the body. A small stick is put into the urethra to keep it open. None of the hijras who had the operation told me that they felt any pain when the cut was made; it was variously described as "a small pinch" or "like an ant bite."

When the cut is made, the blood gushes out, and nothing is done is stem the flow.[4] Meera told me that the blood is considered the "male part" and should be drained off; she stated that this is why it is important to have a hijra dai ma do the operation. If others do it, for example, the "sex change" doctors who are available in Bombay, they try to stop the flow of blood, and this is considered less effective ritually, as well as medically harmful.

The hour just after the operation is considered to be the critical time during which the client's life or death is in the balance.[5] This uncertainly is conceptualized by the hijras as a "tug of war" between Bahuchara Mata, who gives life, and her elder sister, Chamundeswari, "the goddess who sits on a lion in Mysore," who takes life. During this hour the dai ma's assistant secretly disposes of the severed organs, which are placed in a pot and buried under a living tree.

A 40-day recovery period, similar to that of a woman after childbirth, follows the operation. This is the liminal period of the rite and includes behaviors and symbols that express the marginal status of the client at this time and also have a beneficial impact on her health. No stitches are made in the wound after the surgery, and the wound is healed through repeated applications of hot *gingili* (sesame seed) oil and heat to prevent infection. For the first 3 days the nirvan's diet is limited to tea with brown sugar, ghee, and farina with brown sugar. By the fourth day rice and vegetable curry are added to the diet; this induces vomiting, which brings out the "bad materials" left in the body. After the fourth day, *chapatis* (flat wheat bread) made with oil and onions may also be eaten, and this diet continues for the remainder of the 40 days. Pure sugar and wheat bread are also important elements in the diet of women who have given birth; both items are also part of the traditional badhai given to hijra performers, another illustration of the symbolic identification of childbirth with emasculation as rebirth.

At no time during the 40 days is the nirvan allowed to leave the room where the recovery is taking place, not even to go to the toilet. The hijra elders look after her so that all of her needs are met. Apart from the restricted diet, there are other prohibitions: The nirvan is not allowed to see milk (coffee and tea must be taken black), eat bananas, look in a mirror, comb her hair, or see a man. On the third day after the operation, she is given a bath. At the end of the 12th day, saffron is applied to the nirvan's face and her hair is washed; this is repeated on the 20th day, the 30th day, and the 40th day. This is the same ritual as for a woman who has given birth.

On the 40th day the reincorporation stage of the ritual takes place. The facial hair, which by now may have grown very long, is pulled out with tweezers. Turmeric is applied to the face and body and then washed off.[6]

The nirvan is dressed as a bride, and her hair parting, hands, and feet are decorated with mehndi, a red vegetable dye, as those of a bride. She is adorned with elaborate jewelry and new clothes. She is given some milk to drink and then, accompanied by a procession of hijras, late at night, is taken to a body of water—a lake, an ocean, or a temple tank. Now a puja is performed to the Mata; this includes pouring milk three times over the head of the nirvan and three times into the water. This is the final act in the ritual; only now is the nirvan free from the curse of impotence and reborn as a hijra, who can call on the Mata and act as a vehicle of her power.

It is the emasculation ritual that transforms an impotent male into a potentially powerful person. The renunciation of sex and the repression of sexual desire are, in the Hindu belief system, associated with the powers of the ascetic, and it is this association that is at the heart of the powers of the hijra. Hijras explicitly recognize this connection: They frequently refer to themselves as "other worldly" and as sannyasis, people who renounce society to live as holy wanderers and beggars. This vocation requires renunciation of material possessions, the social relations of caste, the life of the householder and family man, and the worldly attachments of normal men and women, most particularly, sexual desire *(kama)*. The importance of chastity to the religious ascetic is that sexual desire is seen as a distraction from spiritual purposes. Also, sexual activity, which involves a loss of semen, results in a loss of spiritual energy. The hijras' emasculation is their culturally defined "proof" that they do not experience sexual desire or sexual release as men. This proof of renunciation is the basis of the hijras' claims on society. As I suggested earlier, and as we shall see later, not all hijras, or even most, live up to this ascetic model; it is nevertheless the most powerful idea that legitimates their ritual functions in Indian society.

THE POWER OF EMASCULATION: CREATIVE ASCETICISM

In Indian reality, the hijra, as an impotent man, is "useless, an empty vessel, and fit for nothing" because he is unable to procreate. But in Hindu mythology, impotence can be transformed into the power of generativity through the ideal of *tapasya,* the practice of asceticism. *Tapas,* the power that results from ascetic practices and sexual abstinence, becomes an essential feature in the process of creation. Ascetics appear throughout Hindu mythology in procreative roles, and of these, Shiva is the greatest creative ascetic.

In one version of the Hindu creation myth, Shiva carries out an extreme, but legitimate, form of tapasya, that of self-castration.[7] Brahma and Vishnu had asked Shiva to create the world. Shiva agreed and plunged into the water for a thousand years. Brahma and Vishnu began to worry and Vishnu told Brahma that he, Brahma, must create and gave him the female power to do so. So Brahma created all of the gods and other beings. When Shiva emerged from the water, and was about to begin the creation, he saw that the universe was already full. So Shiva broke off his *linga* (phallus), saying that "there is no use for this linga," and threw it into the earth. His act results in the fertility cult of linga worship, which expresses the paradoxical theme of creative asceticism (see O'Flaherty, 1973:131). Consistent with the paradox of creative asceticism, it is the castrated phallus that is the embodiment of creative tapas and is associated with Shiva. The falling to earth of Shiva's linga in castration does not render him asexual, but extends his sexual power to the universe. O'Flaherty's comment about Shiva that "[the linga] becomes a source of universal fertility as soon as it has ceased to be a source of individual fertility" (1973:135) bears directly on the position of the hijras, who as emasculated men (whose organs are buried in the earth) nevertheless have the power to bless others for fertility.

This Hindu theme of creative asceticism provides an explanation of the positive role given the hijra in Indian society. Intersexed and impotent, themselves unable to reproduce, hijras can, through emasculation, transform their liability into a source of creative power that enables them to confer blessings of fertility on others. This identification with the powers of generativity is clearly associated with the ritual importance of hijras on occasions when reproduction is manifest—at the birth of a child—or imminent—at marriages, "which anticipate the reunion of male and female in marital sex" (Hiltelbeitel, 1980:168).

One of the most important links of the hijras (as eunuch-transvestites) to the creative asceticism of Shiva is mediated by Arjun, the hero of the Mahabharata, who is ultimately identified with Shiva (see Hiltelbeitel, 1980:156–157). Within the Mahabharata, there is a well-known story involving Arjun, which hijras point to as the story of their origin. Yudhistira, one of the Pandava brothers, is seduced by his enemies into a game of dice in which the stake is that the defeated party should go with his brothers into exile for 12 years and remain incognito for the 13th year. The Pandavas lose and go into exile as required. When the 13th year comes around, Yudhistira asks Arjun what disguise he will take up for the 13th year in order to remain undiscovered. Arjun answers that he will hide himself in the guise of a eunuch and serve the ladies of the court. He describes how he will spend the year, wearing white conch shell bangles, braiding his hair like a woman, dressing in female attire, engaging in menial works in the inner apartments of the queens, and teaching the women of the court singing and dancing. Gopi, the hijra who narrated the story that opens Chapter 2, also told me that whoever is born on Arjun's day, no matter where in the world, will become a hijra.

The theme of the eunuch is elaborated in several different ways in the Mahabharata, and it is Arjun who is the theme's main character. Arjun, in the disguise of eunuch-transvestite, participates in weddings and births and thus provides a further legitimation for the ritual contexts in which the hijras perform. At one point, for example, Arjun, in disguise, helps prepare the king's daughter for her marriage and her future role as mother-to-be. In doing this, he refuses to marry the princess himself, thus renouncing not only his sovereignty, but also the issue of an heir. His feigned impotence paves the way for the birth of the princess' child, just as it is the presence of the emasculated hijras at the home of a male child that paves the way for the child's virility and the continuation of the family line (Hiltelbeitel, 1980:166). The portrayal of Arjun in popular enactments of the Mahabharata in the vertically divided half-man/half-woman form, again highlights the identification of Arjun with the hijras and the identification of both with the androgynous Shiva.

The widespread association of the powers of asceticism with self-castration in Hindu mythology, particularly as associated with Shiva, provides the background through which we can understand the legitimacy of hijra emasculation, which is often conceptualized as self-castration. Indeed, the powerful imagery of the story that opens this chapter—that of the hijra flaunting her power through the upraised male organ—recalls vividly the fact that Shiva worship centers on the erect linga.

Still another important way in which the hijras identify with Shiva, the creative ascetic, is through their powers to bring rain. In Hindu mythology, the production and cessation of rain is a form of creation that results from tapas and chastity (O'Flaherty, 1973:42–43). One of the stories that the hijras tell about their own powers parallels precisely this theme in Hindu mythology as it involves ascetics:

One time there was a king in Hyderabad. There was a great drought during his reign. There were two hijras sitting in the road. . . . The people of the country went and told the king, "Do something about the drought, the whole country is famished and the people are dying." The king said, "What can I do? I can't do anything, you people must approach those two hijras who are sitting there by the roadside." The people spoke to the king with contempt and said, "Why should we ask them instead of you?" The king said, "If anything at all can be done, only they can do it, not me."

So then the king himself went to the hijras and told them, "There is a drought, people are dying, and the city wants rain. If you make rain, you can live here; if the rain doesn't come you must go outside the city to live." The two hijras who were sitting together were mother and daughter [elder and junior]. The daughter said, "Look, mother, so many people have come, let us tell some lies and run away." But the mother said, "Wait, please, I'll do something. God will look after me." So she took the cloth from the upper part of her body and dipped it in a cup of water and gave it to the people to take with them. Then, she said, the rain will come.

Immediately the lightning and thunder came and rain started pouring down; everyone was neck deep in water, it was such a heavy downpour. Then the mother said "enough" and the rain stopped. The people came back to see the hijras but they were gone, and the place they had been sitting in was submerged in water. So the king ordered that wherever hijras were seen in that city they should be respected, and that is why that city is full of hijras.

The centrality of this theme of generative power and its relation to emasculation is seen in what might be called a modern variant of this myth, in which hijras are given the power to make trains stop and start. In talking about the power of the hijras, I was told this story by a hijra elder:

Do you know why we hijras travel free on the trains from Poona northward? There is no rule to ask us for the train fare. Not even the Central Government can ask us. What happened was that there was a hijra who had just got operated on, she had become nirvan. The people, after the operation, put her on a train. It was just the seventh day after the operation. The people traveling in the train were making fun of her and bullying her. The ticket collector and the others made her get down from the train. On top of this, the ticket collector kicked her.

"Mata," she prayed, "if you're true, and it is true that you've given me back my life, and if my procession is to be done after 30 days, if you want to save my life, this train must not start from here. Then only will I realize you are the truth."

Then the signal was given and the train had to start, but it could not start. There was a big crowd around the hijra and the people asked her what had happened. She said, "I'm an old hijra and I've just got the operation done under the name of the Mata. If you want the train to start, put me back on the train." Then they made her sit in the train, but still the train would not start. Then she realized that she had prayed wrong, so she put a cloth on her head and prayed to Mata: "I want this train to start. Then only I can reach my place and also the other passengers can go without difficulty."

Then the train immediately started. From this time on there was no rule to ask a ticket from the hijras on any train. We can even dance in the train, beg in the train, nobody will say anything. From Poona onward, the whole of North India we can travel.

In many ways, then, do the hijras transform their impotent maleness and its associated lack of status into generative power through emasculation.

EMASCULATION AND WORSHIP OF THE MOTHER GODDESS

Whereas at a deeper level the hijras' claim to power is through the ritual sacrifice of the phallus, as the identification with Shiva suggests, at the more conscious and culturally elaborated level, it is the devotion to the

Mother Goddess (specifically Bahuchara, who is one variant of the Mother Goddess) that is the focus of the hijra community and the most explicitly acknowledged source of their powers.

In Hinduism, religious devotion is related to success and salvation and devotion is equated with submission, particularly in regard to the Mother Goddess. The Goddess is compelled to offer help when confronted with the "utter helplessness" and complete surrender of the devotee. This response is part of the larger "universal compulsion" in Hindu society not to deny anyone anything if they beg for it (Carstairs, 1956:160). This universal compulsion to offer help comes from an underlying fear of those whom one rejects: In Hindu mythology, to reject a woman, particularly a goddess, is especially fraught with danger (O'Flaherty, 1980:278–279). The realization of the Mother Goddess's power and the danger of denying her wishes are often explicitly given as the reason for her worship. This underlying fear in worship of the Mother Goddess helps to partly explain, or at least put into context, the willingness of the hijras to sacrifice their genitals to her in response to her call and as evidence of their devotion.

In Hindu mythology and ritual, the Mother Goddess is represented as having both a beneficent and a destructive aspect; this represents an ambivalence toward the real mother that is perhaps universal. But it is the "singular intensity and pervasiveness" of the destructive aspects of the Mother Goddess, which "nevertheless contain the seeds of salvation," that is particularly characteristic of Hindu India and provides the psychological and symbolic context of hijra emasculation.[8]

Hindu mythology—and hijra mythology—abound in images of the Mother Goddess engaging in aggressive acts—devouring, beheading, and castrating—a regular panoply of violent behavior that nevertheless also contains symbolism of initiation and rebirth. This theme is nowhere so obvious as in the myths and rituals of the hijras where rebirth emerges from emasculation. One of the forms taken by this theme is that of the Goddess as castrator of her mortal consort, as in the hijra myth cited earlier (pp. 25–26).

The Mother Goddess as castrator of her mortal consort appears frequently in Hindu mythology and ritual (O'Flaherty, 1980:81–86) and is an example of the many violent, destructive acts that the Goddess perpetrates on those who anger her. One of the sources of her anger, as in the myth cited here, is the rejection of her love by her consort, who attempts to evade her advances by explaining that she is like a mother to him. This suggests that the consort experiences the offering of the Goddess's love as an incestuous confrontation—a confrontation from which he must free himself. How does one flee the sexual advances of a mother? One way is to transform oneself into a child, a form of unmanning that is less severe than castration. Thus, we see that in the hijra myth above, the prince calls the Goddess "mother" in an attempt to seek protection from her sexual demands by retreating into the nonsexual condition of a child.

This attempt at flight from the mother exists in other Hindu myths, which parallel the hijra myth. One of the most popularly enacted episodes of the Mahabharata involves the celestial nymph Urvasi, who falls in love with and tries to sexually provoke Arjun. This episode describes the feminine beauty and grace of Urvasi, who, exhilarated by liquor and excited by desire, seeks out Arjun in his palace. Urvasi expresses her sexual desire for Arjun, but Arjun tries to fend her off by saying, "I bend my head unto thee, and prostrate myself at thy feet. Thou deservest my worship as my own mother and it behoveth thee to protect me as a son" (in Kakar, 1981:77). But this does not work for Arjun, any more than it does for the prince in the hijra myth. At Arjun's words, Urvasi gets furious and she curses him, saying that as he has "disregarded a woman pierced by the shafts of Kama, the god of love" he shall have to spend his time "as a dancer and destitute of manhood and scorned as a eunuch." Subsequently, this curse is modified so that Arjun only need become a eunuch for a year. In the hijra myth also, the goddess is satisfied with nothing less than the complete submission of her husband, represented by the total loss of manhood of the eunuch state.

Sudhir Kakar (1981), in his psychoanalytical study of Hinduism, family, and personality in India, sees in this story of Arjun and Urvasi the increasing helplessness of the child who desires the mother's comfort and care but is faced instead with her sexuality. In his rejection of her, she becomes dangerous and destructive, and it is only through the ultimate submission of emasculation that he can receive her protecting presence. In the hijra myth, also, we see that the Mother Goddess will protect the devotee, in this case her consort, but only after she has castrated him. She will give him life, but only after she has killed him. Whereas in the hijra myth—and symbolically in Urvasi's curse on Arjun—it is the Goddess who does the castrating, in many Hindu, and hijra, myths it is the devotee—son, consort, worshiper—who castrates himself. In this case, the conflict presented by the male's anxiety over his inadequacy to fulfill the sexual needs of the mother is resolved by self-castration in order to appease the mother.

There are many myths, rituals, religious roles, and themes in Hinduism that involve transgenderism in the form of transformations from male to female; asceticism, too, has been identified as a process of heightened identification with the mother. These all suggest that the hijras' emasculation ritual is only the extreme end of a more general continuum of ritual practices which derive their cultural meaning and psychological effectiveness from the Hindu cultural and social context. Kakar's analysis of the relation between Hindu culture and personality seems overgeneralized in its application to "Indian culture" or even Hindu culture, but it has, I believe, a certain cogency in relation to the hijras' emasculation ritual. Though not referring specifically to hijras, Kakar eloquently expresses the relation of hijra emasculation to Hindu culture and personality: He sees the many mythopoetic (and, I would add, ritual) manifestations of bisexuality in India as "express[ing] powerful, living forces in the individual unconscious—dark, ambivalent forces, repressed by most . . . that only the deviant, by means of . . . intense mental anguish, dares to act out" (1981:158).

Viewed in this context, then, the meanings and motivations of the hijras' emasculation ritual can be understood in terms of a wider pattern of culture and personality—motives and forces—in India, which it also serves to highlight. What might these forces and motives be, which are so strong that they do not merely appear in some distant age, or in symbolic imagery, but which are acted on by thousands of persons as part of a religious obligation that no government, from the British to the Indian, has been able to erase? How may the forces that motivate emasculation be understood and related to the cultural context in which they appear? Here again we can turn to the psychoanalytical perspective on Hindu culture suggested by Kakar for a partial answer. Kakar suggests that it is the particular form of the Indian "family drama" that is the source of these "powerful, living forces in the individual unconscious," which sometimes manifest themselves in extreme forms of transgenderism, such as those displayed by the hijras.[9] Whereas in all societies the image of the "bad mother" combines the aggressively destroying and the sexually demanding themes, in India it is in the sphere of unsatisfied erotic needs, in the seductive, provocative presence that the mother extends, that the possibility of psychosexual disturbance most centrally lies.

In India there are several social factors that dispose a young mother to turn the full force of her eroticism toward an infant son. These include the cultural requirement for the repression of a woman's erotic needs; her distance from her husband in the joint family; her increase in status and respect when she bears a son; the closeness between the mother and the son for a relatively prolonged childhood; and the relative abruptness of the break in this extremely close and intimate relationship between mother and son around the sixth or seventh year.

The young boy's ego cannot cope with the sexual demands of the mother nor can he happily accept the separation from his mother that his rejection of her entails. The son's response to the mother's overpowering demands and his simultaneous desire to retain her protection result in a fear of the "devouring mother." This leads to a "vicious circle that spirals inward in the Indian unconscious: mature women are experienced as sexually threatening to men; this contributes to 'avoidance behavior' in marital sexual relations; this in turn causes women to extend a provocative sexual presence towards their sons, and this eventually produces adult men who fear the sexuality of mature women" (Kakar, 1981:95).

The mother's incestuous demands on the son are too strong; they lead him to want to avoid them at all costs, even at the cost of his manhood. But the rejected mother becomes dangerous, and abandonment by her is unthinkable, so close and necessary is her presence. Hence the worship of the Goddess as mother. For it is the Goddess, dangerous as she is, who nevertheless brings blessings, ultimate salvation, and rebirth, just as it is the mother, potentially dangerous as she is in abandoning her son, who nevertheless is the object of the son's deepest longings for reconciliation with her. This, Kakar holds, is the significance of the theme of the devouring mother and the many rituals and extreme devotion shown her in India—a devotion that prominently includes the most abject submission of the (male) devotee and involves both symbolic and, as with the hijras, actual castration.

The variety of mythopoetic and ritual expressions of transgenderism in Hinduism, including, of course, hijra emasculation, suggests that a number of different mechanisms are operating in the devotee's attempts at reconciliation with the mother through the worship of the Goddess. All involve the male's attempt to remove his masculinity—that which he vaguely perceives to be the basis of his conflict with his mother. In one case, as we saw above, the male attempts to infantilize himself in order to flee the mother; in other cases, devotion to the Mata involves transvestism; and in still other cases, in myth and symbolism involving self-castration, the son attempts to remove his masculinity in an even more explicit way. Desperate for reconciliation with the mother, longing for that fusion which represents salvation, the (male) devotee, in rituals ranging from transvestism to emasculation, proves his submission and is thereby assured of the nurturing and life-giving presence of the mother that he desires. In the castration ritual, the nirvan finds a way to both flee the sexually demanding mother and be reconciled with her. The hijra myth makes that clear: After castrating the prince, the Goddess promises her protection but the protection is only offered—and experienced by the hijras—if the castration takes place.

The hijras call their emasculation ritual "rebirth"; this illuminates the view of the ritual as part of a struggle against death, which, because of the "Hindu family drama," takes a characteristically Hindu form of a desire for fusion with the mother.[10] It is this desire for fusion with the mother as a vehicle for the struggle against death that gives Mother Goddess worship such power in India, where the separation from the mother is experienced as a kind of death. As the hijras say, "It is the Mata who gives us life, we live only in her power." In emasculation, the hijra, as a devotee of the Goddess, achieves the ultimate identification with the mother, thereby reducing his anxiety about separation from her—the source of all love and life. "The only unbearable harm that the Goddess can inflict on the worshiper is to abandon him. This, not mutilation, is the source of devastating grief" (O'Flaherty, 1980:280). It is clear that this is true for those hijras who undergo emasculation.

In the hijra emasculation ritual, then, many things are being enacted at once. On one level, the operation transforms impotence into generativity, an "empty vessel, good for nothing" into a powerful figure who inspires both awe and fear (though also mockery and abuse). By giving up their useless male organ, hijras are gaining the important power of generativity. At another level, the ritual is resolving, by culturally patterned acting out, the conflicts over the incestuous mother. At still another level, the hijras' identification with the Goddess through sacrifice of their genitals assures them of her life-giving presence, warding off death.

The psychological motivations of the hijra emasculation ritual are reinforced by more material concerns. As noted earlier, emasculation is not only a religious obligation, but it also distinguishes true hijras from "fake" hijras. This gives the hijra community a way to protect its economic monopoly over certain ritual occasions. This is an extremely important consideration in a society where such economic niches are crucial for survival and where, of course, the social structure of the caste system provides a model for occupational exclusivity. It is to these issues that I turn in the next chapter.

CHAPTER FOUR

🌺 Social Organization and Economic Adaptation

Three thousand eunuchs wearing garish makeup, gaudy saris, bangles, and bells are holding their national convention here. They have gathered for a ten-day festival to proclaim their cult's new national guru. Their former guru died as a result of the Union Carbide gas leak in 1984.
BHOPAL, INDIA (AP)

Earlier we saw how the hijras function as a religious cult; now we will see that they also function like a caste, that is, a community organized around a traditional occupation, through which they are integrated with the larger society. Like other subcultures outside the mainstream of society, both in India and elsewhere, the hijra community replicates many of the beliefs, roles, and behaviors of the larger society. Thus, the themes of hierarchy, respect, respectability, and reciprocity are important here as they are in Indian society in general. In this chapter I look at the social organization and cultural norms of the hijra community, showing how these serve them well as a means of adapting to the larger society and permit them not only to survive but to flourish.

SOCIAL ORGANIZATION

The census of India does not count hijras separately, so it is difficult to make reliable estimates of their numbers; the most common unofficial figure cited is 50,000 nationwide.[1] Hijras live predominantly in the cities of North India, where they find the greatest opportunity to perform in their traditional roles, but small groups of hijras are found all over India, in the south as well as the north.

The effective working group of the hijra community is the local level communal household, consisting of anywhere from 5 to 15 members. Even in a location peripheral to hijra culture like Bastipore, there are at least five such communes; in larger centers of hijra culture like Delhi, Bombay, Ahmedabad, or Lucknow, there may be scores. Hijras sometimes live alone, but even then, they keep close ties with the hijra communes in their locality. Whereas a few hijras live alone because of a temperamental preference for the isolated life, others do so because by virtue of their talents and ambitions they make an excellent living and feel secure enough in their work to want to be independent of the restraints of communal living. A hijra who lives on her own does not have to share all of her income, but only that part of it she earns when working with a hijra group. And some hijras who have acquired "husbands" live with these men in a house of their own.

Hijra households are structured around a core of relatively permanent members. But at any given time every household also contains some transients who have come from other places to stay for variable periods of time. Sometimes these visiting hijras are short-term guests who have come from other cities for a social visit. More often they are younger members of the community who, feeling "fed up" with their life in one place, decide to try somewhere else for a while.

The hijra household is organized as a commune: The members contribute part or all of their earnings to the household, and they may also help with household chores. In return they get a roof over their heads, food, protection from the police, and a place to carry on their business, whether this is performing, begging, or prostitution. Thus, the hijra household functions as both a residential and an economic unit. The hijras living in a household are subject to its rules, more or less strict depending on the region.

Crosscutting the distribution of hijra households in space is another dimension of social organization, which divides the hijras into "houses." (These should not be confused with households. Households are communal living groups; houses are symbolic descent groups.) Every hijra joins the community as a member of the house of her sponsoring elder or guru. These houses are a structural principle of organization; they do not have a spatial dimension. They may be thought of as symbolic descent groups, like clans. Members of the same houses can, and do, live in different households. There are seven named houses into which all hijras are divided: Laskarwallah, Chaklawallah, Lalanwallah, Bendi Bazaar, Poonawallah, Ballakwallah, and Adipur. These named divisions exist with some slight variation from region to region all over India. The main function of the houses appears to be to divide the community into groups in order to facilitate intracommunity organization. The houses are not ranked, and there does not seem to be any advantage in joining one over another. Indeed, it is difficult to find any meaningful distinctions among them, though each house has its own story of its founding (about which most hijras are not knowledgeable) and some rules special to it. For example, members of a certain house may not be allowed to wear a certain color clothing. When a hijra dies, it is the elders of her house who arrange and pay for her funeral.

Nor are the hijra houses exclusively associated with any particular way of earning a living. Members of all houses engage in all kinds of work. Hijras speak of the house as analogous to a family: "Just as a mother will have ten children, each of whom will do a different profession, so it is among us. Like a mother with ten children one child will do business [prostitution], one child will do badhai, one child will go to the shops [to beg], but the whole house is under one roof. Like a family we also have people in the same house doing different things."

In the division of the hijra community into houses, an analogy is also made with *jati* (caste). As one hijra explained it to me: "There is only one caste of eunuchs all over India, all over the world. But for convenience, like in one family there are six brothers, it's like that, we have kept these houses also." Hijras also describe their houses "like the five fingers on the hand" or like different nations with the same origin, such as England and America.[2] This organization replicates the pattern of jatis within the caste system or lineages within a jati; it emphasizes both the segmented branching and the related nature of the houses; and it helps reinforce the community's solidarity as it assimilates to its structure the relationships of real families, lineages, and caste.

Each house within a region has a leader, called a *naik* (chief), and it is the leaders of the houses in a region who get together nationally from time to time to decide on policy for the hijras in India as a whole or to celebrate some event of national significance to them, such as the death anniversary of a famous hijra leader. But the most important functions of the naiks are at the level of the local community, which might be thought of as a city, like Bastipore, or, in a large city like Bombay or Delhi, an area of the city. For any important occasion within a locality, whether the initiation of a new recruit or the resolution of a dispute, the naiks, as the heads of the seven houses locally, get together in a *jamat,* or a "meeting of the elders."

The term *jamat,* along with its functions, derives from a Muslim cultural pattern. The jamat is the coming together of the elders to make decisions for the group and thus is similar to a village *panchayat* (council). "From the Muslims we hijras got the idea that we should have our own seven houses where our leaders come together to sit in a jamat and decide on the good things and the bad things," is the way one hijra put it. Another said that the hijra organization is modeled after the Muslims where "all people come together for social occasions and the men come together to decide things. Like the Muslim jamat, we hijras also spread a white towel on the floor and keep a plate with *pan* (paan) leaves [the traditional Indian offering of hospitality] and fruit on that, and make our decisions."

One of the most important decisions made by a hijra jamat is sanctioning hijras who violate community rules. One of the most important norms in every hijra commune is honesty with respect to property. With so much geographic mobility among hijras, it is necessary that individuals be trustworthy, for if something is found missing from the household or from an individual's private possessions, the accusations and conflict that follow are very disruptive to the harmony of the household and, ultimately, to its economic success. Furthermore, in their performances for marriages and births, hijras may need to enter the houses of their audiences; therefore, maintaining a reputation for honesty is necessary for their profession. Drinking alcoholic beverages is not specifically against hijra norms, but it is not generally done by "respectable" hijras, and drunken, abusive behavior is not tolerated in a "good" house.

The sanctions for misbehavior may be fines of varying amounts. For serious infractions of the rules, a hijra's hair is cut as a way of publicly stigmatizing her within the community since hijras are obliged to wear their hair long like women. In the most serious cases, such as abusing or assaulting one's guru, the sanction may be expulsion from the community. If a hijra has been expelled from the community, she can be readmitted only in a meeting of the jamat.

Expulsion from the hijra community is a powerful sanction. The outcaste is not welcome in any hijra household; nor can she move to another city and try to join another household, as her reputation will follow her. One of the functions of the nationwide social network of naiks is that it works as an effective blacklist. Because both urban and rural space is divided into territories allotted to different hijra houses, it is difficult for an unaffiliated hijra to find a place to work that is not already owned by some hijra group.

Beyond the organization of the hijras into households and into houses, there are no caste or other ascribed social differences that are formally significant in hijra social organization. In some places, such as Gujarat, Hindu and Muslim hijras live in different communes, but today in most cities Hindu and Muslim hijras—and Christians as well—live peaceably in the same households. Nineteenth-century reports claim that individuals "become Muslim" when they join the hijra community (Ibbetson et al., 1911:331).[3] Although I found no formal procedure for this, nor any formal requirement that they do so, Islam has an obvious influence on many of the patterns of contemporary hijra social organization and culture. For example, the founders of the seven houses are all said to have been Muslim, and each of the present leaders of these houses in Delhi and Bombay, as well as the major national leaders, is Muslim. Many of the Hindu hijras I met said that they planned to "become Muslims," though none ever did that I knew of. Many Hindu hijras, as well as Muslims, said that they keep the Muslim fast for *Ramadan,* describing it as "our most important holiday," but, in fact, only the Muslims did so. Whereas in the past Muslim rulers of Indian states were generous patrons of the hijras, the main patrons of hijra performances today are Hindus. As one Hindu hijra said, "We are Muslims, but we earn from the Hindus."

The reverse situation, that of Muslims becoming Hindus, did not seem to occur at all, and what seems a great contradiction—the prestige accorded Islam in a community that centers on the worship of a Hindu goddess—did not seem to pose any problem for the hijras I met. Nor did any of the Muslim hijras I knew seem to have any problem belonging to a community whose religious aspect centers on devotion to a Hindu goddess and other rituals that are contrary or even offensive to Islam.

I am not altogether clear why this bias in favor of Islam exists. It may have something to do with the importance of eunuchs in the courts of the Muslim princely states. Hijras often talk nostalgically of the honor and respect they were given by the Muslim rulers in the native states during the British period (1765–1947). They compare this to what they see as a decline in respect for them in the present era. The egalitarian ideal of Islam, as compared with the hierarchical nature of the Hindu caste system, was also frequently and favorably mentioned to me as an explanation of hijra inclinations toward Islam.

This integration of Muslim and Hindu cultural elements within the hijra community is not new. Nineteenth-century accounts, for example, allude to hijras having Hindu names and worshiping Hindu goddesses while reporting that "although hijras come from any caste upon emasculation [they] take the names of Musselmanee [Muslim] women, and as such, live and are buried." In Gujarat, the British noted that Muslim and Hindu hijras lived separately and did not eat together, though in all other respects they were alike, whereas in Poona, in the state of Maharashtra, Hindus of all castes and Muslims lived together (Preston, 1987:377). It may be that the restricted interaction in Gujarat is related to the fact that this is the location of the major temple of the hijra Goddess, and thus hijra behavior there is more constrained by Hindu orthodoxy. In his historical study of hijra land rights, Preston (1987) notes that because the hijras drew on all sectors of society for their membership, their community was characterized by religious and communal syncretism as they "borrowed rather freely from the cumulative social backgrounds of those who joined." This was a source of great confusion to the British (as it may be to the Western reader), who were anxious to "nail down the Indian social order into fixed categories," but it does not appear to be a problem for the hijras.

Members from all castes are welcomed into the hijra community, and hijras do not follow any castelike rules regarding purity or pollution in connection with, for example, intercaste dining. A study of 100 hijras in Delhi counted about 50% of the Hindu sample coming from scheduled (previously called untouchable) castes (Ranade, 1983:75). On the other hand, the caste origins of the hijras I worked with in Bastipore, Delhi, Bombay, and Chandigarh all indicated a middle or low, but not a scheduled, caste background. Many of the hijras I spoke with specifically commented on the inappropriateness of caste distinctions within a group that is itself so much on the fringes of society. In any case, like others who take on "other-worldly" roles by breaking with their families, the hijras have renounced not only their own caste status but the relevance of caste as well. This is precisely parallel to the essence of initiation in many Hindu religious sects, which also deemphasize caste and follow a policy of open recruitment (van der Veer, 1987).

Nor are class lines clearly drawn within the hijra community, although there is definitely a prestige, or ranking, system based on how individuals earn a living and to some extent, their standard of living. The major division here is between those hijras who engage only in the prestigious work of badhai and those who earn a living through prostitution. Reputation, based on personal qualities such as honesty, generosity, wisdom, fairness, and amiability, is an important basis for self-esteem, but it does not operate in any structurally significant way within the hijra community. The major formal principle of hijra social organization, which does indeed establish a ranking system, is that of seniority, judged not by age but by the time of entry into the hijra community.

THE HIJRA HIERARCHY: GURUS AND CHELAS

Seniority, as the major principle of social organization and social control in the hijra community, is expressed in a hierarchy of *gurus* (literally, teachers) and *chelas* (literally, disciples).[4] Every hijra has a guru, and initiation into the community occurs only under the sponsorship of a guru.

When a new recruit is about to join the community, her sponsor, who will become her guru, calls a jamat to which the leaders of the seven houses are invited. A plate with pan leaves is placed on the floor.[5] Each person sits and covers her head with the end of her sari or a scarf. Then the elders ask with one voice: "Whose jamat is this?" The guru sponsoring the initiate answers with her own name and the name of the house she belongs to. The elders then ask the newcomer if she is willing to become the chela of that guru. When she answers affirmatively, the sponsoring guru puts five rupees on the plate that holds the pan leaves. This is the public confirmation that establishes the guru's claim on the individual now recognized as her chela. The elders then clap their hands in the traditional hijra manner and shout *"deen, deen, deen"* (the Urdu word for religious duty). This is the seal of initiation, and the newcomer is now a formal member of the community. She is given a new, female name by her guru and vows to obey the guru and the community rules. This is similar to the essence of initiation in many Hindu religious sects, in which the initiate loses his secular name and that of his *gotra* (lineage) and takes on a new religious name and clan name of his guru. In this way a spiritual family is formed by the disciples of a guru (van der Veer, 1987).

As part of the initiation, the new member pays a sum of 150 rupees (about $12) to her guru, which is divided among the naiks at the jamat. This sum is called *dand* (dund), which literally means a "fine" but appears to operate more like a fee, which essentially gives the chela the right to work "in the name of her guru." Because gurus control work, both through their house's "ownership" of the territories where hijras work, as well as acting as employment agents—whether for ritual performances or prostitution or asking for alms—the connection of guru to chela is the foundation of the economic benefits gained by joining the hijra community. Freelancing by hijra imposters, or by hijras who do not have a guru's permission to work in a particular territory, is strictly controlled; trespassers, if caught, will be beaten or fined or both.

Munni, a hijra performer from Chandigarh, related several incidents to me where this had happened:

> One time, when I was with my guru, a troupe from a different area came into our territory, so we had a big fight. That troupe was beaten by us and we cut their hair also. This happens a thousand times. Once some troupe tried to come into our area in Sector 9. We all went to that place and had a big fight. We broke someone's leg, someone's arm, and someone's head. Someone's face was broken, and a lot of injuries were suffered. We had a stabbing, also, with knives. Everybody has to fight for the respect of the territory. My chelas, they will also fight for me until death to hold this territory.

The chela is tied to the guru economically in another way, because the guru, not the new chela, pays the 150-rupee initiation fee. Thus, the new chela starts out in the community owing her guru this sum. Ideally, a hijra remains a chela of her original guru for life, and because gurus accept only chelas who are willing and able to earn for them, they have every expectation that they will easily recoup the small initiation fee, and much more, in return. However, procedures have developed for changing gurus (by which one automatically changes one's house), and these procedures ensure that the guru will always come out a financial winner.

If a chela wants to change her guru, she must compensate the original sponsor for doing so. The assumption here is that the original guru has not only invested the initiation fee of 150 rupees, but also other monies in the form of gifts, as well as the time and energy in training the chela and setting her up in some economically profitable enterprise. The guru must get her investment back.

Thus, when a chela wants to change gurus, she must pay her original guru double the initiation fee, that is, 300 rupees. This fee is paid by the new guru, not by the chela herself, thus incurring a new cycle of debt. If after changing to a second guru, the chela again wants to change, her new guru will have to pay double the price—600 rupees to the former guru—and so on. The changing of gurus occurs in a ritual similar to the initiation. The chelas discards her old clothes, giving them to the former guru, and puts on a new set of clothes—petticoat, blouse, and sari—given to her by the new guru. As one hijra said, again making an analogy with the family, "This is like your parents give you a new dress after your marriage. Whatever you are wearing at the time, when you leave the old guru you have to give to her. Then whatever the new guru gives you, you must wear that."

The provisions made in the hijra community for changing gurus appear to be a wise adaptation to the inevitable conflict of personalities, particularly to the conflicts over earning and sharing, which are also characteristic of the Hindu joint family; here, however, unlike a family, change is possible, though expensive. Generally speaking, changing houses is looked down on, and chelas who make too many changes may be considered to be more trouble than they are worth. On the other hand, a guru may be willing to pay 600 or 1,200 rupees, or even more, for someone else's chela who she feels will be a good earner and pay an ample return on her investment.

While the guru-chela relationship has important, perhaps even critical, economic dimensions, it is also more than merely an economic relationship, at least ideally. The guru-chela relationship is both modeled after and a substitute for the family relationships that the hijra has renounced. In addition, it has the quality of the traditional guru-chela relationship of spiritual master and disciple. Because the guru-chela relationship is modeled after traditional family relationships—and serves many of the same functions as these relationships—it is often highly idealized. Although involving hierarchy and a strong economic component, a guru-chela relationship is always conceived of as reciprocal, multidimensional, and mutually satisfying. The guru is expected to take care of the chela as a parent does of a child (chelas are often referred to and addressed as daughters or children), and the chela is expected to be loyal and obedient to the guru. As in families, too, the guru, as elder, is the center of the chela's social relationships. Through a web of fictive kinship a chela automatically takes on the "relatives" of her guru, thereby expanding the chela's social, emotional, and economic life.

The importance of the guru to the chela is illustrated by a conversation I had with Kamal, a hijra performer in Bastipore whose guru lived in Bombay. Kamal had moved back to Bastipore, partly because it was her home and partly because she had tired of the restrictions of respectable hijra life in Bombay:

In these Bombay houses there are so many jobs to do . . . like cooking. I never wanted to do those jobs, I was more interested in going around. After coming home from the whole day job, then I had to cook and do other household chores. And if I did the household jobs during the day, then I wouldn't have time to go out and the whole day would be lost.

In these houses with the gurus things are very strict. If you don't keep your hair covered with your sari, if you don't cook properly, if the house is not spotlessly clean, for all these things they give you trouble. You can't just throw your dirty clothes down anywhere, you have to wash them immediately and hang them up. If you don't serve on the proper dishes, they will shout, "What, are you a man that you cannot do these things properly?" So, for these reasons, I came away from my guru's house back here to live on my own. I can earn my living with my feet and prefer to live independently.

Still, I have good relations with my guru and send her money from time to time. I visit her in Bombay also, and whenever anyone comes from there, she always inquires for me.

I then asked Kamal, since she was doing so well on her own, why she could not do without the guru altogether.

Never, it cannot be. Even though my guru did not teach me anything—all the singing and dancing I learned on my own—you cannot be without a guru. Just suppose you are without a mother, how will you have a position in society. Everyone will say, "See, she doesn't have a mother." Only because you have a mother can you live in this world, dress properly, go about. If you don't have a mother, how can you come to exist?

It's like that with us, if we don't have a guru. Just as with you people [nonhijras], a daughter is known by her mother, we are known by our guru. How can we live like this in a sari without a guru? It is not possible. To belong to the hijra community you must have a guru; otherwise, you will have no respect in society.

While it is clear from Kamal's words, as well as from interviews with other hijras, that putting spatial distance between oneself and one's guru lessens the economic responsibility to the guru, the idealization of the emotional, social, and material dimensions of the guru-chela relationship replicate, and are drawn from, the ideology of the Hindu extended joint family. The following comment from Alan Roland (1982:239) is a striking aspect of hijra social organization: In the Hindu joint family "the person lower in the status relationship within the kinship or work group needs the nurturance and protection of the one higher up, and will therefore show the proper deference and loyalty to the superior in exchange for consideration and being taken care of." The emotional need for such a relationship is even more evident among the hijras than in many Indian families today because the hijra commune is both a kinship group and a work group. One has, therefore, so much more to gain or to lose by fulfilling, or failing to fulfill, the expectations of others. Because these relationships among hijras only imitate family relations, hijras may be aware of their greater fragility; this helps explain why they are so explicit about the need for maintaining the obligations inherent in such relationships.

This emotional and economic dependence on one's group shows itself among hijras in a way similar to Indians' talk about their families: a strong reluctance to criticize one's elders and the regular verbal presentation of the guru-chela relationship as a highly idealized one. On one occasion, I asked Savitri, a hijra who was living separate from her guru, whether this was due to some quarrel or perhaps to a flaw in the personality of her guru. In connection with this, I also asked her if there were any ways she thought hers could have been a better guru and if that would have kept her from leaving. Savitri regarded my asking her to consider her guru's shortcomings with amazement, giving me the same shocked look I had often encountered when I asked people in India to talk about the possibility of their parents having shortcomings. Savitri answered:

> We never think of such things as which guru is best or of any shortcomings in our guru. We never think of that at all. One guru might give his disciples diamonds to wear, while our guru might give us copper or brass to wear. Whatever it is, we accept it. We never think of some other guru.
>
> Once we join a group, we're not concerned with what others do. The guru is like a mother to us. When we go out and return to the house we cover our head and touch the guru's feet, we bend down at his feet and kiss them and the guru gives us his blessing [a common way of showing respect for significant elders in India]. In the morning when we wake the guru, we kiss his feet and wake him up. When someone goes out begging, or we go to perform with our drum, we will always touch the feet of the guru before we go.

Hierarchical relationships, though mutually satisfying in many respects, do not always run smoothly, however, whether within familes or between hijra gurus and their chelas. Underlying the verbal idealizations of the guru-chela relationship there is often ambivalence, particularly among the junior members of the hierarchy. This ambivalence, however, is rarely handled by outright rebellion, as any assault on the guru would be punished by expulsion from the community.

As noted earlier, the guru-chela relationship provides not only an economic nexus to the community, important as that is, but a social one as well. Chelas of the same guru are "like sisters," and the kinship relations of the guru become relations of the chela. Thus, a guru's guru becomes a "granny" (mother's mother), and a guru's "sister" becomes an "aunty." These social networks are the foundation for the geographic mobility that is so characteristic in the hijra community, especially among its younger members, and so useful as an element of economic adaptation. This ever-expanding network of fictive kin permits a hijra to move from place to place, because it provides a welcoming environment and a base from which to earn a living wherever she goes. It also means that if there is some quarrel in a hijra household, especially where some latent anger might be potentially directed against the guru, some of the household members can temporarily shift to other households and let the conflict die down, before it can move to some irreparable breach.[6]

Still another advantage in joining the hijra community is the economic security it provides in illness or old age. An ill or elderly hijra in good standing can always find a place to stay in some hijra household. When she gets too old or too ill to work outside the house, she can earn her keep by performing small domestic chores within the household to whatever extent she is able. Whereas some ill or very elderly hijras may return to their natal families (some hijras do continue these ties, though many do not) to recover or to die, those hijras who have nowhere else to go must turn to the hijra community for aid.

This dependence of hijras on their community is entirely consistent with the values and organizational principles of Indian society: a willingness of individuals to submit to hierarchy, a combining of resources and expenditures (as in a joint family) as a means of economic adaptation, and a conviction that there is no security without a group. This holds for men as well as women in India, so that most hijras, regardless of the extent of their feminine orientation, find these values and organizational principles congenial and appropriate in cultural terms.

These values and organizational principles may seem very restricting to Americans, for whom independence and individualism are culturally valued ideals. But for hijras, being independent of the group means not freedom, but social suicide. In India, especially in such a marginal subculture as the hijras, the societal values of hierarchy, dependence on the group, and tight social networks built on reciprocity remain paramount. Group cohesion, not individualism, is adaptive. This helps explain why hijras hardly ever think seriously about severing their ties with the community and going out on their own, although younger ones often complain (to outsiders) about the restrictions and hardships of their life.

EARNING A LIVING: TRADITIONAL OCCUPATIONS

Like every caste, the hijras are primarily associated with a traditional occupation, which helps ensure individuals an economic niche within Indian society. This economic niche has a spatial dimension. In cities, each hijra guru has control over a particular neighborhood, and her chelas ceaselessly comb the houses and maternity hospitals of their "territories" to find out when and where a child, particularly a male child, has been born or where a marriage is about to take place. When they come across such a home, they put their distinctive mark, or sign, on the doorway in chalk. Each hijra house has such a mark, and this is a notice to other hijras that this location is "taken" and no other group may peform there. The group marking the house returns on the baby's naming ceremony day (the 12th or 20th day after birth, depending on the health of the mother and child), or may come back on some other specifically requested day. In some cases, a family will call the hijras to come, but this is usually not necessary, as they invariably show up on their own.

A hijra performing group ranges from three to five or more persons. A performance may be merely a short song and a blessing; a more elaborate performance involves singing, dancing, and clowning. In both cases, these performances are always accompanied by someone playing the dholak, the two-sided drum, which is necessary to their dancing and singing. In some hijra performing groups, the person who plays the dholak is a hijra; if the group does not have a drummer of its own, it will hire a nonhijra for this role. The dholak is sacred to the hijra community, and the drummer's role within the group is a prestigious one.

In each area of India there are more or less fixed payments that the hijras demand for their performances, varying somewhat according to the social class of the family. These payments include both a sum of money and certain goods—sweets, used or new clothing, and perhaps rice or some other grain. Hijras are reputed to never be satisfied with what they are offered, and a certain amount of negotiation may go on between the family and the hijras, but people most often try to send the hijras away satisfied because of the fear or shame of their abuse if they are angered.

It is in the hijra demands that they be allowed to perform, and in their negotiations over payment, that one sees the ambivalence toward the hijras and the ways hijras use this ambivalence for their own economic advantage. In Chapter 1 I suggested the element of extortion sometimes experienced by hijra audiences. Here I will elaborate on this theme as it relates to hijra economic adaptation.

G. Morris Carstairs, in describing the hijra presence in the village in Rajasthan that he studied, calls them "an abomination in the sight of respectable people [because of] their shamelessness in parading their perversion before the public gaze. . . . They would perform travesties of women's songs and dances, and when, as invariably happened, they were abused and threatened, they would utter obscentities and expose themselves in a grossly indecent manner until the wedding party flung coins to them in order to be rid of them" (1957:60–61). While a certain Victorian righteousness pervades Carstair's language, there is no question that he gives an accurate sense of the negative feelings some Indians have toward the hijras. I found some of this negativity, but it was not by any means universal or, as Carstairs suggests, so intense. On the other hand, one does see, from time to time, articles in the newspapers about a rampage of hijras abusing the residents in some locality where their demands to perform or collect alms were not met.

The effectiveness of extortion through public shaming by hijras is legendary. In the early 19th century a series of letters between British district officers who were trying to put an end to many "immoral" aspects of Indian culture recorded that "the Hijera . . . proceeds to the different villages and demands payment from the Ryots [peasants], who, forthwith, produce the pice [money], under the dread founded, apparently of experience, of a refusal to render prompt payment, being followed by the whole of the wretches lifting up their Soogras [petticoats] and outraging the feelings of the females of his family, by the most shameless and abominable exposure of person." It was further noted that hijras resort to "still more disgusting and cruel" practices for the purpose of extorting money:

"For the Hijera is supposed not only by the common people, but even by intelligent Brahmins, to have the power of detecting impotence. This belief affords a ready means of extorting money from the married and childless, who, aware of the contempt and derision which a charge of impotency, coming from such a quarter would subject them to, are glad to purchase secrecy at any price" (Preston, 1987:378).

The British authorities attempted to criminalize such "indecent" practices and the extortion associated with them but with little avail. The combination of Indian tolerance for such practices and the obvious economic advantages to the hijras of engaging in them countered British efforts at change, and not only had little effect on the practices, but also little deterrent effect on hijra recruitment.

This extortion is also associated with a second traditional and public occupation of hijras, that of asking for alms, either from passersby on city streets or, more commonly, from shopkeepers. In every city, specific groups of hijras establish their exclusive areas for this activity, each area being under the control of a naik, or local guru. The areas are further subdivided chronologically by days of the week; and a structured round of alms seeking by different hijra groups is followed. In some cases, shopkeepers, anxious to avoid the kind of shameless and abusive behavior described above, settle on a "contract" with one hijra group; they agree to give a fixed sum of money weekly, or even monthly, to avoid harassment by this hijra group and others. On festival days, the hijras will expect, and receive, more than the usual sum.

In some communities, the hijra procession that follows the "birth" of a new hijra also passes through the main street of a locality, demanding some extra contribution from the shopkeepers along the way and threatening them with the curse of impotence if they do not give.

Earning a living asking for alms is considered unpleasant work by most hijras: In order to earn an adequate amount, one must ceaselessly roam the streets, which is both tiring physically and makes one vulnerable to the ridicule or abuse of the public, especially small boys and rowdies. Begging can be a steady source of income, however, particularly in larger cities, and is consistent with, and even reinforces, the hijra self-image as religious mendicants.

This self-image, and the hijra claims to entitlement to perform their traditional occupations, finds historical support in the edicts of Indian states, which officially granted them these rights. In each district of the Bombay Presidency (an area under British rule, covering what are now the states of Maharashtra and Gujarat), there was one hijra who was the holder of a hereditary right to collect food and small sums of money from each agricultural household in a stipulated area. Indeed, so implicated were the native governments in this matter, that even after the British took control in this region a new hijra could be initiated only with the permission of the local Indian revenue officer (Preston, 1987:380). The granting of rights to hijras to beg for alms, and protecting their territorial rights to do so against other hijras, was consistent with the Indian concept of the king's duty to ensure the ancient rights of his subjects. Not only were the hijras' rights to collect alms affirmed by the Indian states, but the states also gave them grants of land, which legitimately succeeded from guru to chela.

Ultimately, the British government refused to lend its legal support to "the [hijras'] right of begging or extorting money, whether authorized by former governments or not," hoping thereby to discourage "the abominable practices of the wretches." Through a law disallowing any land grant or entitlement from the state that "breach[ed] the laws of public decency," the British finally were able to remove state protection from the hijras (Preston, 1987:380, 382). Hijras today in India often refer to these traditional entitlements; though these entitlements obviously have no contemporary effect, they confer a historical legitimacy on the hijras' occupation of begging and are thus an important source of self-esteem.

The historical and contemporary picture of the traditional occupations of the hijras demonstrates that they have succeeded in carving out for themselves a viable economic niche over which they exercise considerable control both within their own communities and in their interactions with outsiders. As individuals who have left their families and renounced caste, hijras, like other renouncers, transcend networks of social obligations and thereby threaten the social order on which established society depends. Because of this, they generate anxiety and often fear among those with whom they come in contact. More specifically, the hijras have used their position as sexually ambiguous figures outside the normal framework of society to manipulate and exploit the cultural norms of proper behavior to their own advantage. As a group at the lowest end of the Indian social hierarchy, and having no ordinary social position to maintain within that hierarchy, hijras are "freed from the restraints of decency" and they know that their shamelessness makes people—not all, but surely most—reluctant to provoke them in a public confrontation. Unconstrained by behavioral norms that regulate the lives of ordinary men and women, hijras are particularly invulnerable to social control by outsiders.

Hijras are stigmatized by their outrageous behavior (or the potential of such behavior), but this stigma functions as an effective strategy of economic adaptation. They trade on their disreputable image, exchanging the respect due restrained behavior for the control over their clientele. Believed to have special powers because of their sexual ambiguity, and daring to do what others will not—cannot—do because such acts are so shameful, hijras have to a large extent cornered an economic market.[7]

Hijras have also shaped their social organization so that it functions effectively in maintaining internal control. The organization of hijra territoriality is well maintained; any disputes over work in the community are never referred to the police but are handled by the jamat. The explicit and functional hijra hierarchy, with its economic and social security backed up by the threat of expulsion from the community, helps keep a tight rein on its members. And yet the hierarchy is sufficiently flexible so that both geographic and social mobility are possible: Both of these mechanisms leave room for those who get restive and want to either move around or move up.

Through their organization into communal households in which income, chores, and resources are shared, through their strategies of reciprocity based on the guru-chela relationship and expanded through fictive kinship beyond the local community, through their maintaining of an effective national blacklist and enforcement of their sanctions for conflict and misbehavior without using state courts, the hijras have resisted losing control over their internal political and economic affairs.

Hijras have also managed successfully to maintain their economic predominance, if not total monopoly, of their ritual role. Defined by the larger community as emasculated men, they have clearly seen that it is in their interest to preserve that essential definition of their role, which they do by making loud and public gestures to denounce the "frauds" and "fakes" who imitate them. They thus reinforce in the public mind their own sole right to their traditional occupations and also increase their credibility.

And yet, with changing times, and like other Indian occupational groups, or castes, not all hijras are able to earn a living through their traditional occupations. Hijras complain that opportunities for their traditional work seem to be declining, partly as a consequence of family planning—Indian families are having fewer children. They also complain of a loss of respect compared to what they enjoyed under the Mughals and even the British. It does seem to be true that with increasing urbanization, education, and Westernization of values, the role of traditional ritual figures like the hijras becomes less compelling. Some Westernized upper–middle–class families I met refused to allow the hijras to perform at marriages or insisted they curtail their performances to a bare minimum. In response to this decline in the market for their services, the hijras have raised the price of their performances dramatically. They have also attempted to expand the occasions on which they claim their performance is necessary, for example, at the opening of hospitals or business establishments. These claims that they do not have the opportunities they need to earn a living through their traditional occupations justify, for many hijras, their practice of prostitution, an occupation that accelerates the loss of respect accorded them in society.

EARNING A LIVING: PROSTITUTION

There is no question that hijras widely engage in prostitution; indeed, it may be their major source of income. In spite of this, however, it is also considered "deviant" and stigmatized within the community. Apart from the generally low standing of prostitution in India, as a sexual activity it goes against the wishes of the hijra Mother Goddess, who is herself celibate. It also contravenes the cultural ideal of the hijra as a sannyasi, an "other-worldly" person, and a religious mendicant. Thus, hijras are reluctant to admit that they engage in prostitution, and most are defensive about it, at least initially.

All hijra prostitutes I met claimed they engaged in prostitution because it was the only way they could earn a living. And the demand for sex with hijras appears to ensure them of a living. But while it is true that prostitution can be a very lucrative source of income—some prostitutes claim incomes of over 30,000 rupees a year, a sum perhaps comparable to the salary earned by a middle-level executive and almost triple that earned by a college professor—it is more likely that the guru, rather than prostitute herself, benefits the most financially. Prostitution has low status among hijras for other reasons. An individual prostitute has almost no control over her working conditions. She always works under the control of a hijra elder (sometimes her own guru, sometimes a hijra who runs a house of prostitution and who is perhaps not the guru of any of the prostitutes), and she must "take on all kinds of customers, whether it's a businessman or a policeman." Prostitution is experienced as physically demanding work (though not as demanding as begging and certainly much more rewarding financially), and in spite of the demand for it, many prostitutes do not live well.

Hijra prostitutes are generally attached to houses of prostitution that are for hijras only. Sometimes these houses, or flats, are located in red-light districts of a city; in other cases, such as in Bastipore, houses of hijra prostitutes are located in ordinary working-class neighborhoods, while nonhijra prostitutes are located in separate areas throughout the city. From my conversations with and observations of hijra prostitutes, it appears that although some of their customers, such as those they may pick up at night walking the streets, mistake them for women, the customers that come to their houses know that they are hijras and prefer them over female prostitutes for a variety of reasons, which are suggested later in the text.

Prostitutes working out of houses of prostitution are often exploited by their gurus, or "madams," who take a fixed portion of their income, which can be anywhere from 50 to 100%. A prostitute must also pay a minimum daily amount to the house manager (in 1985 in Bastipore, it was 60 rupees a day) whether she earns that much or not. Although some gurus or house managers return a fair amount in living space, clothes, food, jewelry, and money for special occasions, there is little recourse against a guru who is not generous. Prostitutes are carefully supervised to see that they do not malinger or run off with a customer, and they may be expected to do onerous domestic chores as well.

In spite of these difficulties, however, few hijra prostitutes work on their own. This is because the community of gurus and prostitutes provides their working space, a steady source of customers, a minimum assurance of physical security in case customers get rowdy, and someone to pay off the police so that they are not arrested, because prostitution is illegal in India. Not unimportantly, it also provides them with a social life.

Prostitution presents the hijra community with a conflict. It is considered a low calling, offensive to the Mother Goddess, one undermining of the hijra ritual role in society, but it is far too lucrative a source of income for it to be prohibited by hijra gurus, who are the ones who benefit most by it. And so, a compromise has been reached. In large cities that are centers of hijra culture, like Bombay and Delhi, prostitutes are not allowed to live in the "respectable" houses where hijras earn their living by performing in their traditional ritual capacities and where the "big gurus" live. In Bombay, for example, hijra prostitutes live together in flats, often in the red-light district. Otherwise, however, these hijra prostitutes are considered full members of the community. They are invited to social functions, maintain relations with their gurus, and participate in hijra fictive kinship networks. In other, smaller cities, more marginal to hijra culture, hijra prostitutes and performers reside together, and one individual may both perform traditional hijra rituals and engage in prostitution.

Hijra prostitutes today appear to be recruited from the zenana class; it is these individuals who pay the initiation fee to join the community, a fee that "born" hijras—hermaphrodites—do not pay. So while on the one hand, hijras publicly condemn those "who are men and join us just to make a living," on the other hand, they also allow them to join. In this way the hijra community absorbs some of its own competition and benefits financially from the zenana's earnings. Some of these zenana may eventually become real hijras by undergoing the emasculation operation (see Ranade, 1983; Sinha, 1967).

Whether as performers or as prostitutes, hijras have effectively adapted to the society that surrounds them. They have successfully constructed their own world out of the one presented to them—a special cultural world made over to suit their own needs. The hijras may be only "half a caste"; indeed, some seem to be, as one observer described them, "among the poorest of mendicants, . . . lead[ing] a wretched existence, despised by everyone," but they have nevertheless managed not merely to survive, but to adapt, by creating an organized yet flexible society for themselves and by maintaining control over their traditional occupation.

The hijra world may be considered a deviant world; surely it is outside the bounds of respectability, but it is not outside of Indian society. Although becoming a hijra means making a commitment to a stigmatized identity in some respects, it is a commitment that nonetheless gives social support and some economic security, as well as cultural meaning, to their lives, linking them to the larger world rather than isolating them from it.

CHAPTER FIVE

🪷 Kamladevi: A Prostitute

Kamladevi is a prostitute. She attended a Christian convent high school until the ninth standard (eleventh grade) and speaks fluent English, in addition to Hindi and Tamil, her native language. She is from a small city in Tamil Nadu, and her father is a police inspector. When I first met Kamladevi, she was about 35 years old and had been a hijra since her late teens.

Kamladevi has a vivacious personality and a delightfully malicious sense of humor. Unfortunately, she does not seem to have been able to use her considerable insight and intelligence to carve out a contented life for herself. Although Kamladevi dances and sings whenever the opportunity presents itself, she mainly earns her living as a prostitute. Partly because she has a restless temperament and partly because she has a quick temper and easily gets into quarrels, she does not stay long in one place.

When I met her, in early 1982, Kamladevi was shuttling between Bombay and Bastipore, staying several months at a time in each place, living in communes of hijra prostitutes. Whenever she talked about her life among the hijras, she seemed to alternate between viewing it as having authentic ritual validity and as being merely a convenient niche in society for gender "misfits" like herself. More than any other hijra I met she had an ironic view of her own life.

When I first met Kamladevi, she was staying in the neighborhood of Temple Road, in a hijra house of prostitution that was attached to a *hamam* (hamam: public bathhouse), as several hijra communes are in Bastipore.[1] At one time the house was run by Raj Dev, who was the most important guru in Bastipore. Some years ago he had become seriously ill with a paralyzing disease, and for what remained of his life (he died sometime between 1982 and 1985) he was a total invalid. In his last years he lay on the floor in the part of the house used for the hijras' domestic life and was cared for by whoever was not busy at the time.

The person in charge at the house was Lalitha. She dominated the house not merely by her position but by her personality. Lalitha was remarkably tall, over 6 feet, and had classically beautiful Indian features and extravagantly thick, jet black, straight hair, hanging below her waist. She wore chiffon saris and diamond earrings along with many gold chains and wrist bangles. Lalitha was famous, or rather infamous, in Bastipore for having, in Kamladevi's words, "just walked in off the street one day in a shirt and *lungi* [sarong worn by men] several years back, and now look at her, how rich she is, that is the ladder to come up."

Lalitha ruled the Temple Road house with an iron hand, at least when it came to making sure "the girls" were working and collecting the money. Another hijra, Sonia, managed the bathhouse part of the business. Sonia was enormously fat and quite masculine in appearance, with extremely hairy arms and a tattoo on her wrist. Unlike almost all of the other hijras I have met, she wore no jewelry. Whenever I came to the bathhouse, Sonia would be sitting quietly smiling in a corner, like some gigantic Buddha.

In addition to these two senior people, there were three other hijras who regularly lived in the house. Thangam was a beautiful, feminine-looking hijra who lived with her husband at night, but came to do housework and cooking at Temple Road during the day. Zarina, a be-jeweled and bedecked Muslim hijra, came from another hijra house in Bastipore because she had quarreled with her guru. Kumari, a slightly built hijra, was, like the others, from South India originally and had been living in this house for several years. Thangam claimed she no longer did prostitution or went out dancing "because her husband didn't like her to," but Zarina and Kumari, along with Kamladevi, worked regularly as prostitutes. From time to time, when I visited the house, there were other hijras staying there for various lengths of time. One was Gopi, a fat, loud-mouthed hijra with a demanding manner. She had just come back from a stint working as a fortuneteller at a temple in a nearby city. Another was Rekha, a prostitute who was a special friend of Kamladevi and who, like her, shifted back and forth between Bastipore and Bombay. I soon got over my surprise at seeing the household composition change frequently.

Kamladevi had come to Bastipore in January, 1982, and planned to stay a few months. I was able to talk with her at length because she spoke English and in addition was witty and bright. From our first meeting she was responsive to my interest in learning about the hijras. Having been one for almost 20 years, she was a mine of information. In addition, she quickly picked up that, as I had been talking to the other hijras when Lalitha was roaming about the house, I was "probably told all lies." I did not think I had been told "all lies," but I certainly appreciated and encouraged Kamladevi to tell me her version of the life and relationships in this house, as well as about hijra life and culture in general.

Having traveled back and forth to Bombay so much, Kamladevi was also able to provide me introductions within the hijra houses of prostitution in that city. I greatly appreciated this because these hijra prostitutes are busier than those in Bastipore, which made it more difficult to meet and spend time with them. As it turned out, near the end of that year's visit to India, when I returned to Bombay, Kamladevi herself also returned there, so I was able to continue our relationship.

In Bombay the house from which Kamladevi worked was much less of a "community" than were the houses in Bastipore. Here, in the midst of the red-light district, the hijra prostitutes paid the household head a fixed sum for the rental of the work space (a curtained off bed in a room that held four beds and a washing up area). So long as they paid this fee, they were pretty much on their own to do what they liked with their time. Thus, in Bombay I was able to meet Kamladevi many times privately over the course of a month, in parks, or in tea shops, where she could talk more freely for extended periods of time.

BEGINNINGS

When I asked Kamladevi to tell me how she came to join the hijras, she answered me with a long story about her childhood and adolescence:

I'll tell you about us hijras. We dress like girls because of the sexual desire [for men]. Why else would we wear saris? We are born like full human beings, from the womb of our mother. But at 5, or 8, or 10 years old, you come to know that you are different. We are born as a boy, and we grow up. One in a hundred people will know we are not a boy, but a hijra. Someone who has already had a relationship with a hijra, he will come to us and show us the state of his desire. Then we are attracted.

There are two types among us. One type has relationships only with men, the other type has relationships with men and women. Those who say they have no sexual interest are all telling lies. Those who say they have less interest—that they like only to sing and dance—they are the aged people. When they were young, sex was their main desire. Now they say, "Oh, I think only of God and religion," but that's all nonsense. When you enter the "dragon" of this life, you get the bad habits first; then when you become old you become less desirous of this sexual interest and think more of religion. It is only from getting older.

I'll tell you frankly how it happened with me. I am a Protestant, and we speak English at home. I did my schooling at a convent school in Cantonment where I continued until the ninth standard (eleventh grade), when I left and took a correspondence course to complete my matriculation. After I passed my matriculation I joined an industrial training institute for the sheet metal and welding course. But I didn't like that so my father had me join the college for my Bachelors of Science certificate. After 6 months of college I started going out with hijras and became like this, but from my childhood itself, I had a lot of feminine tendencies. My behavior was always different from others. My parents even sent me to Bharatnatyam classes [a school of classical Indian dance] although I was a boy.

But although I was a boy, I refused to wear pants, even in the Industrial Training Institute. I used to wear only lungi. Even if they stitched me pants, I would buy the lungi with my pocket money. I used to cut my sister's small skirts and make a half petticoat and wear the lungi over it. I never wanted to wear pants.

I would take an eyebrow pencil and *kajal* [eyeblack used around the eyes of young boys and girls for both health and beauty] and make up my eyes and put on a little lipstick when I left the house to go to school, and then take it off before I came home. I would shave the hair off my face, but my brothers would throw away the blade so I couldn't shave. They would catch me and draw a mustache on me with the eyebrow pencil. When I went to the college my father would send his orderly from the Police Department to accompany me to make sure I didn't do these things. My father at this time was a sub-inspector of the police in the Crime Section. My uncle was also an inspector with the police.

When I was in the fifth standard (seventh grade) at Warden Road School, there was one Anglo-Indian fellow. He noted my activities. He was one of the students, but an older fellow. I was then 11 or 12 years old. When the bell rang for the recess, I would not go. Only after everybody had gone to the toilet and come back, only then I would go to the toilet, even if the bell had already rung. He used to come at that time to the toilet. He told me, "You look like a girl, your activities are like a girl, I like you so much." I told him, "Don't tell me I'm like a girl, I don't approve of it." But still, he was persistent, and it was he who spoiled me and gave me the first experience.

After that, a physical education instructor also noticed me. When the physical education period came, I used to join only the girls' group. I used to play volleyball, ring toss, girls' games only, I would not join the boys' group. So the physical education master told me, "Why are you joining the girls' group? You must go and join the boys' group, you are the sub-inspector's son, you must keep up the respect. Don't join the girls, your activities will be spoiled." But still I stayed with the girls' group.

He noticed my activities like this for 2, 3 days, and then one day he told me to meet him after the physical education period. I was wondering why he was calling me, for there was nothing for him to tell me after the class, unlike the other subject lecturers. I was confused about this, and even in the class period I was thinking about this only, without concentrating on the lessons. When the bell rang, I started to leave the class, but the master was opening the door to the classroom and asked me, "Why are you going? I asked you to come and see me." Then he made me sit on his lap and told me I looked very nice. Then he also spoiled me. After that there was another lecturer in the school and he also spoiled me.

After some time I dropped out of the school and started going for my matriculation at the night college. Around this time I came into contact with the hijras. They noticed me, they saw me going to the college every night. Then one of them approached me and said, "Oh, you are also like us, come in and spend some time." But I knew I was being observed by my father's constable so I used to scorn them and go away. But slowly, because they persisted, I devised a plan and went to their house, cutting my college classes. For 6 days I went continuously to their house.

There they were bringing the customers for prostitution, telling them about me, saying, "Some nice new girls have joined the gang." One of my customers was one of my father's own constables. The first time he was shocked, but he returned for me the very next day and two times after that. I was very scared doing this prostitution. I would close my eyes in the dark room and go through the experience. Like this it went on for 6 days.

I always had the fear that my father would come to know. It happened that our gardener's son came to this house as a customer. He told his mother about my being in the hijra camp doing prostitution and she told my mother. My mother almost shed tears of blood, she was so upset. Seeing her, I also cried and was very disturbed. That night I acted as if I was asleep and heard my mother telling my father about my being in the hijra camp and doing all the bad things. My father pulled me out of the bed, put my head into a barrel of water, and beat me with his uniform cross belt. I was in bed from that beating for 3 days. Then they changed me to the day college and somehow I graduated. Then they put me in the technical course. But still my connection with the hijras was there, and one fine day I ran off with them for good to Bombay. That lady who was the head of the hijra house there, it was she who took me to Bombay.

When I came to Bombay, I was given my name by one Maulama, my guru's guru, an important leader in Bombay. All of the gurus sat in a circle and they put the five rupees in the center. I covered my head with my sari. They asked me, "Have you come to Bombay before?" I answered, "No." They asked me, "Will you be Raj Dev's chela?" (This one who brought me there was also the chela of Raj Dev.) I said, "Yes." So then I had to pay the 150-rupee fine, which this Maulama paid for me. The big gurus took the 150 rupees and gave 5 to me. Then all the gurus clapped their hands three times and I became a chela to the group. Those seven gurus divided the 150 rupees among themselves, and we had tea and coffee and biscuits for the group.

If you go to Bombay on your own, whoever calls you first to her house becomes your guru. Even if she only gives you a glass of water, that glass will cost 150 rupees. When a newcomer comes, they are not accepted right away. Only after testing for 20, 25 days, only then they'll make you a chela.

While Kamladevi was telling me this story, I was sitting with her and Zarina and another individual who was a stranger to me. He was a handsome, slightly built young man with a shoulder-length pageboy haircut and a light mustache, wearing a lungi and a shirt. Kamladevi suddenly pointed at this young man and said, "See this fellow, don't tell lies, say the truth, that for you this function was not done." It seemed that Kamladevi had, in the last year, made the decision to take a chela of her own, this young man, Amudh, who was sitting beside her against the wall. Still pointing at him, Kamladevi said:

> See, I took this fellow to Bombay with me. I dressed him up as a girl, gave him a sari, and made him take off his mustache, because in Bombay the elders won't like us to dress like that. This boy lives with his parents, he is 28 years, and sells bananas side by side with his mother on the bridge over the city railway station. His parents are very affectionate to him and let him be as he likes. But they are very interested in his welfare and want him to live at home. They worry about where he is at night and whether he is eating properly. Maybe after they are gone he will join the hijras permanently. He came to Bombay with me, but got homesick after a month and came back before they could perform the [initiation] ceremony for him. He lived with me and I gave him a name, but—why should I tell lies?—he lost courage and came back here.

This was the second time this had happened with Amudh, and Kamladevi seemed to have resigned herself to having to look elsewhere for a chela. After saying this about Amudh, she continued to tell me about her entry into the hijra community:

> See, this testing is necessary. We test both the character of the person and whether they are willing to earn a living. We see, can the newcomer do work in the household, can they dance or sing well, can they clap their hands for money in the shops, can they play the dholak [drum] . . . can they do any of these things? If you don't have any of these qualities, they will also see whether you can do prostitution. If you have that capacity, it's all right, they will take you as a chela. But if there is no income, how will they make you a chela? It is for these things that the person is tested to become a hijra.
>
> We also test to see whether the person behaves like a "lady," how they conduct themselves. These people, the elders in Bombay, they are very strict. If someone new comes to the house they test them strictly. There are a great many rules. You cannot shave, you must only use the tweezers. If you use the blade, they fine you 50 rupees, because with the blade your face becomes rough. You cannot wear full white clothing, like white petticoat, white blouse, and white sari, while your guru is alive. You can wear some white clothes, but not all white. [There is a similar restriction for a woman whose husband is still alive; all white clothes are for widows.] If you are in Poonawalla house, like me, you cannot wear blue color. No blue blouse, blue bangles, blue sari. You should not swim in the water, you should not ride a bicycle. For swimming and riding a bicycle the fine is 51 rupees. If you wear caps or turbans, for that also the fine is 51 rupees.

If we break these rules we get a lot of losses [punishments] and ill health. But I know all the tricks to get away from the fines. I know how to behave.

Now these hijras today have at least a little freedom. When I joined, the elders in Bombay were too strict. If the sari was tucked too high, they would beat us. If the upper part of the sari moved away from your head, they would beat us. "Are you a man," they would say, "why are you doing all this?" When you go out you must cover your head with a sari. Suppose a customer gets friendly, you can't be talking with him more than 5 or 10 minutes or the elders will say, "Oh, you want to have him permanently as a husband, is that why you are doing all this?" and they would beat us.

WORKING LIFE

It seemed to me that Kamladevi and the other prostitutes in this house did not have an easy life. Kamladevi frequently complained about her situation but did not seem to be able to find a way to get out of it.

This life is very troublesome. Yesterday I went for a badhai, a baby had been born to some Sindhi family over near Munshi Marg Road. Fat Manjula, she lives in Market Lane, she called me to come with her, she is my "grandmother." She is a very comic entertainer. In this badhai, Fat Manjula acts like a pregnant lady and imitates all the difficulties the pregnant lady goes through to have the baby. She puts a big pillow under her sari, and then finally comes the confinement and she takes the baby—the pillow—from her stomach. For this program they give only an old sari, and Fat Manjula sold it to me for 30 rupees. Generally I like a bright yellow sari, this was a multicolored one, but it had yellow predominating so I took it.

I earn quite a bit of money, but I don't have any wealth. I want to go to Bombay, but I took a loan of 500 rupees from the pawn shop and I have to finish paying that loan before I can go to Bombay. I don't know how long that will be. Some days I pay 20 rupees, some days 30, and some days I can't pay anything. Robbers and prostitutes, you can't say how much you'll earn in a day.

Lalitha fixes the price for us. Sometimes she'll say three rupees, sometimes five or ten. This becomes a problem for us because once Lalitha has fixed the price, the customer will refuse to pay more. Not only that, but he'll go and speak bad about us to Lalitha if we ask for more. And we pay Lalitha three rupees for the room, so for five rupees what do we have left? Only two rupees. Whichever customer pays high, like 50 rupees or so, immediately Lalitha will say, "Oh, I'll take this one." Like, for instance, there is this one man from Hyderabad who comes. He brings a cassette and occupies the room quite a long time and wants the partner to do twist dancing to the music. Whenever he comes, Lalitha says, "He's my husband," and goes with him because he pays sometimes even 150 rupees. I feel like dying, I am so bored with my life.

One day as I was sitting in my house with my friend who was accompanying me as a translator, I was surprised by a visit from Kamladevi and Kumari. I had not given any of the hijras my specific address, but the house we were living in was a very special and well-known place—in the center of the town—and thus Kamladevi had no trouble getting a taxi driver to find it. Kamladevi and Kumari were a little hesitant as they stood on the doorstep, wondering, obviously, how they would be received. In fact, I was delighted to see them and immediately asked them to join us in our morning tea and biscuits. After her first cup of tea, Kamladevi began with her litany of woes about her life:

I was lying down for the last 4 days because I didn't feel well and Lalitha was so cross about it. So to please her I satisfied two customers before I went to the hospital today. I had to go to the hospital because I am having a problem with my eyes. Two customers I had, whereas the others did not even have one since morning. Every time we are absent from the house it means a loss of money to Lalitha. So you must never tell her that we came to visit you like this. When some customers come and ask for me specifically and I am out, then Lalitha gets furious; if they come and ask, "Where is Kamladevi, where is Kamladevi?" and I am not there, Lalitha gets so angry because she is losing money.

I used to be at Yusuf's house [another hijra commune in Bastipore], but there I never had peace of mind. Even if you earn 1,000 rupees and you don't have peace of mind, what's the use. And if you earn only one penny, if you have happiness and peace of mind, that's better. Yusuf's house was full of conditions, the whole world's strict conditions were there. And he takes away the whole money also. You can't even earn a *paisa* [penny] from him. For your food you have to pay five rupees, while here, at Lalitha's place you pay three rupees for your food and you are free to eat as much as you want. For staying, we need not give anything. You can have your bath free also, but for expenses like soap, you have to buy yourself. When we take the customer in the back room and use the lying [down] position, you have to pay three rupees, but if the customer wants to do it in the bathhouse, you pay only one or two rupees. And the rest of the money, whatever the amount, you can keep. But in Yusuf's bathhouse, it was not like that. He wanted 15, 20, 30 rupees, like that, he takes the whole thing. He does the black magic also, which is why I came away from that place.

But here at Lalitha's also, life is so hard. Yesterday I had 20 to 25 customers and still, if I take a rest, Lalitha will say, "You're going on sitting and chatting, you're wasting your time and not looking after the customers." Yesterday I was so tired, 25 customers I pleased, and still she was after me.

Even before Lalitha, with Raj Dev, it was not easy. One time when I was there, this was before Raj Dev became ill and before Lalitha came, Sushila was very sick. She had a husband at this time, and her husband was giving her 10 rupees daily and taking her to the doctor. One day she came in to rest and Raj Dev abused her and beat her. She was so angry then that she pulled his hair. These elders don't like us to have husbands. It means less income for them. Not only that, but when you have a husband, he will tell you, "Why are you giving all your money to the elders? Save some for your old age." He will give you advice. Also, sometimes, when the husband is in difficulty, he will take 20, 30 rupees from us, and this means less for the guru. In this case, Sushila's husband was making sure she went to the doctor. This Raj Dev thought that I had instigated Sushila to fight so at about midnight, Raj Dev put my suitcase outside and told me to get out. I had not instigated the fight, and Sushila told that to Raj Dev and took my suitcase inside and told me to get inside. Then Sushila left that house.

We continued talking about these things in general, gossiping a little about the different hijras I knew in Bastipore, when suddenly Kumari, who was normally very quiet, burst into the conversation:

These people [the gurus] are now only interested in money. Here in Bastipore there is no unity and no strictness. Even men can come into the group. You know this Meera, at Gasworks Street, she is a real man. She had a wife and daughter and she had a boyfriend, and got that boyfriend married to her own daughter. In Bombay the hijras will not allow a man to come into the group, they will not let a man leave his family and join them. To be a hijra you should not have any relations with a woman. We may earn money by having boyfriends or customers, but we will not do any wrong things. You may go after a male as a boyfriend, but we hijras will not go after women.

Kamladevi nodded her head in vigorous agreement and laughed uproariously at the shocked look on my face as I digested this news about Meera. She was obviously delighted to be able to tell me something I did not know about Meera—something, indeed, that I had never guessed at. Passing on this information to me gave Kamladevi the chance to downgrade Meera in my eyes and also to show me how important a source of information she herself was to me.

Because Kamladevi was so frank about her work as a prostitute, we had many conversations on this subject. I was particularly interested to know more about the men who were the hijras' customers. At one time, I asked Kamladevi why she thinks men come to hijras rather than to female prostitutes.

See, there is a proverb: "For a normal lady prostitute it is 4 annas [cents] and for a hijra it is 12 annas." These men, they come to us to have pleasure on their own terms. They may want to kiss us or do so many things. For instance, one customer will ask us to lift the legs [from the position of lying flat on her back] so that they can do it through the anus. We allow them to do it by the back but not very often. The people who know the knack, like me, they will put their hand below the anus so that the customer, thinking it is the anus, he will do it. They will put it inside, but it will just be our hand. Without their knowledge we do it that way, and the water [semen] will pass off down into the ground where we hide it with the cloth. The customer will never know. We try to avoid doing it by the back and mostly do it between the thighs. If a customer only gives me 2, 3 rupees baksheesh [tips], I do it between the thighs, but if they give 20 extra I do the above method. I can manage this, but not everyone can. For them, it is a real hardship, they have to do it through the anus only, and it is initially quite painful. Such is our life.

Having heard so many times from Kamladevi and other younger prostitutes how difficult their lives were, and how much more difficult it was to work for someone else and turn over one's hard earned money, I asked Kamladevi why she didn't strike out on her own.

We haven't enough courage to do that. I am especially afraid of the rowdies. Rowdies do come here and they'll either ask for money or ask to come and lie down with us. I'll silently go and sleep with them because I am afraid not to. When they come we try to look sickly before them so that they won't pick us up. See that "girl" [hijra] who came yesterday, she had that long scar running across her face. She is from Yusuf's house, some bullies gave her that scar with a knife. When we go to the temple we bring back a small lime [a talisman] for protection. I get so afraid in the night that I have this lime near me and pray to the Goddess that no rowdy or bully should come and disturb me. The police take money from Lalitha, 15 policemen take five rupees a day, so we don't normally get harassed by them but even the police will not protect us from the rowdies.

If we do anything wrong, the police catch us, but they give us concessions. Like suppose some hijras are doing prostitution here and there in the night, loafing around. If the police catch us, they ask us, "Why are you doing like this?" with sympathy. They are interested also in why we do this. Then we explain that we don't get much money—we get 50 cents or even 25 cents, so what shall we do for eating? Sometimes men come to us, thinking that we are ladies. Then after they find out we are hijras they give us only one rupee or two, and go away. So we must dodge the police like that, by getting their sympathy, then they leave us without prosecuting us. Once they caught me in Bori Bunder here in Bastipore. At that time I was very pretty and fair, that was before I had the operation, and like this I talked to them and they let me go.

One time the police caught nine of us hijras in one night. Meera was there, and I was also there. We could not come out of jail because we didn't have the bail money so they took us the next day to the court. I talked to the judge in English. They wanted my name and I said, "My name is Kamladevi." The judge asked me, "What did you do?" All the hijras told me to talk to the lawyer in English because it would have a good effect. I told the judge that I was going for prostitution at night, but that I did not steal anything and did not do any crime. So he asked me, "Are you a boy or a girl?" I told him, "If you want to see and know the answer, I will show you."

The lawyer told me with surprise, "You talk fantastically well." I told the judge and the lawyer, "You brought me here like this, even when I have paid the money to the police. From each person the police received 50 rupees and even then they did not leave us alone, they took us to this court." So the lawyer scolded the police: "What, you didn't catch anybody so you brought these hijras here!" The police answered very politely, "They were loafing around in the night so I brought them." And the lawyer told them, "Hereafter, don't bring these hijras here, just scold them and leave them alone. You haven't caught the real prostitutes, you have only caught these hijras." See, we lost the money to the police, but still he brought us to the court.

When they caught us, if those other hijras would have asked me, I would have told the police our side of the story and won their sympathy and we would have escaped. But before I could say anything, all these hijras took out money from their jackets to give to the police and asked them to leave us alone. Of the nine hijras they caught, my name was the last. I convinced the lawyer that I did not do anything wrong, but was only trying to earn my food. I talked for five minutes like this to the lawyer, and he gave us all coffee and sent us home in the police lorry. In the police station they tested us, whether we were a boy or a girl. At that time I was new from Bombay and looking young and fair. Then they asked us to do a dance for the night duty people, but then they beat us for roaming in the night like prostitutes. But after that we became happy and danced for them all the night.

In Bombay the situation is different. In Bombay I can go in bra and panties, or without bra also, and roam about at 3:00 or 4:00 in the morning and no one will bother me. Suppose any rowdies come and bully us, I'll write up the petition in English and give it to the inspector of police. I will explain to him that the rowdies bully us to give money we ourselves earn, a rupee or two, standing in the street. They ask us for a bottle of beer and 50 rupees. We tell the police inspector, "We've come from a different city to earn. How can we give this money to these local rowdies?" So I write this all down and give it to the police inspector because they won't have time to listen to us. I'll sign it Kamladevi and give it to them.

THE OPERATION

Kamladevi had undergone the emasculation operation about 1½ years before I met her. She expressed ambivalence about it, alternately speaking of it in terms of its importance to being a hijra and cursing herself for having done it. Kamladevi spoke many times of her bad luck and ill health, which continued even after the operation. She thought this might be because she had not yet gone to the temple of the Mata near Ahmedabad. Recently, she had had a dream of the Mata telling her to come to the temple, and she talked about going there after leaving Bastipore:

> It is because I have not gone to the Mata's temple that I am having such troubles and conflicts in my life. If I pray to the Mata, these troubles will go away. This is why I had the operation also. My life was going badly so I decided that this would change my luck. I had to wait so many years because the operation is very expensive. You must give so many rupees to Meera, including seven saris. Meera was the one who did my operation.
>
> It's a sort of a fate. Even if you have one *lakh* [100,000] rupees on hand, you may not be able to get the operation done. And also, if you don't have a single cent, but you have the moral courage, you will get the operation done through some means. So much . . . I paid so much for the operation—27 saris, 20 petticoats, 27 blouses, 2 dance dresses, 1 big tin box, 9 stone nose rings, 200 rupees, all the costume jewelry for the ears, neck, hands, and nose—but I was so obsessed that I thought I must get this operation done or die. After living so long, this was the only thing lacking in my life.
>
> Some people do it with only 1,000 rupees. For instance, when Meera wanted the operation done she took 500 rupees to Chaniput [a small town near Bastipore] but still she did not succeed. Then, when she didn't even have the money, she sold her radio for 200 rupees and got the operation done. For Thangam, it was 1,000 rupees. She got operated on in Ahmedabad, not in Bombay, and still she had to go back three times because she did not have the courage the first two times. For me, the operation was in Bastipore, in a small place near the suburbs. They [her hijra elders including the guru] had taken a small house there the second day after I reached Bastipore from Bombay.

I asked Kamladevi on several occasions why it was so important for hijras to get the operation done. Once she answered me with the story that opens Chapter 3. This day she answered me in another way:

> See, when you go for a dance, some people may ask, "Are you a hijra or are you a man?" So that way, if you have had the operation you can show them. Only those who have had the operation are real hijras; they are called nirvan, nirvan sultans [like a king, that is, a very important

person]. If you want to be a *pukka* [pure] hijra, you must have the operation. So, like when you might go out of station [take a trip] with a group of hijras, and when you are sleeping in the night your clothes may go up, but you need not bother if you have had the operation. Otherwise, people will make fun of you and the local rowdies will say, "Oh, this is a man, he has got male organs, he has come to dance with the hijras only for the sake of earning money." For that we lose respect and they will abuse us also.

Having lived so many years, if I didn't get the operation done, it would be a great "black mark" for me. Meera did this operation for nine of us here, just as she did it for me. For Meera herself, one dai ma operated on her. One should not even call these people gurus, they are even higher than that. The Mata's power comes on them. It will come in their dreams. The Mata will appear wearing everything green—green bangles, green blouse, green sari. The Mata will ask that person, "Give me back my nose ring, where is my nose ring?" If that happens it means you have the sanction to operate.

I could not help but comment again that it seemed both a very expensive and somewhat dangerous enterprise. I also expressed to her that it seemed like a very final kind of thing to do; an irreversible change of sex must surely be a decision not undertaken without a great deal of thought. As to the painfulness of the sex-change operation, she assured me that this was not a difficulty as the male organ has already become weak and useless: "Once we are spoiled by these relations with males," she said, "the nerve in the male organ breaks and it is not good for anything." As for the expense, she said,

I did not think I am giving these things to Meera, but I gave it to the Mata, to Bahucharaji [the hijra Mother Goddess] so it is not too costly. It is the Mata that comes upon the dai ma, who gives her the courage and the moral support. All the persons Meera operated on were operated on properly. There was no infection. Actually, it is not the healing that is the problem, the main thing is to see if you can pass urine freely. I should not say lies, with Mata's grace, my urine flows very free, more than before the operation. There is no failure in Meera's hand.

When we are operated on we become the favorites of the Mata and only the Mata's power will come on us, no other godhead's. For those who are not operated on, any godhead can come on them, any other Mata, Shiva, any. Even if we feel sad sometimes and want to curse somebody, we can only curse with the power of the Mata. Those who are not operated on can curse with the power of some other godhead. After all, we are eating Mata's food, we are living in her power. For hijras the true goddess is Bahuchara Mata. She is the only goddess for us. If you go to her temple and worship her and leave two cocks, all your karma, any of the bad things which you have done, will go away.

For those who are operated on, like me, Tuesday is the holy day. On that day we wash our hair and in the evening we pray to the Mata. We keep all fruits for her, and she especially likes watermelon. If you offer her that in the puja [prayer ceremony], you can see her smile in the photograph because she is so overjoyed. So every Tuesday we keep all the fruits, the pan leaves, fried *gram* [chickpea] four, puffed rice, however much you wish to eat in a frenzy, the same you can offer to her. I want to go to see the Mata's temple near Ahmedabad but I have no money. When I earn money here in Bastipore, I will go to the temple.

I asked Kamladevi why she was so short of money—after all, she had been working steadily at prostitution both here and in Bombay.

See, I have just come away from Bombay with just one sari on me, I came without taking anything. Then I had to buy three saris, one for 30 rupees, one for 40, and one for 200. I take it by the scheme of paying in installments. I've already finished paying for two saris, only one is remaining. I came away from Bombay in great frustration, just 6 months after having the operation. The doctor said I'm having jaundice, I'm having typhoid. Then some doctor said I'm having TB, they even said I'm having cholera. I went on having treatments. For three injections they charge 20 rupees in Bombay. I went on taking these injections, but it only gave me temporary relief. I could not even bear to take coffee or tea. Only cold water was bearable to me.

I assumed that these ill physical effects Kamladevi was feeling were a result of the operation, but she corrected me:

No, it is not like that. I had made a lot of vows to the Mata and I did not fulfill them. The Mata even came to me in my dreams and asked for the fulfillment of the vows. I prayed to her—there is a proverb: Poor people's vows take 7 years to complete, the vows of sannyasis take only 2. I am a poor person so my vows are also delayed. I told the Mata, "I'm only a poor person. In this operation you have taken my life and given it back to me. Should you also put me through difficulties like this? You have to keep me well, only then can I come to your temple." I argued with her. She told me, "You are supposed to come in 1 year, you haven't come yet [it was already 1½ years]." I answered, "You have not kept me well, whatever I earn is going away. If you keep me well off, then I'll come to you. If you are not doing this, then you can take my life which you did not take in the operation."

Now I did feel better. Only after the dream I got all these health troubles. On the Ramadan day I wore a polyester blouse, polyester sari, and dressed so well. But 2 days after Ramadan, I fell ill.

On one of the days when I was sitting with Kamladevi in the house and she was talking about the operation, Zarina joined us and she and Kamladevi both bewailed their decision to get emasculated:

Why did we ever have this operation? Now we are feeling bad for having it done. Before the operation, even when we went out at night, we never had a fear. But now, suppose we see a drunkard, or a rowdy; now after the operation, we get frightened. If there is even a knock at the door at night or a drunkard approaches us, we get frightened. The local rowdies and bullies come at night, knock at the door and wake us up, and forcefully have their way with us.

"But still," Kamladevi said, "we must do it."

I could not get Kamladevi to elaborate in a clearer way why she regretted her decision to have the operation. On some occasions she related her regrets to her weakened physical condition, in spite of having earlier assured me this was not so. On other occasions she just seemed to feel that it had not changed her luck the way she had hoped it would. On still other occasions she evaded my question, in her merry distracting way, and sometimes she simply denied that she had any regrets at all.

AN ENDING

When I returned to India in 1985, I went first to Bombay and, eager to see Kamladevi again, went to the place where she stayed. I was met outside the building by a hostile-looking hijra who told me that Kamladevi was no longer there, that she had died. I was shocked and tried to find out some details, but none were forthcoming. When I went to Bastipore, the first thing I did was go to the house where Kamladevi had lived to inquire about her. That day, Lalitha was not there, but Premlata, a good friend of Kamladevi's who I had met in Bombay, was there. I asked her about Kamladevi, and she also said that she had died, of some respiratory illness. She could not give me any more information.

When I went to see Meera and Sushila, I immediately asked about Kamladevi. They said that Kamladevi had married a Muslim while in Bombay and then came back with him here. They added that he had squandered all of her money and that she did not get enough nourishment. "Because of her past life, drinking and eating anywhere, her health deteriorated," they said. Sushila added:

Kamladevi and I were friends for 20 years. She came back to that house in Temple Road, but then she went to Sanakpur [a small town near Bastipore], where some of these hijras from Raj Dev's house have gone. Those people at that place are very bad; they are not cultured and it is not a good place to go to. If you go to that place, you won't even leave with your dress on. They don't spare us either, even with our being of that group. Innocent people go there and get duped. So Kamladevi's health failed because she went to that place and stayed with those people. Even though she had an educated husband, he would eat off her hands only and didn't contribute toward the household expenses. This made Kamladevi fall ill, and she had had asthma before, so she passed away. This happened to her because she swore falsely on the Koran. We don't know if she is dead or not, but when she left from that place, to go to her parents' place, she was a gone case.

I was unable to learn any more about Kamladevi's fate. When I returned to India in 1986, I again went to Bombay to look for her, but no one at her old flat knew anything about her. As I did not return to Bastipore that trip, I could not inquire for her there. I hope to return to Bastipore next year, and I will try to look for her. I have a small hope that maybe she did not die and that we will meet again.

Hijras perform for a marriage.

A chela fixes flowers in the hair of her guru.

Hijra portrait.

A hijra in ordinary dress.

Three hijras on their way to a temple.

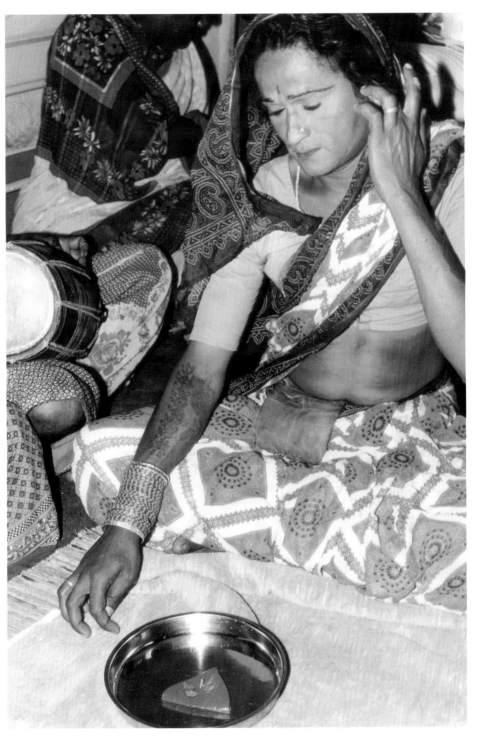

A hijra at a jamat.

A hijra dancer at a college function

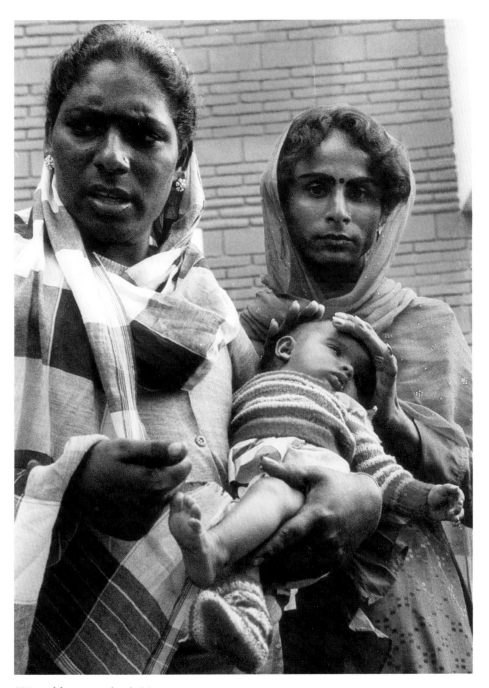

Hijras bless a male child.

A hijra in repose.

CHAPTER SIX

🐚 Meera: A New Guru

Meera, at 42 years of age, is on her way to becoming a successful guru. I met Meera in the following way: Told by some hijras in Bastipore that I must go to Gasworks Street, where I could visit a house where all of the hijras had the operation, I set out immediately with the two men who at that time were helping me in my work. One of them was a taxi driver named Ramesh. The other was a single middle-aged man named Anil who had apparently, in his life of drinking and partying, met with the hijras in their occupation as prostitutes. He was a bit of a flirt and was able to establish good rapport with the hijras in the way that their customers do. Perhaps he had been a customer of theirs himself: He never admitted this to me, but he seemed familiar with the hijra places of business and had mentioned introducing many of his friends from the Middle East to them. In any case, he and Ramesh were quite willing to pursue this lead, so off we went in Ramesh's taxi, to find the Gasworks Street house.

When we arrived in the neighborhood and asked for the hijras, we were immediately directed to a public bathhouse on a side lane off the main thoroughfare and were told to go upstairs. After introducing ourselves to the few hijras sitting there, and explaining that I was from America and interested in knowing about the hijras, one of those present immediately caught hold of a small child who had appeared in the room and sent her to deliver a message to someone outside. In scarcely 5 minutes, Meera appeared. She made an impressive presence and was clearly the leader of the group in some way. Without our even asking, she immediately announced that "we are all operated here!"

We sat on the floor and Anil began to flirt with Meera, showing her a costume jewelry ring he had with him. Ramesh, too, was very much at home; it was a friendly, sociable gathering. Different hijras came, were introduced, and left; some worked in the bathhouse downstairs and could only take a few minutes off to see what was going on. Meera, who had taken charge of the occasion, pointed out that some of the hijras lived in the room in which we were sitting. Others apparently lived nearby. After a half-hour of small talk, we left, fixing a time for me to return the following day.

That next morning Meera was again not present when I arrived but was immediately sent for and quickly appeared. This time, and on all of my subsequent visits to this house, I was accompanied by a Tamilian friend of mine, who acted as translator. My friend's warm personality endeared her to everyone; I think the fact that she and I were both married women with families was especially important to Meera, for whom family life was very significant.

Meera was openly enthusiastic about my interest in the hijras and said to the others gathered, "We must tell everything, so that this lady gets the right information." When I mentioned my willingness to pay those hijras whose time I took up in conversation, knowing that I might be taking them from other work, Meera refused, saying, "Even a prostitute can take money—we will do this for friendship." And so my relationship with Meera started in the most friendly manner, and it continued this way throughout that year and on my subsequent visits. In fact, however, Meera did not "tell everything," and some of what I learned about her, I learned only from other people. For example, Meera never told me she was married, though subsequent to my learning this through Kamladevi, other hijras confirmed it. Whenever I attempted to bring up the issue, Meera denied it in an evasive way, by referring to the normative prohibition on hijras having relations with women. Although I found this an unsatisfactory response, I eventually dropped the subject.

Over the next 7 months I visited this bathhouse regularly, which allowed me to observe its ongoing daily life as I talked with whoever was free at the moment. Sometimes I would give a day or two's advance notice of when I planned to visit; at other times I just dropped by at different hours of the day. No matter when I came, I was led into the room on the second floor and a few minutes later Meera arrived, beckoned by some instant grapevine. She seemed to have endless amounts of time to spend with me, unlike many of the other hijras who worked in the bathhouse, went out begging for alms, or engaged in prostitution, which kept them occupied on a fairly continuous basis. Clearly, one of the privileges of hijra rank is leisure time.

Meera is a bright, articulate person, who appeared self-confident and assertive. She was meticulous in her dress and conservative in her ordinary demeanor. On the days when I took posed photographs, she adorned herself flamboyantly with makeup and fancy clothing and showed herself to have a flair for the dramatic pose. Normally, however, she dressed in a feminine manner, more like a middle-class housewife than a "drag queen," which is the impression many other hijras give, with their exaggerated and garish femininity. Meera was exceedingly neat and clean, and much concerned about respectability and her reputation. She did not drink or smoke, and although she could shout raucously, was generally restrained.

Tall and large-boned, Meera towered over most of her companions. She had a masculine-looking face and wavy black hair. Of all the hijras I met, she expressed the most complete and intense feminine gender identity, a subject she repeatedly returned to. She was the one hijra I met who was taking hormone treatments[1] so she could "be more like a woman."

I liked and admired Meera in many ways and was pleased when, during my visit with her in the summer of 1985, she suggested "we become sisters." This took the form of a small ritual, and although she was younger than I, she said she would be the elder sister because she had, of course, seniority in the hijra community. An exchange of gifts is customary for this ritual, and she seemed very pleased with mine to her: a fancy, heavy, pure silver key holder. This is something that every prosperous proper Indian matriarch possesses, and I thought Meera appreciated the symbolism of it as much as its monetary value.

Born in Malaysia, of parents from a middle-level agricultural caste, Meera returned with her parents to Tamil Nadu when she was very young. In response to my question about how she came to join the hijras, she stressed the elements of cross-gender behavior in her childhood and adolescence.

BEGINNINGS

As early as 4 or 5 years old, whenever my parents went out, I would put on *bindi* [the decorative colored dot that all Indian women except widows wear on their forehead] and would imitate the work of the women. I would pretend I was a girl and put a sway into my walk. Because I was an only child to my parents, they didn't object when I wore bindi and dressed up in girl's clothes. They said I could lead any life which suited me.

As I got older, sometimes boys would come and ask me out for a picture, and so we would go. And when we went for a picture, the boy would take me and kiss me. . . . At first I was scared of men, but after the first scare I started to get interested in them. After that first experience I started going out regularly with boys. This is how it happens for us hijras; even those who tell you they have no sexual feeling. When we do this going out with men we meet hijras and they say, "Why don't you come and join us?" So we do.

See, it is like in an ordinary Indian house. There is a girl in the house and generally she doesn't go out with a man. Then she is given in marriage, and after that she goes to live with her husband. Gradually, she develops a feeling for this man. So, it is the same way with us. We go out with a boy. The first time it may not be a pleasant experience. We get scared of him. But after the first time, we go out with other men and the sexual attraction builds; from one man we go to another man.

I asked Meera to tell me about her first experience with a man.

See, there was this boy, he used to live across the street from me, in the same village. He used to watch me dressing up and putting flowers in my hair and doing up my face. We were friends, I liked him, we were just friends. He was in high school and was sitting for his high school finals, and then he was sent away to college for 1 year. I was about 13 or 14 at the time. When he was in this college he was told about people like me, people who are men but who . . . When he went away to college that year, he had had a "boyfriend," and I guess he had "relations" with him. That was how, when he came back, he started saying that he liked me, and why don't I come out with him. And then we kissed, and then one night we had "relations." Of course we couldn't have relations in the normal way—we had it from the back. In that way I came into this life.

Subsequently, according to her story, Meera took up with "a man in the military" and he took her to Madras, where she met some hijras, one of whom took her to Bombay. This hijra, who had been living in Bombay, had a boyfriend from a rich family who had come to Madras with her. So Meera, this hijra, and her boyfriend all went to Bombay together.

When I went first with those people to Bombay, they left me with all Lalanwallah people in Falkland Road [a red-light district]. After 3 months there I returned to my own home and stayed with my father. After that I again went back to Bombay, but then I went to Great Palace Street [another hijra area of prostitution]. I was a sort of supervisor over the girls who were "spoiled" down south and were being sent to Bombay for the purpose of doing prostitution. As a supervisor in these places, it was my duty to watch over about 10 girls [hijra prostitutes] to see that they didn't run away and that the business was carried on properly. I was a "watchover." The business house was run like this: We collect the money first so the man can't run away without paying. After all, we have to run this business house on the payments collected. Or, for example, there is a boy, and he comes to see this girl in the house. He falls in love with that girl, but even if he wants to entice her away, we do not allow him to do that. So that the girl may not run away, we keep watch over her. We pay a heavy amount to buy these girls for prostitution. When an old customer comes, the girl who's always had a go with him, if some other girl takes him, she will have a quarrel. This quarreling and fighting among the girls is not allowed; we prevent such fights and put the girls in their proper places.

In Great Palace Street the guru was not a good person, and I found life very difficult. We were not very well looked after in that house. We never got food at the proper time, and we were not allowed to sleep until 2:00 in the morning. It was very troublesome for me so I came back to my father's house. At my parent's place I used to have everything to eat and drink, from milk to fruits, but in Bombay we didn't have anything. But still, again, for my pleasure, I ran away from my parents and went back to Bombay and stayed another 3 months. I repeated this same thing three or four times. On one of these occasions I left my guru's house and slept in a railway station, where all the street urchins used to trouble me.

After returning several times to Bombay, Meera finally decided to leave for good, saying that "the people in Bombay are too greedy, all they think about is money." She came back to South India, this time to Bastipore, to stay with Raj Dev, the most important guru in the city. He was in charge of a hijra bathhouse and house of prostitution. But Meera did not find life at this house agreeable either because "there were too many restrictions and Raj Dev made us work too much." So she left.

> After I left Raj Dev I had a lot of difficulties. I had no money and no place to get food and boarding. No one here in Bastipore speaks Tamil [her native language], and I couldn't understand one bit of what they said. Nobody admitted me into their fold, and I used to sleep in the railway station. Finally, I took up a house here in Gasworks Street, paying 100 rupees per month for rent. Then these girls [her current chelas] started joining me. If I said they could stay, they were allowed to stay; if I had any other ideas they were not allowed to stay. I used to keep these girls inside my room and safeguard their interests. We had a built-in bathroom, so there was no need for them to go outside. This present hamam was there, but these hijras all wore shirt and lungi [referring to the fact that some hijras, in order not to call attention to themselves in public, wear men's, rather than women's, dress]. The agent of that bathhouse called me and told me that I shouldn't wear a sari, that I should be wearing a lungi and shirt like the others, but I told him, "I was born like this and I am used to wearing only saris." So he said, "It's all right then, but lead a respectable life."

I asked Meera why she thought men came to hijra prostitutes rather than to women prostitutes.

> These men who come to us, they may be married, or unmarried, the father of many children. Those who come to us, they have no desire to go to a man. . . . They come to us for the sake of going to a girl. They prefer us to their wives. See, there's many a customer whose wife has already had three or four children and he still longs for sex, which his lawful wife won't be able to provide [she no longer satisfies him]. But the hijras can do this [sex] from the back, from behind. These people are attracted to the hijras because they get the satisfaction from the back or a satisfaction from between the thighs. These men prefer us to their wives. . . . Each one's tastes differ among people. . . . It is God's way; because we have to make a living, he made people like this so we can earn.
>
> Also, those regular [women] prostitutes, they have all sorts of diseases because they go to all sorts of men, but we hijras don't contract disease.[2] Some of these hijras, like Kamladevi, and all those people at Raj Dev's house, as far as my knowledge goes, they do this [sex] by the mouth also, but in my case the Mata has not permitted me to do that. Those

hijras who do that have endless difficulties because it's not nice and it's not the wish of the Mata. Those people down there at Raj Dev's have been undergoing endless difficulties because of this. I won't even take a glass of water from them.

HUSBANDS

After Meera had been at Gasworks Street in Bastipore for a while, she found a steady boyfriend; but a few years later he left her. She then met another man, Ahmed, with whom she has had a relationship for several years and whom she calls her husband. She now lives with him in a house separate from that where her chelas practice prostitution, and it is this house where I visited her many times in the summer of 1985. Ahmed is a central person in Meera's life. She divides her time equally between being a wife and being a guru. The two roles are not incompatible; in fact, the money that comes to her as a guru has allowed her to provide a comfortable setting for her marital relationship. This relationship causes some gossip because Ahmed is at least 10 years younger than Meera, and her strong attachment to him is considered unbecoming, especially for a woman like herself in middle age.

> When I first came to this place, I selected a boyfriend. He was a Brahmin boy, well read and intelligent. He could repeat anything he heard said the very next minute without a fault. But then he left me with almost nothing except the sari and the blouse that I was wearing on my back. This Brahmin boy is married now and has two children, but he still comes here to visit now and then.
> After this boy I met Ahmed. He lived with his parents just up the street. This Ahmed's parents never wanted him to be with me. They tried to beat me and kill me and thought they could separate me from Ahmed. Then [in 1979] I had the operation. It was after Ahmed saw the difficulties I went through to have the operation that he developed a liking for me. He sleeps with me, but I can never bear him a child. I am sure that if he wants, he will marry someone else who will bear him a child, but he'll never give me up.

Sometimes the relationship between Meera and Ahmed does not go smoothly.

> Ahmed never comes home on time. For dinner he goes to the hotel [restaurant] close by. He sits there and he passes the time with his friends. They go loafing around to the hotel to have tea, and he never comes home on time, and I'm waiting with his dinner. I will wait even till 1:00 in the morning. Then when he comes home so late I'll have to get up to give him his food. And then we have a quarrel.

One time Kamladevi and I went out and danced in one of the colleges, and Ahmed and another boy came to watch the dance. I had dressed up very attractively for the dance sequence, and I did not know that I was being watched by him. After the dance was over there was a lot of riot. First, Kamladevi and I had performed on the stage, and they paid us for that. After, they asked us to perform on the bare ground. If we had just gone home then it would have been all right, but Kamladevi wanted the extra money, so she said, "Let us dance on the bare ground also." Then the rioting started. I had been operated on but Kamladevi had not yet been operated on, so we ran away. Ahmed saw all this and told his parents. They got very angry with me and asked me, "What made you go there, don't you have enough to eat at home, don't you have enough clothing, don't you have people who are looking after you, aren't you ashamed of yourself? And then they beat me black and blue. Among Muslims, if a married woman goes out to perform, they punish her. After that I did not perform at all, that was the end of my performing days.

In the beginning, when I selected my man, Ahmed, I felt that this life was not the life for me. I felt really dejected. At that time Ahmed was in love with another girl. She was 12 years old then, a Hindu girl, and my man is a Muslim. He was a playboy before, one among the rowdies. But after he became friendly with me he became more well behaved. And he's very clean. Even so, I don't leave him be. If he is at fault in a quarrel, I beat him and also receive beatings from him. "I have sacrificed for you," I tell him, "therefore, you should also sacrifice for me." I tell him, "Now you have married me, why do you have eyes for someone else?" Sometimes we have hand to hand fist fights, but then we make up. Once he had beaten me so hard that one of my ribs was broken and I was in bed for some time. That time, his friend had come and they had a liquor party here at home. I told him, "Go to a bar or a hotel and have your party, not here at home."

I was head over heels in love with him but he acted as though he loved me just for the sake of the money, since I would give him 50, 60 rupees [about $5] whenever he asked for money. So at this time, when he had also kept this girl, I said, "Then leave me and go." But he said, "No, I won't leave you," but he still continued to see this girl. He never came home for his food or drink, he was always roaming about. Once he squabbled with that girl and then he asked me to beat the girl. I wouldn't do that, so he beat the girl himself and then left her.

I asked Meera whether Ahmed's friends ever tease him about his relationship with a hijra.

No, they don't make fun of him because he is the head of a gang of rowdies and they are all afraid of him. His friends come to our house. They all come home and eat food in my house, and they talk to me like a sister and don't make fun of me.

Given all the quarrels with Ahmed that Meera spoke of, I asked her how she felt about marriage.

It is like a sparrow having a husband for itself who is a male sparrow, and an ant for an ant, the same way we also want a man. If we go to Bombay we are given respect because we have stuck to one man, who also earns and looks after us. In Bombay the hijras must earn and sustain their men. In Bombay the man is given five rupees for his expenses, apart from food, tea, and shelter. This man goes out and only returns late in the evening in time to be in the company of the hijra. The whole morning the hijra goes out to work and comes back in the evening again to start the household chores and to feed her husband. It is not like that for me.

Once you make up your mind to do it, you cannot let it go. See, if I feel dejected and there are tears in my eyes, then Ahmed will ask me, "Why are you so depressed? What do you want? What has happened to you?" And if Ahmed is not well, even with just a headache, I will sit by him the whole night tending to him, massaging his head, his feet, his body. For 1½ years, when I lived with Old Rekha at Nehru Road [another hijra locality in Bastipore], while Ahmed was away working in Kuwait, I had a lot of difficulties.

See, Serena, my life is not like yours. The urchins there at Nehru Road, they used to rip off my sari and I had to show them what was underneath. They teased me so. But Ahmed is like a God to me, because when he came back he saved me from all this humiliation. He's guarded me so well. If anybody teases or disturbs me, he gets very angry. He does not allow his parents to say anything bad to me. Even to do the housework he keeps a servant for me. Even when I keep after him, scolding, "You went here, you went there, you went everywhere, you have been talking to so and so [other women]," even then, he won't say one word back to me. When he is not here the police and the urchins bother me, but when he is here, everyone is silent. When Ahmed is not here, nobody will respect me even as much as a five-cent piece. If he is there, I'm the lord of everything. . . . If anybody troubles me, Ahmed will thrash them and send them away. God and he are one to me. I used to be so thin, as thin as Sushila. I had asthma, and I was always short of breath. Ahmed didn't mind that at all but would always make me sleep beside him.

After my operation even his parents gave me their sympathy when they saw how much I suffered. We were very happy; now when we quarrel, I tell him, "Leave me alone so that I can continue my own life and you can be free to do what you like." Then he tells me, "In the beginning [right after the operation] you were so thin, very frail, and looked as though you would die at any time. Because of me you are now nice and healthy."

I was seriously ill after the operation, I was on the verge of death, but Ahmed looked after me and nursed me back to the condition I am now in. Daily he would bring 20 rupees worth of meat for me, all the nourishment I needed. He would make me eat food and saw that I had my full quota of nourishment. So even now, he doesn't leave me but takes very good care of me. I'm the one who suspects him, thinking that he goes to the prostitution houses and other places not worth visiting.

Among us hijras, if we keep a man as a husband, we must live with him. If we are deserted then it is death to us—we die. If Ahmed goes away to another lady or another hijra, then I would shave my head and burn myself, like the widow who commits *suttee* [suicide]. It is because we don't want to go to another man that we immolate ourselves or we kill ourselves.

Working in this hamam, so many men who come here as customers say, "Why don't you select one of us? We will look after you well." For this we answer, whether the man is attractive or not, whether he's dark or fair, it's no concern to us, we answer, "No, my man is my man." We good hijras don't have eyes for these men, we won't even touch them. But some of these girls [hijras], they do go and have an affair with everyone, even Sushila does this, but I won't go. If a man leaves us and goes away, we may take to drinking out of sheer dejection, and in this way we may try to end our life. If my husband is not at home, I switch on the light at night and keep awake the whole night either reading or listening to music till he comes home.

Some of these hijras will do anything [implying prostitution] to please the public, to gain wealth. They are mercenary people, but we others [good people], we don't go about like that. At this age [middle age] we would like to be more respectable and lead a respectable life. So after some time we fall in love with a man, and eventually we marry him and lead the life of any normal housewife.

THE OPERATION

When I first met Meera, she was eager to talk about the operation and described it to me in great detail, as something she had undergone herself. Subsequently, I was told she had performed 18 operations, which she confirmed to me in 1985. I then understood that her detailed knowledge of the operation and the recovery period came from her experience as a dai ma. For Meera, the most important motive in having the operation was "to be more like a woman," but she also viewed it very much as a religious ritual.

I was talking with Meera one day early in the summer of 1985, thinking about how I could broach the subject of my having heard that she was a dai ma, when she brought it up herself. We had been talking about Ahmed, her favorite topic.

See, Ahmed had told his parents that it was his wish and will to see me, so let them not interfere. Then by and by he fell in love with this girl somewhere up this lane, and I had a quarrel with that girl. When I fought with that girl Ahmed said, "You're a man and I'm a man, so how can you have anything to do with me?" When he said that, I thought I would take poison and die, I wanted to end my life. Then Ahmed told me I should have the operation. So I went for the operation at that time. But just before that, some hijra had died during the operation, so I got afraid and ran away. Then Ahmed told me, "If you're afraid, then don't have the operation." But then, after a while another dai ma came here, so I had the operation. And now even I do this operation. I have done 18 operations. But now I have left off performing this operation because it is a sort of ill omen for me. The Mata came to me in a dream last year and told me to stop performing this operation. I am paid handsomely for doing this operation, but the money doesn't last long as it is a curse.

I asked Meera how she had decided to become a dai ma.

See, the Mata's power came to me in a dream. The Mata was wearing green bangles, green blouse, and a green sari. The Mata asked me, "Give me back my nose ring. Where is my nose ring?" This dream came on a Tuesday and a Friday [the special days of the hijras' Goddess], for three consecutive days. That is the call we get from the Mata which gives the sanction to perform this operation. This dream also signifies that someone is coming to get the operation done. It is essential that we receive the permission from the Mata to operate; otherwise, the operation will not turn out well.

All of Meera's 18 operations have been successful. Meera believes that the success of the procedure is not in her hands, but rather is up to the Mother Goddess. Her reputation has spread far and wide, and people have come from other cities to have her operate on them. Even her detractors admire her skill. Meera takes very good care of her clients and personally supervises the 40-day recovery period herself. This helped explain a puzzling event that occurred near the end of my first stay in Bastipore.

I had given a garden party for the hijras I knew in Bastipore. It was to be a very festive occasion, and everyone was looking forward to it with great anticipation. On the day I came to pick up the hijras in Meera's neighborhood, she was nowhere to be found; I got only the most evasive replies to my inquiries as to where she was. Sushila told me that she would definitely be coming, but when she at last arrived the party was almost over. At the time Meera told me that the taxi driver had trouble finding the house and that he had to circle the neighborhood for hours. Now, she admitted that she had been taking care of one of her clients on whom she had operated.

I knew it must have been a very important reason for Meera to arrive so late, especially since she was always so reliable about appointments.

When I asked Meera why she had had the operation, she replied:

Why I got operated on was, I wanted to be like other women, to be very attractive. Before the operation, Ahmed and I were never even talking to each other, but when I got operated on, he and his family looked after me. Then he permanently had me. He can decide to marry me now, that is his wish and will. Our feelings are like women, only. After the operation we become like women.

I am taking these hormones now. See, we have spent so much money to get the operation done, we can spend some more money and become full-fledged women by developing breasts. See how nice and fat I have become. Before the operation I was so thin, like Sushila, now I am nice and fat, like a woman. It is only for this purpose that we get operated on.

We have the same feelings you people have. When any male touches us, we also get a sort of excitement out of it. When we sleep with our men, after the operation we can sleep without any clothes on because we resemble women only and no one will know that it is just an operated part. Those people, like Sushila, who haven't had the operation, they can't remove their clothes in front of a man because they still have their male organ.

Now, also, when we go on the road and these bullies harass us and they say, "There is a man dressed in a sari," we can lift our skirts and say, "See, there is nothing there like a man." We want to show them that we are women, dressed like women. We are not like those men who stay with their parents, dress like men, go to restaurants, public urinals, and go to men, contact men. We are like women, we dress like women, we leave our parents and join this group. We are not like those men.

When I returned to see Meera, in 1985, she showed me a small baby she was taking care of that she had "adopted." She then told me that after her years of taking hormones she was able to produce breast milk. She demonstrated this by massaging her breasts, and a jet stream of milk appeared. "But," she said, "the baby doesn't take milk from me, so I just remove the milk from my breasts and throw it out." Meera expressed great satisfaction with her life at this point:

I have now stopped doing this operation. Ahmed told me to stop. I gave away the Mata's picture to someone else so that I shouldn't be feeling that because the Mata was there I was bound to do these operations again and again. After I gave away the photo, I don't get the power of the Mata on me to perform these operations.

I have put some money by, but I'm not very avaricious. If God has designed that I should get money, I get it. There was a man here, he was running a club. He had a lot of money but suddenly he died: Was he able to take his money with him? He died in a very bad way, bleeding in the nose and mouth and endless suffering. I was given a lot of respect for doing these operations; even in Bombay I was famous. But now my only wish is this, that my husband should be all right, my chelas should be all right, that God gives us enough money to sustain ourselves. God is great.

CHAPTER SEVEN

🌺 Sushila: Achieving Respect

Sushila was born a male, of a Tamil family in Malaysia. In 1981 she was about 35 years old. She is a lively, dynamic, feisty person, though she admits that she drinks and fights too much. Her father is a middle-level civil servant in Madras, and she has three brothers and two sisters. She has been a member of the hijra community for 18 years.

When I first met Sushila, in 1981, she was living with her husband in a small house in the same working-class neighborhood of Bastipore where Meera lived. The area was known as a red-light district for hijra prostitutes, one of several in the city. Although Sushila lived on her own—not in the bathhouse with the other hijras, who, like her, used it for their prostitution—she was perfectly friendly with them, visited them often, considered herself as a member of the community, and participated actively in their affairs.

From our first meeting, Sushila was outgoing and receptive to my interest in the hijras. Because she was largely supported by her husband and didn't need to work as regularly as the other hijra prostitutes, she also had more time than many of the others to talk with me. Maybe it also helped our rapport that I smoked, a slightly deviant act for women, at least respectable women, in India. She also smoked, one of the few hijras I met in Bastipore who did so. She began our first conversation by saying, "I'll tell you about this business—why should I lie?—I am also a prostitute."

Sushila is an articulate, fluent speaker and was not above a bit of gossip about the other hijras. This was helpful to me in providing a framework for evaluating her personality and also as a check on what others told me. Of all the hijras I met, I liked Sushila the best; she not only incorporated those qualities of hospitality, generosity, and friendliness that make India such a delightful place to work, but she was also entirely frank, once trust had been established. More than this, however, what I identified with in her was her seemingly constant struggle on the one hand to be herself, say what she thought, and act however the impulse moved her, and yet at the same time live up to the norms of her society and establish herself as a respectable person in the community.

After I first met Sushila in August, 1981, I visited with her at least several times a week over a period of 7 months. Not all of these sessions involved long or structured conversations. One of the problems of interviewing people in India, especially with a group as communal as the hijras, is that it is not easy to get anyone alone. During my first year, I only spoke with Sushila in the common room of the bathhouse; when I visited India again in the summer of 1985, she invited me to her own house, where we were able to close the door and have relatively private conversations for an hour or two almost every day for the time I was there.

Sushila often spoke to me about her quick temper; she has a hard time backing off from a fight and often initiates them, particularly when she has had too much to drink. It is interesting to me, in this connection, that she started the story of her life with an event involving her aunt, her father's sister, who, while in Malaysia, killed the Chinese plantation foreman who had made a sexual advance to her. It sounded to me, as Sushila narrated this story, exactly like something she would do herself.

Sushila shows a great deal of spunk and determination: She has managed, with much imagination, to carry out the life plan for a woman of her culture, in spite of the fact that she was born a man.

Sushila was born in Singapore. When she was 3 months old her mother left that metropolis for India, together with her, her father's sister (paternal aunt), and her own brothers and sisters. Sushila's father was working at a rubber estate, and when the aunt killed the plantation foreman, the whole family had to leave. When they came to Madras, Sushila's grandfather (her father's father) built separate houses for each of his six children, including Sushila's father.

BEGINNINGS

Without being asked about her mother, Sushila volunteered the information that it was her father's sisters, who also worked on the rubber plantation, who used to take care of her:

> My mother never used to carry her children on her lap, fearing they might spoil her clothes. My father's sister, she was the one who reared us. My mother would just be sleeping on a cot and if a child cried, she would ring the bell for my aunt to come from the rubber plantation and attend to the child. We were brought up on tinned milk, and my aunt would mix the milk for us, feed us, tidy us up, and then go back to her own work.
>
> My mother didn't like messy children. If we had messed ourselves, then she would just drag us along with the bedsheet and put us down without touching us.

This apparently changed when the family moved to India, as Sushila remembered that her two younger brothers were cared for by her mother, who breast-fed them, unlike the other children. At some later point, Sushila's father, narrowly escaping Japanese patrols, walked through the

Malayan jungles and eventually joined his family (sisters, father, wife, and children) in Madras.

When I asked Sushila how she came to be a hijra, she said, "I was born like this. My parents felt deep sorrow when I was born abnormal." I asked her about her childhood.

> From my earliest school days, I used to sit only with the girls and not with the boys. I asked the teacher's permission to do this. The boys used to tease and pinch me during the recesses. One day one of the boys in my class dragged me by the hand to tease me and he pushed me. I retorted and pushed him back. His clothes got dirty [from the horse-play], and he went and complained to the teacher, and the teacher told the headmaster. My clothes also got dirty, so I went home and told my parents all that had happened at school. They changed my clothes and sent me back to school. When I got there, my class teacher beat me and sent me to the headmaster, who also beat me for having pushed that boy in my class. I went home crying at noon, and I told my mother all that had happened and how the teacher and headmaster had beat me. Then my aunt [her father's sister] and my mother both came to the headmaster and asked him why he had beaten me. He told my mother I had pushed that boy and that's why I had to be beaten. Then they told him that they would not send me to school anymore if the children were going to torture me, so they stopped me from going to school.

Following this episode, Sushila tried a number of different occupations over the next several years. First, she was sent to a small town in Tamil Nadu where an elder sister lived and where she learned to stitch clothes on a sewing machine. This did not suit her, however, and she was then sent to a place in Madras where she worked in an electrical wiring shop connecting wires to plugs. Of this time she particularly remembers using her small wages—plus the few cents tips she received—to buy some flowers, or blouse material, or curry for her mother and sister.

In talking about her mother at this time, she said:

> My mother would always wait for me for lunch or dinner until I came home. She would appreciate the gait [at this point Padmini, her real cousin, who is also a hijra and was staying with Sushila, demonstrated an exaggerated, swaying, feminine walk] with which I walked down the street. I used to come home at 11:30 and 12:00 at night, and my mother would stay awake waiting for me.

Around this time, when Sushila was about 12 years old, her mother died, and soon after that she herself became ill with typhoid. She was then cared for by her aunt, and she stopped working at the electrical shop, because—she said—the doctor told her she was too weak to continue. After she recovered her health she was sent to work with a bookbinder, who attempted to teach her that trade. She did not like it, however, and quit, and was put to work as a watchman. She disliked that work as well and "ran away from there," after which she was put to work in a rubber factory manufacturing tires. She cared for this work as little as her previous jobs, despite the fact that it only required her to work 4 hours a day. So after 4 months she took the 150 rupees that was coming to her and left.

At this time Sushila ran across some hijras "like me" who invited her to join them in selling fish in the market, which she did. She was now living with her father's sister and the sister's husband. Several times Sushila specifically mentioned that her own father never beat her, comparing him to the uncle who did, because "he didn't like me degrading myself selling fish."

At this time (about age 13) Sushila said that "I felt I would like to have a man," and in the market she met a fisherman with whom she developed a sexual relationship and whom she referred to as her husband. He lived in his own house with a wife, his mother, a sister, and the sister's husband. Sushila moved in with them.

Sushila said that although there were so many people in the house, "My mother-in-law always entrusted me with the money and the keys to the cupboard."

> I would run the house. Whenever they went out I would give them their jewelry to wear, but when they were at home, it would be in my safekeeping. My mother-in-law used to earn 200, 300 rupees and more a day, and my sister-in-law's husband, and my husband's sister, were all earning, and all the money used to come into my hands. And when I left that place I handed over the keys and came away with just the clothes that I was wearing. To this day they remember me and are sad that I left them.

> I asked Sushila how she came to leave that place.

> My father-in-law's sister had a very handsome son who had been away in the Andaman Islands. He came to visit and brought with him a tape recorder. Although he had come to visit his parents, he came to visit us very often. When there was nobody else [besides her] at home, he would bring the tape recorder and record all my conversation on that. I was attracted to him, but since I never spoke to any man, I only slowly got used to talking with him, but then did so very freely. He also felt the same attraction for me and recorded all that I was thinking and saying to him. He had recorded my story from the beginning, and we were involved with each other. If I didn't see him for one day I used to feel very bad. I would even risk going to his house and seeing him and talking to him there. My mother-in-law came to know of it and called me, along with my sister-in-law. They asked me what was going on with this man from the Andamans—was it true what they had heard? I didn't answer them, I felt so ashamed that I left that place.

I asked Sushila if her family knew where she was at that time, and she said:

Yes, they knew, but they didn't bother to come and contact me. It was an embarrassing situation for them, to come to a fisherman's house in search of me. Even though I wore a lungi, I used to wear a bindi and kajal [feminine makeup]. My family didn't like this since they had felt that I was more a boy, they treated me more like a boy than a girl. They felt this [her being like a girl] embarrassing for them. But still, then I went home on my own.

Sushila stayed at home for only a short time, perhaps a year or two, and then left.

How I left my house is a story. I had gone to the beach with an ex-minister's son, and he made me sit in the car with him and did so many things [sexual things]. When I went home he gave me 60 rupees. I had kept it in the hipfold of my lungi. Then I went to sleep for the night. My elder brother had kept some cash under his pillow and had gone to the toilet. My younger brother took 20 rupees from that. In that young age, even, he was lending money on interest and took the money for that purpose. Nobody in the family but me knew that. They all scolded me the next morning, saying that I had taken the money. All the house scolded me saying, "That pottai has taken the money and is putting the blame on this young fellow." I cried and tried to convince them that I didn't take it.

Then my brother asked me, "why do you have to take my money? After all, you are a pottai. Go and give your anus somewhere; you'll get all the money you need." I got furious and I said, "You want *paisa* [money]? Here, I have 60 rupees from giving my anus to someone, take the money." And I flung the money at his face. He put his head down in shame and went inside. After this incident I was feeling very frustrated in my house. Feeling very bored I went to a movie one day and there I met a hijra. She asked me if I would come to Bastipore with her. I asked her why should I want to do that and she said, "There you can always wear a sari and live, so come. She said we could go begging in the shops in Bastipore and earn 50 to 60 rupees a day. I hated my house so much that I came to Bastipore with her.

When Sushila first came to Bastipore, she was taken to the house of Yusuf. But she did not like this house—there was too much hard work there.

I stayed with Yusuf from about 6 months to a year and gave all my earnings to her. She gave me these silver anklets, of the type Muslims wear, with bells and all that on them; there were four pairs of them. Then, one of our own people [Hindus] came and took me away to

Bombay. Without Yusuf's knowledge, I ran away with them. At Bombay they left me with some hijras. People started calling us to join them. If I had set a foot in any one of those houses and had taken even a glass of water, I would have become the chela of that guru. For this reason we are prewarned by the person who takes us to Bombay not to drink water, tea, or anything, at anyone's place. Even if we are somewhere and we are thirsty, we are supposed to go back to the house where we are staying and drink water. The person who had taken me to Bombay was Raj Dev's guru, Raju. He put me on to a *nani* [a female kinship term often used for an elder hijra who is not one's guru] and told me that I could be Raj Dev's chela. We had a jamat and I put five rupees in my name and in Raj Dev's name by proxy, and that's how I was joined with my guru.

But I did not like that place. We had wheat balls to eat, but that didn't agree with me. I don't eat wheat [people from South India have rice as their staple], and this food didn't agree with me. The work I did there was to go to the shops. I ask you, who will like that work? So because of that and also because of the food, I ran away from that place and came back to Yusuf in Cantonment. But Yusuf said I could not be his chela because I had run away from him, and that I could only be Raj Dev's chela [Raj Dev and Yusuf were the only two gurus in Bastipore], so he sent me to Raj Dev. I became Raj Dev's chela and began earning from Raj Dev, and stayed with him.

Soon after that, one time my uncle's son [referring to Padmini] came to Raj Dev's place at Temple Road—he's also a pottai—and he stayed with me there for a week. Then he went back to Madras and told my "housepeople" that I am here. Then they wrote a letter to me at that address, and I started writing to them. Then my aunt's son, who is an inspector in the police, and my younger sister's husband, came together to Raj Dev's house in search of me. The day they arrived I had gone to the temple and had washed my hair and was drying it outside. There I was, nicely smoking a cigarette when these two people came straight to me and asked me, "Where is Ram Chand [the male name given to Sushila by her parents]?" not knowing I was that person. "Who is Ram Chand?" I asked. They said, "His name is Ram Chand. Here I believe he is called Sushila." They did not recognize me, but of course I knew them and I was shaking with fear, thinking my uncle would beat me. Then I told them that Sushila had gone to Bombay yesterday; I was afraid because that man [the aunt's son] is a police inspector. They started to leave and had reached the end of the street, but I felt so bad, I felt I should reveal the truth. I clapped my hands to call them and attract their attention and I said to them, "Come inside at least, sit down and have a coffee. Then I said, "This Sushila is a very good person around here, so you must at least take a coffee." Then when they were leaving I asked my younger sister's husband, "What, you can't recognize me?"

"*Okkalla* [motherfucker]! I'll be damned, it's you, I could not recognize you!" he said. Then they stayed for 4 days.

Another time my brother—the one who had abused me—came. He is a clerk in a Hindi school. He came with my sister's husband. They both came in and my brother said, "Who is Ram Chand, where is Ram Chand?" I had gone out to order coffee for them. I was just entering as my brother had asked for me, so I just stopped at the doorstep, to hear what they were saying. Then my brother-in-law answered, "Oh, your sister has just gone out, here is your sister." Then I came in and my brother looked me over from head to foot, and he put his head down and cried for 2 hours. I told him, through my brother-in-law, "Ask him to drink his coffee, it's getting cold." I made him stay there for 2 days. That evening I brought brandy for him; he ate and drank some brandy and took the rest with him. Then my guru, Raj Dev, said that since my brother has come I should wear fine jewelry and he gave me all the jewels to wear before him. My brother always considered me as a male child, and he was still crying over my wearing a woman's dress and wanting to be with men. My brother asked my brother-in-law if my hair, which was very long at that time, was my real hair. My brother-in-law said, "Oh, it's the real hair of your sister, see for yourself." But that very night I lost the whole head of hair, because that night one pottai was smoking and accidently the ashes fell on my hair. I was sleeping next to her, and I lost the whole head of hair. My brother said to me, "Come home," and I said, "I'll come like this only [that is, dressed like a female]. If you're interested I'll come home." He said, "No, we're such a big, honorable family, how can I let you come home this way?" "Then I won't come," I said.

And so Sushila remained in the hijra commune in Bastipore.

Then 10 days later, after my brother had left for Madras, I received a telegram saying my sister was seriously ill. So my guru gave me 2,000 rupees cash, and I went to the shops and bought some clothes, for which I had borrowed money from the moneylenders. I bought about 1,000 rupees worth of clothes, and with that and 3,000 [rupees] cash and two suitcases, I left for Madras. I arrived at my sister's place, and she was carrying a pot to draw water for drinking purposes. I had come in a taxi and the people in the houses all around had come to see who alighted from a taxi. They were talking about a famous film actress, Bhanumati, and comparing me to her. My sister did not even recognize me as she passed by carrying the pot of water. After having paid the taxi driver, I clapped my hands to call my sister. She came to me and asked me what I wanted. I slowly told her, very gently, "Don't you recognize me? I am Ram Chand." She put the pot down and immediately took my two suitcases and took me home. The people who come early in the morning to put the *rangoli* designs [chalk designs that Hindus have drawn on their doorsteps for auspicious purposes] in front of the house asked my sister who the visitor was, but she didn't answer them. I really felt like laughing, but it was not worth laughing in front of them—that would have been bad manners. So I covered my mouth with my sari and got behind my sister. She told my father, "I have brought Ram Chand," and my father opened the door and took me inside. The people living in the house opposite, when they heard my name mentioned, immediately collected a crowd to come and see me. There were two rooms in the house, each opposite to the other. My father and brother both requested me to get inside one of the rooms and to change my dress into a lungi and shirt before these people could see me. I told my father, "If you people feel ashamed of me because I am wearing a sari, I don't want to embarrass you. Allow me to go away here and now." They didn't have an answer, they just kept quiet. At that time I stayed only for 2 days and went back to Bastipore without seeing my uncle because I was afraid of him.

WORKING

I'll tell you the truth, I'll not lie, in those days when I was with Raj Dev, I was also a prostitute. At first I was very afraid, and I felt like I wanted to run home to my parents. I did run away once but this person, Raju [Raj Dev's guru and the one who brought Sushila to Bombay], she brought me back and taught me the trade. I told her, "I am afraid, I don't like this," but she said, "Since you've got into it, I'll teach you how to go about it." And then I settled down to prostitution at Raj Dev's hamam.

I'm not bluffing, you can ask the others about me, how much wealth and jewelry I had. The customers would come asking for me only; if I was not there they would go away. I used to earn 200 to 300 rupees a day in baksheesh and give even that to Raj Dev. I had to give all my earnings without holding back even a single penny. Even for a string of flowers, I had no money. At 9:00 in the night [hijras say "our houses close at 9:00"; no men are allowed after that hour], Raj Dev would call me and say, so nicely, "*Beta* [son] come here, give me the money bag," and I would immediately give it to him. The amount would be 300 to 350 rupees. Other times she would take the money and throw the empty bag at me. She would snatch away all the earnings and give me just a four anna bit. After 10:00 at night we were sent to Tilak Road. There was a bar there where we used to earn from 500 to 1,000 rupees a night. At 12:00 we would return home and go straight to the hamam and wake the guru and hand over these earnings to him—it would be anywhere from 300 to 1,000 rupees.

There is a hotel near the picture house there, where we also would go and earn. There were three other girls with me. So many rich men would come to us, but they all would select me first before the other girls. We three Indian girls would dress in a sari, but there was also an Anglo-Indian girl there who would be dressed in a frock. The people in the bar would always ask me first to receive the customers, so in this way I earned a lot of money, all of which I gave to Raj Dev, my guru.

Rehanna [an older hijra in that house] used to advise me, "Why are you giving all your money away to Raj Dev?" Because in return he would give me only four annas for coffee. It was with my money that all the needs of the house were taken care of—the guru's drinks, cigarettes, extra expenses, visitors' expenses, and gifts to the guests who come here, in addition to what we must pay toward the expenses of the house. After paying for all this I must also have 200 to 300 rupees in my bag. If I don't have that, Raj Dev would get very angry and curse me with such abusive language.

In those days, also, things were very strict. Nowadays the pottais have a little freedom, but when I joined, it was different. We would constantly be bullied by these gurus. When we left the house we had to cover our heads with our saris. If we talked too long to a customer, we would be beaten. My guru, Raj Dev, had beaten me so much in those 6 years you could see the marks all over my body, just because I had that man as my husband [Sushila's first husband, a taxi driver].

One day I was in a very thoughtful mood, shedding tears, feeling very sad. I was thinking how we hijras earn so much, but even for a cup of coffee we don't have the freedom to drink. That day I had a headache, so I asked someone to bring me a cup of coffee, and I took a tablet for my headache. Raj Dev came and kicked me, and the whole cup of hot coffee poured over me, and the glass broke. He abused me so: "What is the caste of your mother that you only want to relax like this without working!"

Depending on the day I spoke with Sushila, she would have different memories of Raj Dev and the time she spent with him. Some days she was bitter, at other times, more nostalgic.

Though Raj Dev is dead and gone now, I still remember him for his generosity. Raj Dev did not cheat me completely. Whatever I earned, Raj Dev gave me in the form of jewels, to half the amount. He made me a gold chain for 25 sovereigns and then another necklace for 12 sovereigns and earrings for 1½ sovereigns. You ask anyone about the jewels I had. But then what happened was that Raj Dev's niece was getting married and he wanted to get her a few jewels made. I told Raj Dev that I had a pair of earrings that he had given me which could be given to the bride, and he could get new ones made for me later. Then later on, Raj Dev's brother's son got married. Raj Dev didn't ask me for my chain, but I myself gave it to him for his brother's son's wedding to be given as a gift to the bride. It had five strands of gold with a stone-studded pendant. He pledged that chain with the pawnbroker for cash to help get his brother's son married. Then Raj Dev's younger [other] brother died. I gave away my other necklace to Raj Dev to be pledged for the funeral expenses.

I asked Sushila why she was no longer at Raj Dev's house.

The last fight I had with Raj Dev came because of my ex-husband. I was sick at that time. My husband was giving me 10 rupees daily and taking me to the doctor. I went to the hospital one day and then came home and lay down. Raj Dev came and told me, "Oh, your husband has given you brandy, you are taking that and laying down in the guise of sickness." He took my hair in his hand and beat me. At that time I could not bear any more, so I pulled his hair back. Raj Dev thought that Kamladevi had instigated me to fight him, so at about 12 midnight, he told her to get out and put her suitcase outside. She did not instigate me and I told Raj Dev, "Don't send her out, send me out and I will go. Why should she go, has she not given the income to you?" I had lived at Raj Dev's for 5 years by this time, I had equal rights in the hamam, so I told Kamladevi to take her suitcase and get in. Then Raj Dev got frightened thinking I would beat him up and went inside. That very morning I left the place without telling anybody and came here to Gasworks Street.

Then Raj Dev came the next day and took me back. But soon there was another fight with one Lata, who had come from Bombay, and again Raj Dev pushed me out. There were a lot of people around when he did this so I was very ashamed. Then I felt furious. I told him, "I have earned so much every day, this is my hamam, so you get out." Then he calmed down and went away. He came later in the evening and was sitting outside. After an hour he called me and asked me to come and sit near him. Then he asked me, "How can you do such things to me?" So I told him, "How can you do this to me? If you humiliate me, I will also humiliate you. Look how much I have earned for you. You've put me to shame before so many people." Raj Dev should live long to suffer!

By this time, Lalitha had come to the hamam. During this time I had again quarreled with Raj Dev. I told him, "Look, you have taken away all my jewelry, promising to get them back for me, but up till now you haven't given me anything." Raj Dev promised that he would retrieve all the jewels for me, and he went to his hometown to sell away his lands and get some money to retrieve the pledged articles. While he was away Lalitha did some black magic and Raj Dev got paralysis. My husband went to ask the fellow who owned the hamam for the jewelry that Raj Dev had pledged with him, but the fellow said that Raj Dev owed him 5,000 rupees so he would not give the jewelry. At this time the hamam was taken over by Lalitha; she was in charge of the accounts and did some tricks and got the whole thing in her hands. So that is when I came away here.

HUSBANDS

After coming away from Raj Dev's to Gasworks Street, Sushila also changed husbands. Sushila's first husband was a scooter-taxi driver. After they separated, she took up with the husband she had in 1981, when I met her, a Brahmin who was a chauffeur for a large corporation that had its headquarters in Bastipore. My questions to Sushila, about the kinds of relationships hijras have with their husbands, led her to compare her own attitude toward her husband with that of others:

> Some of our people are mad for their husbands. They have "husband fever." When they come to know their husbands may be going to see someone else, or are visiting some other house of prostitution, they may even commit suicide. But take my case, I just leave my husband with a very careless attitude. He is not the type to go elsewhere, it's true, but I also don't doubt him. If he doesn't return one night, I have the phone number of his company, and I ask someone to ring up for me and find out where he is. The shopkeeper will tell me, "It is a business affair, he is working, he has gone out of town with the car." Then I will not even mention it to him.

> But these other people, even if it is 2:00 or 3:00 in the morning they will go in search of their husbands and won't sleep until he returns. If that fellow talks to another girl, they'll immediately doubt him and fight with him. One day like that in a fight, Meera poured kerosene over herself to burn. Luckily she didn't strike the match before everyone came and calmed her down.

> Even now, though I have a husband I do business [prostitution]. I don't like lying and thieving. I never hide anything. My husband says to me, "Why when I am earning 500 to 600 rupees each month which I am giving to you, do you have to go and do prostitution?" But I tell him, "Suppose you leave me, I have to do that to earn my living. Now all these other hijras think I'm something, but if you leave me I'll have to go back to this business." That's how I treat my husband. Even if he is standing outside the hamam, I'll first finish my business with the customer and only then go to him.

In spite of her "careless attitude," Sushila spoke very warmly of her husband and was disconsolate because she could not give him a child. She very much wanted this for him, because she thought it was necessary that he lead "a normal family life." Toward this end she told me that she was trying to find him a wife and had written to an orphanage in Madras to see if there were any girls there who would be suitable. When I left Bastipore in 1982, there had been no progress, however. But when I returned to Bastipore in the summer of 1985, Sushila had quite an achievement to tell me about. She was now a mother-in-law and a grandmother! How had this come about? She proudly told me that she had adopted her [former] husband as her son and had arranged his marriage with a neighbor's sister. The girl was poor, but respectable, and quite pretty. The couple now had a son, making Sushila a grandmother. They were living with the boy's mother in another part of the city, but they visited Sushila nearly every day and I often met with them. Since her "son's" marriage Sushila has found another husband, a man who does not live with her but often comes to spend the night.

Once or twice when I came to see Sushila in the morning, she would have bruises on her head or arms, which she claimed she got from beatings her new husband had given her. I asked her why she quarreled so much with him, and she answered somewhat ruefully:

> It is not he who scolds me. I'm the one who is short tempered and who fights with him. When he comes we usually drink liquor and when I'm drunk, I abuse him profusely and there is a fight. I always call him a son of a bitch and fight with him. I met this man while I was at Raj Dev's. I had known him for 10 years. While at Raj Dev's, I kept him at a distance. There was one girl there also at Raj Dev's, one Malika. She kept this man for herself, they were staying in a separate house. She had been operated on so he used to go and sleep with her. I went there and fought with Malika and brought him back here.

When I first met Sushila, she was with the group for whom Meera had announced, "We are all operated on here." Soon after that, however, when we next met and Meera was not present, Sushila told me that she had not had the surgery, though she had assisted at several operations.

> Since I had my mother's spirit in me, I did not have the operation performed. If I had the operation, then the spirit of Bahuchara, the Goddess, must come upon me and not the spirit of my mother. But now my mother's spirit has left me, it has gone to my sister. This is how it happened. When I was still a girl, with my father in Madras, I was lighting the lamps and had lit some camphor during the puja. Suddenly I fell down unconscious, dropping the lighted camphor on the tray. Then they brought a certain *pandit* [priest] who told my father that my mother's spirit had come upon me. Now it has left me because I don't perform any puja and besides, I have a Christian man here [her present husband], so the spirit has gone to my sister.
>
> I'm trying for an operation now that my mother's spirit has left me. I want to get the operation done, and even my husband wants me to do it. If I get operated on I will be like Meera. Meera was like me, very thin, before she got operated on. It will cost 2,000 rupees for the operation. Meera did these operations and she told me that I could get it done for 1,000 rupees, but she doesn't do them any more. I'm waiting for a loan that my husband will get shortly to meet these expenses. I've kept it a secret from everyone; after the money comes, I'll get the operation. My husband wants me to get the operation done so I will look robust and

nice, like the others. Now I am so thin and not nice to look at, he wants me to be like the others. Even my own people—the hijras—tease me because I am so thin.

I asked Sushila if people in the street tease their husbands when they go out with hijras.

No, mostly the husbands go out alone. And even if we go with them, people don't pay attention to us at all. People don't say anything about their connection with the hijras. When our husbands are outside on the streets, talking to their friends, if Meera or I go out, they just bow their head down and pretend not to see us. But it's not like that with my husband. He takes me out and I go out with him. Only then their parents will ask them about this, because naturally, they want their sons to be more respectable, ordinary, normal human beings. So our husbands tell their parents that it is their own choice and let them not interfere.

Recently, my husband and I had been to my daughter-in-law's place. He wants me to be with him always so we are thinking of shifting elsewhere to a quieter place. We haven't as yet told anybody, but we've already taken a house just outside Bastipore for us to live in. He's given me a month to wind up my establishment here. He says, "I want you to come away so that we can always be happy and enjoy ourselves. Then there'll not be any more quarrels, I can promise a happy life for you."

He always wants me to be well dressed and enjoying myself. After my daughter-in-law came, I stopped using makeup or putting on any stylish dresses, or using turmeric [face powder] or bindi or anything at home. Only when I go out I use all this. If I am dressed up at home my daughter-in-law may not respect me, thinking that this prostitution is going on here and that I may be in it. It is not a nice thing if my daughter-in-law views me with disrespect.

By this visit, in 1985, Sushila seemed to speak more of herself as a woman, perhaps in connection with the new family roles she had taken on:

See, we hijras are like women, we dress like women, in sari, and we like to use cosmetics, makeup, plenty of flowers in our hair, to look more attractive. Even at home we could use makeup and try to look more attractive, but outsiders who come to see us will not respect us, thinking that we are prostitutes. Now I'm like this, as you see me [referring to how she looked that morning, wearing an old sari, with no makeup, and her hair hardly combed], but when I go out I make myself very attractive by using makeup and dressing up in all my finery.

People hereabouts have been asking me how is it that you respectable people [referring to myself and my translator, who at this time was a highly respectable Brahmin lady of late middle age] have been coming to see me. I said you were a lady friend from America. People don't bother me, they know I command respect here. Now at least you know why we don't dress up in all our finery when you come here, for the reason that some people may stamp us as prostitutes.

Sushila then returned to the subject of her husband:

If I want my man, I must go where he wants me to go. After my daughter-in-law comes, I will leave her with her husband for them to continue the household and I can live with my husband. My husband doesn't like this place because there is a brothel here and prostitution is raging rampant, but I like to stay here. Once when I got in a fight with my husband, he went to Meera's house—you know she runs this house of prostitution down the lane—and a neighbor of Meera's came and told me. I went and brought him back and now he comes here only. He promised not to beat me, and when one of my teeth got broken in a fight with him, he went and got a new one made for me.

I asked Sushila about the qualities she finds attractive in her man and the qualities she thinks make a good wife.

What I find attractive in my man is the way he has taught me to be clean. He likes to see me well dressed, tidy, with flowers in my hair, with a bindi, wearing new clothes, keeping the house clean, and not using bad language.

For a housewife, she should look clean, wear good clothes, comb her hair neatly, put flowers in her hair, wear bindi on her forehead. I have my husband's lunch ready by the time he comes home. I tend to his house and am at home instead of going in the streets. You see how many people come and sit here with me to chat [referring to some of her neighbors who would stop in to say hello]. If I was disrespectful, they wouldn't come to me and sit in my house and have a chat with me. Now that I am respectable and talk to people well, people come and sit with me.

My daughter-in-law comes and I am the queen of the house. I only fetch vegetables for her to cook for our meals. The rest of the work is done by her and I relax. I don't even wash the dishes.

Sushila went on to talk about the difference between being a prostitute and leading a family life:

Now I have my husband and he's the only man for me, instead of all the men visiting me from all walks of life and entering my home at all odd hours. Therefore, I am respected. Now I'm leading the life of a respect-able woman with a husband, an adopted son, a daughter-in-law, and a grandson—and running a house. For this we get some respect outside.

CHAPTER EIGHT

Salima: An Outcast

When I first met Salima, she was living on the street, sleeping on a tattered bedroll with not so much as a plastic lean-to to protect her from the monsoon rains that fall so heavily in Bombay. Her clothes were dirty, as were her hands and feet, and she had a several days growth of beard. I was told about Salima by the young man who was my research assistant in Bombay; as she lived near his hostel, he had passed her every day for several years and thought she might be willing to talk with me. The interviews were difficult to manage; as she had no house, we were obliged to have our conversations in a nearby park. Between 1981, the first time I met her, and 1985, her condition seemed to get worse.

Salima is a Muslim and was born in Bombay. In November, 1981, she was in her early 30s. She is a "real" hijra, born intersexed. Accepting that she was "neither one thing nor the other," Salima joined the hijras when she was about 10 to 13 years old. Because she was born intersexed, Salima did not undergo the emasculation operation; as she said, "There was nothing there to operate on." Instead, she had a very elaborate nose- and ear-piercing ceremony (which was once also a regular part of the traditional hijra initiation, but is now only practiced in a much reduced form and perfunctory manner for most hijras at their point of entry into the community).

In her early teens Salima, along with a group of her "sister" hijras, began to be sent out to both beg and perform. She played the dholak, a prestigious function in the group. All day, every day, Salima and her group would go either to the big Bombay vegetable market to beg cash and kind from the stall keepers or go around to their exclusive territories in Bombay, seeking out families where a wedding was taking place or where a child had been born. Salima was the leader of this group of chelas; she had not only been a hijra longer than most of them, but also was a "real" hijra and the favorite of her guru since she had been with her as a child.

This was Salima's life for about 15 years. During those years she found herself a husband, Ibrahim, a man who was Muslim, like herself, and with whom she lived for about 6 years, until he left Bombay. After a period of time, during which Salima saw Ibrahim on the sly, her guru discovered the relationship. When Salima convinced her guru that this attachment would in no way undercut her own loyalty and economic contribution to the group, Salima's guru arranged a "marriage" ceremony for them and gave her blessings for Salima to live with Ibrahim. The couple lived in a separate house from the hijras, but Salima continued to work with and earn for them.

After Ibrahim left Bombay, Salima moved back in with her guru, who by this time was living with a husband of her own. After some years, the guru fell ill and returned to her native place to recuperate. During this time Salima remained in the guru's house, as did the guru's husband.

According to Salima, this man made sexual advances to her, which she repulsed. In an attempt both to get back at her for this rejection, as well as to undermine Salima's credibility and presumably inherit the guru's considerable material assets for himself, this man forced Salima to have sex with him. He then made this public knowledge and turned the Bombay guru elders against her. Subsequently, Salima was thrown out of her guru's house and effectively cast out from the hijra community.

Formal ostracism from the hijra community is a very serious matter; any hijra who would work with Salima, talk to her, or even so much as give her a drink of water, would be exiled from the community herself. In order to gain reentry, Salima would have to pay a 500-rupee fine to the jamat. Unable to earn, much less save, this amount, Salima has lived on the streets of Bombay for the last 7 years. Occasionally, with other hijra outcasts, she begs in Victoria Railway Station, but if they are seen by other hijras they are chased away. Sometimes Salima joins up with a group of zenanas (nonhijra female impersonators), and they walk all the way to the outer suburbs looking for work performing badhai or begging alms. This gains them only the most meager income.

At present, Salima lives on a street corner under a makeshift tent, in the neighborhood where she grew up. She occasionally takes care of some of the neighborhood children to earn a few rupees and is given some food by her neighbors. When the monsoon rains come, she sleeps under a bus or truck. She sometimes borrows money from her parents, with whom she has kept in touch, but more often she has to lend them money. She is also subject to harassment from the local rowdies who hang out in the neighborhood. Salima would consider doing prostitution, but as she so pathetically says, "No customers are coming to me." When one sees her in her present state of dishevelment, with 3 days growth of beard, and her dirty hands and feet and clothes, it is perhaps not hard to understand her lack of clientele. Salima hopes some day to be able to raise the 500 rupees she needs to pay her way back into the hijra community where she would again have a roof over her head, her prestigious role as drummer, and the congenial company of the hijras. When I returned to Bombay to see her, in 1986, things had changed.

BEGINNINGS

When I asked about her childhood, Salima began by emphasizing the sad fate of her birth:

I don't remember much of my early days. I remember only the days after my mother married her second husband. I consider this man my father. This man had four children with my mother, and I consider them to be my brothers and sisters.

My parents felt sad about my birth, but they realized it was their fate to have me born to them. They were looking forward to my birth—I was the eldest child—and they were sad that I was born "neither here nor there." From my childhood I am like this. From my birth, my organ was very small. My mother felt, as I grow up, naturally it will grow also. But it didn't, so she tried taking me to doctors and all that. But the doctors said, "No, it won't grow, your child is not a man and not a woman, this is God's gift." I am a real hijra, not like those converts—those men who have the operation.

If I was a girl they would have nurtured me and made me make a good marriage; if I was a boy they would have given me a good education and started me in a good job seeing that I was well placed in life. They would have got me married off and would have had a nice daughter-in-law in the house. But I have been of no use to them. My mother feels she has done what she could for me, the rest is my *kismet* [fate]. My parents don't consider me a man, they think of me as the eldest daughter.

When I was young my mother took me to various holy places, like Ajmer, and made a vow in these places—wherever my mother was at any time she would make a vow at each place, but nothing turned out fruitful. It is God's will, some women give birth to lame children, some to blind children, it is God's will, even it is the gift of God. When I was born and my father came to know I was neither a boy nor a girl, he went mad. He also started to make vows at different places, but it was all futile.

I asked Salima whether she thought of herself as a boy or a girl when she was younger.

From the beginning I only used to dress and behave as a girl—I never went to school. Even when I was sent off to study I used to run off to Chowpatty [a beach and public amusement area] and start begging and fooling around. I wasn't interested in studying; I just used to enjoy playing with the girls. So much so that I used to get my hair pulled and get thrashed for it, but still I couldn't be cured of this desire to play with girls. I never thought of myself as a boy, and I never thought that I should behave like a boy or dress like a boy. I only used to behave like a girl.

I used to sit with the girls, playing with them, playing with girl's toys, sweeping the house, cooking, doing all these female activities. I never used to like playing with boys. I would put on girl's clothes and go out. I used to do up my hair nicely and put on kajal [eye black] and rouge. I would ask everyone I knew for these girl's clothes. People thought of me as a girl, and I would get plenty of clothes in this way. I would put on their clothes and dance. Even today, they still laugh and joke with me, and the childhood bond is still there. When people ask why they are friendly with me, they answer, "We are childhood friends. It is not her fault, God made her that way. She doesn't have any masculinity in her; God has made him a woman."

I never thought of myself as a boy. My parents had given me a boy's name, but whenever anyone called me by that name, I would say, "Get lost, don't call me that." Then they would say, "What should we call you?" and I would give them a girl's name. I would say, "Call me by this name or any girl's name and only then I will come; otherwise, I won't listen to you." If anyone called me by a girl's name I would come to them, but if they called me by a boy's name, I would ignore them.

In school I would never talk to the boys, but only to the girls. The teachers would always be after me, saying, "Since you are a boy, why are you sitting with the girls?" But I never would listen to the teacher, and I continued to sit with the girls. For this reason I stopped going to school.

The boys in the neighborhood would tease me and I used to abuse them, as a girl would, and complain to their mothers. Their mothers would say, "Don't complain to us, when these boys tease you, thrash them yourself." So I would abuse and beat them, and these boys stopped teasing me. They would say, in my hearing, "Why talk to him, this *sala* [sister fucker] this *harami* [son of a bitch]? He is always abusing us."

These boys, they would call me hijra, hijra. My mother would tell them, "Why do you tease like this? God has made him like this, and if you tease him, he can make your food go bad. So just leave him alone." Then my mother would also tell me that God made me like this and that when those boys teased me, I should ignore them.

I was sent to my mother's womb by God, that is the gift my mother got. Like any child, I am a gift for her. My mother would calm me down, saying, "Don't feel annoyed when people tease you. You are God's child, and those children do not know your value." When I got older and the children would tease me, I would tell them, "See, today you are doing like this; tomorrow God will punish you for this." When the children would throw stones at me, I would tell them, "This is not good, God will punish you." I would want to abuse them more harshly, but my mother would calm me down, saying, "Never utter anything bad from your mouth, just let it go. Judgment will be given by God."

I asked Salima when she had joined the hijras. She did not know her exact age but guessed it to be around 10 or 11.

At the age when one becomes *syana* [aware of sex], it was then that I went with the hijras. They had already seen me and told me, "We'll make you a disciple of our guru." They used to take me along with them when they went begging. At that time my family was in financial trouble, and I used to help them by giving them the money that I got on my begging trips with the hijras. The hijras had come in the evening to beg for food at my house. They came into the house and inspected my body and said, "You're neither a man nor a woman, but you are born this way." So they started accepting me; they would come to see me, bring with them various foodstuffs and other things. What could my mother say? She said, "Since you are born this way, do whatever you want to do, go wherever you want to go, do whatever makes you happy."

In the beginning I was very scared of the hijras, but they used to talk to me so kindly and gently. I used to run away and hide sometimes, and I never used to listen. Then one of the hijras took me to a hotel; she gave me tea and biscuits and was very nice to me. I said, "You are very nice; you don't beat me or ill-treat me like children say that you usually do." So then my heart opened up to them, and after that whenever they used to call me, I used to go running to them, and the pain in my heart was lessened.

They took me to their guru at Factory Compound, and then I started to live with them. They talked to me very kindly and treated me very well, sometimes even better than my mother treated me. My mother used to beat me at home and scold me, and they never did. In the beginning they never let me go out; I only did work in the house, like sweeping, cleaning, and cooking. They kept me like this until my hair grew long, looked after me, gave me food. Until my initiation, they didn't want me to go out of the house. I wasn't allowed to talk to men or other people. They kept me like a girl, protected. When I was working in the house and I caused some damage or breakage, I would fear a beating from them. I would get scared, and they would ask me, "Why are you scared?" I would say, "I'm scared because I've broken these things. Aren't you going to make me pay for them?" And they would say, "So what if it is broken, never mind."

Sometimes I would miss my parents, and even when I was working I would sit and start to cry. They would ask me, "Why are you sad?" And I would say, "I'm missing my parents. I want to see my mother." They would take me to meet my mother and would give me 100, 150 rupees to give her, along with a sari that they had received. They would say, "Take this, give it to your mother."

When I first went to the hijras my hair was very short. When my hair grew long enough for it to be tied into a small braid, then the jamat came and sat for my [initiation] ceremony. My guru distributed cardamon in my name [an auspicious way of sending an invitation in the hijra community]. Everyone was to know that my guru Sona was taking Salima—that was the name my guru gave me—for her disciple. On a Sunday everyone collected—all the hijras and naiks. My nose and ears were pierced. I wore a sari, and they applied turmeric and mehndi to my hair and hands and feet. They dressed me up just like a bride, gave me a name, and pierced my nose and ears.

Three days before my nose and ears were to be pierced, my guru announced to everyone that Salima's initiation would be taking place. From that day they made me sit in the house; they wouldn't let me go out or do any work at all. Everything was brought to me; my movements were restricted. I was not allowed to eat chili [peppers]. They would not give me anything saltish or too spicy to eat. The only things they gave me to eat were milk, curds, yoghurt—only these sorts of things [such restrictions parallel those before the operation; the foods are considered cooling and are similar to those given to a woman after childbirth].

They made me wear a green sari, green blouse, and glass bangles. For my piercing ceremony, they called the Marwari [a member of a merchant caste originally from Marwar] jeweler and he himself came. They made a paste out of rice, and in front of the rice they put plantains, pan leaves, betel nuts, and some flowers on a plate. Then on another silver plate, they kept one needle made out of gold and gold wire. I sat on a low stool just like a bride [and like a person about to have the emasculation surgery]. All the hijras that were there gave some money, 5 or 10 rupees. Whatever people feel like giving they put on the rice. After this was over, the rice was taken by the jeweler along with the coins, like a token gift.

The night after my nose and ears were pierced, all the rich, important people came and gave presents. The presents that were given to me in my hands belonged to me. It all belonged to me except the coins and small rupee notes that were put on the rice, which belonged to the jeweler. But these presents given to me, I must give them to my guru. They put a garland of flowers around my neck and made me sit in the midst of everyone. All these "big people"—the naiks—gave me something; one gave silver anklets, others gave a sari, bangles, or eight anna coins, whatever they felt like. So, in this way my nose and ears were pierced and they gave me a name. They celebrated this with a great deal of pomp and show, and after this I started going out for the singing and dancing with them. Everyone came to know that I was Sona's disciple.

After her initiation Salima became a full working member of her commune:

From that time I would go out with the other chelas of my guru. I played the dholak. Every person has some specialty. Some sing and dance, some play the dholak. While I'm playing the dholak, I might sing along with the others, but I never put bells on my ankles [danced]. People would come to our house to tell us where we were wanted for a performance on such and such a day and then, on the appointed day, we went.

For those of us in the group of our guru, we don't get a share of the money. Only if you come from outside the group, then you get a share of the money. In front of the house itself, when the guru is given the money, she will give an equal share to all, but as soon as the outsiders leave, we who belong to the guru are expected to return the money to our guru. It is our wish whether we give it to the guru or not. But then we realize that it is he who looks after us and cares for us. I always gave the money back. In any case, when all our needs are looked after, what need do we have for money? Everyone gets an exactly equal share, not a cent more or less.

We never quarreled in our house about the money or anything else. In fact, I never thought I'd have a quarrel with my guru about anything. I was pampered all the time, so it was unthinkable to have a quarrel. I was the oldest of my guru's chelas, and we chelas also never quarreled with each other. If they had any quarrel with someone outside, they used to come home and sit quietly. Sometimes they might say, "It was that one's fault or this one's fault." But then the guru would say, "Child, treat the other person like your brother or sister. If other hijras see you fighting, they will laugh and make fun of you and we will lose respect." In this way our guru used to explain all these things to us.

IBRAHIM

In the course of the many conversations we had, Salima frequently referred to Ibrahim, her husband. It appeared that shortly before I first met Salima, he had gone away. But Ibrahim was still obviously an important person in Salima's life.

Only after leaving my house and joining the hijras did I meet Ibrahim. It was at the market where I used to go to beg vegetables and things that my eyes and those of Ibrahim got locked with each other. This was in the Byculla fruit market. He used to run a fruit stall. As soon as my eye caught his, he started to give me things—oranges one day, sweet lime the next, one or two kilos of apples, or sometimes a grapefruit. In that same bag that he put the fruit, he would also put 20 or 25 rupees. He put it in the bag so that no one would know he gave so much. He did not want me to go from shop to shop. He would say, "In going from shop to shop [to beg] no man should tease you, you are very young."

We would sit together in a tea shop, and I would tell these hijras to take the things and let my guru know that I have come to the market also. I told Ibrahim, "If you don't let me beg, then when I go home and the shares are divided up, then won't my guru ask me, "Where is Salima's share? What did you bring?" I will be caught in my dishonesty." This is what I told him.

But these hijras told my guru that I was sitting with Ibrahim in the tea shop and he was giving my share for the group. Then my guru asked me, "Is it true?" And I said, "Yes, this is a fact. I do meet him. He has told me not to beg. He told me, 'I cannot bear to see this because I have been desiring you from the time you were very young. Ask your guru if he doesn't mind I will exchange garlands with you [an important part of a marriage ceremony].' "

I told all this to my guru and my guru said, "All right, if this is what you want, then you go and tell him to come and meet me." So the next day I went and told Ibrahim that if he wanted to continue meeting me, then he should come and meet my guru. So he agreed. He showed a lot of respect to my guru and did everything properly. He said to my guru, "My mind is to her, and I'm prepared to exchange garlands with her and I want to keep her." So the guru said, "See, if you want to keep her, then take up a house somewhere, live with respectability."

Ibrahim agreed and also agreed to pay for the expenses for the wedding. There is a person, we call him the Bombay *bazaar kazi* [a kazi is a Muslim religious functionary or wise man who can perform marriages]. He comes to our place and performs the marriages. Whether you are Hindu or Muslim, this priest comes to perform the marriage for us hijras.

After this marriage Ibrahim took me to his hut. I stayed with him as his wife and looked after his every need. I used to cook his food, I used to fill the water, wash his clothes. In the evening when he would return from his business, I used to massage his hands and feet. He would get ready-cooked food to eat in the evening. I did everything a wife does for a man—things it is only a wife's prerogative to do. I used to wear a *burka* also, like married Muslim women wear [a long black cloak that covers the woman from head to toe, including her face]. Like this I stayed with Ibrahim for 7 years.

During this time of living with Ibrahim, Salima also kept up close contact with the hijra community and her guru:

Why shouldn't I keep contact with my guru? Why should I not go and see him? When there was a wedding taking place, I would go with them [the hijras]. Sometimes at night I used to go with them or else go for some special function. I would not go every day. But if we were called for a wedding or a night of singing, I would go. Ibrahim himself would tell me to go. The money that I earned from the singing and dancing I would give to my guru. I never brought any of it home with me. But the money that Ibrahim gave me, I did not give any part of it to my guru. That was my husband's earning, so why should I give it to my guru? But if there was a festival or something and I would go to pay respects, my guru would give me something and I would also give something, like a box of sweets. From the guru I would get a nice sari or 51 rupees.

I asked Salima what happened to Ibrahim.

Ibrahim had told me, "Even when you die, I will pay for your shroud. Don't think that I have taken a young person just to fool around; I'll stay with you till the end. But I used to say, "You're saying all this, but your mother and father will never let you abide by your words." So Ibrahim used to say, "Even if my parents force me to leave you, I won't listen to them." So everywhere they tried to fix a marriage for him, he used to go and attempt to break off the marriage arrangements.

But then his brother, that bastard, and his parents, they came and took him away. They told him, "You are not giving us money to run the house; all these years you have spent in Bombay, you never sent any money and we had no news of you." His parents had come from his native place to check on him. When they learned that he got married to me they took him away. Our house was sold, along with everything else. I just took my household belongings and tied them up and brought them back to my guru's house. Again I had to do all the singing and dancing, as well as looking after the dholak and looking after my guru's house. I did all that—I settled down in my guru's house.

Salima said that if I ever met Ibrahim in Bastipore, where he now lived, "You could ask him all these same questions and he would release a flood telling you of all these events." I was not sure whether I believed her or not.

OUTCAST

When I first met Salima she told me that she had been thrown out of the hijra community by the jamat. When I asked her why, she first told me that her guru refused to give her some money to give to her sister on her marriage and that she got so angry, she hit her guru. When I returned to Bombay to meet her in June, 1982, Salima had a different story as to why she was expelled from the hijra fold. She told this later story in great detail and repeated it during several conversations in 1982 and when I met her again in 1985:

After Ibrahim left me, I went back to live with my guru. At this time she was living in a suburb of Bombay. There she became very sick and went to her native place. After that she came back to Bombay, and then she died. It was one minute that I had a house, and the next minute I was houseless. These hijras—my guru's chelas junior to me—then stopped asking for me. For them, I ceased to exist. The share from my guru that was due me was swallowed up by them. They wouldn't let me protest; they tried to swallow up my share. Why should I say "tried to"? They did swallow my share. The guru had left everything to me, but they tricked me out of everything left to me and made sure I left. If I had stayed on everything would have been mine. Everything they did to me was to make sure that they gained all the property left behind by my guru.

The people responsible for this were one of my guru's chelas and my guru's life companion [husband]. This husband of my guru used to burn up with jealousy over my relationship with my guru. In fact, my guru used to tell me, "Child, treat him as your father and think of him as your father," but I never thought of him as my father. I used to resent him a lot—the very sight of him used to irritate me. He used to say of me, "I can't get rid of this person [because Salima was so close to her guru]. Even if I finish this bastard off, it will be a smirch on my character. Neither will the stick break, neither will the snake die. If I make her lose her reputation, I will also lose my reputation."

This husband of my guru never liked me at all. In fact, a few times he carried false tales about me to my guru. Next to our house there was a liquor seller; he accused me and this liquor seller so badly to my guru, that my guru thrashed me so hard that my head split and I was in the hospital for 15 days. The liquor seller's name was Shankar. One day my guru went and asked him, "Is it true that when Salima comes to fill the water jug in the morning she meets you? Does she meet you in the morning?" Shankar, who was a Hindu, said, "No, your holy book is the Koran and my holy book is the Gita, and I swear on the Gita that I have never even spoken to that person you are asking me about." So then my guru started to feel some enmity toward this husband. She asked him, "Why did you let my disciple get beaten up like this? Because of you she got a terrible beating."

This husband of my guru would not only make false accusations against me all the time, but he also used to keep me under his eye with the view to "spoiling" me [use for sexual purposes]. But I didn't give him a chance. So often he used to come home drunk also. One time my guru had gone out for some function and I was alone in the house and this husband came home drunk. In fact, one day he was lying down on the bed and he had removed his underwear and his lungi was completely up, exposing everything.

Whenever he would come into the house I used to walk outside. I never even used to cook the food when he was in the house. My guru used to come and say, "Child, why haven't you cooked the meal?" I ask you, he would come home in a drunken stupor and lie down on the bed and I should cook the food while he was lying there? If anyone came in, what would they think! Won't my name be smirched! So I told the guru, "Either he stays in the house or I stay in the house. When he's in the house don't expect me to stay. From today, if he's in the house, then don't expect me to stay. If you leave in the morning then take me with you. When this man leaves or dies, only then can I stay as a chela at your house or even work as a servant."

Then around this time, my guru got seriously ill and went to the hospital for 15 days. During that time my guru was very sick and after he returned from the hospital he got a paralytic stroke. After he got paralyzed he lost the use of his legs, he couldn't move, he could not even get up to use the toilet in the morning. When he got up, I used to take that enamel pan they use in hospitals and take that to him so he could pass urine. Then I would take that thing and throw the contents quite far away and then would come back and with my own hands I used to bathe him, dress him. I used to look after my guru completely.

My guru used to say, "Child, I've left everything to you; I've written it in your name. I'm going to my native place. If I get well there, I will return and stay here. In case I die everything is yours. If you give any of the others anything as their share, then it will be your goodness of heart. If you don't give anyone anything, and you take over what doesn't belong to you, that's your will. But if you do this, remember all the hijras will lose respect for you. You have small chelas [junior to her]; if you take care of them well and look after them like I have looked after you, then these people will also treat you well. It has been my kismet that you have been with me."

I told the guru, "After you die, I will treat these people exactly as you've treated me. If I eat well and give them stale food, if I eat mutton and fish and give them only *dal* [beans, the poorest and most ordinary food for poor people], or if I wear a nice sari and give them only torn ones to wear, it will be the fault in me. After all, they are like my sisters. Your disciples are now my disciples, and since I am the oldest I will treat them like my children. I will think of them as if I have given birth to them from my own stomach." This vow I made to my guru.

So then my guru went back to Hyderabad, his native place. Now I was left in my guru's house. Before, Ibrahim used to take me out in the evenings, but now I was alone. This guru's husband, he used to come with drink in him, any time of night, 11:00, 12:00, even in the morning at 6:00; he'd come at any time and just bang on the door. After I opened it I had to help him in to go and sleep on a plank, or sometimes he would ask me for water.

One day, as I was sleeping, he came and I helped him to sleep on the plank. Then I went away myself to sleep. Since at this time I was only thinking of Ibrahim, I could not get proper sleep. Suddenly I found that this man had fallen down from the plank, and he came and slept next to me. I woke up suddenly and moved away, and he did not like this. He insisted on my sleeping next to him. He asked me, "Why are you avoiding me?" I said, "I'm here to take care of the house only, and I have my respect for the guru."

He told me, "If the guru is not here, what does it matter? You are the head of the household now." I told him that it is a big sin if I would sleep with him and told him to remember that he is like a father to me. My guru had told me to look after the house as if I were a daughter, and I told this man, "She has not given me permission to sleep with you. If my guru had instructed me to sleep with you, I might have done it, but she has not told me that." Then he hit me, and I hit him back with the rolling pin. After this incident he would not take food from my hand, but only take it from another chela.

After my guru came back from Hyderabad, I explained all this. Immediately my guru said, "That son of a bitch," and she told this man, "I am Salima's mother and you are her father. She is just like a child born to us, and as a father you are doing this!" She was very annoyed with this man, and she stopped talking to him. Then, holding my hand, she said, "My child, you must stay in this house. I know all about how Ibrahim's parents have come and taken him away and now you are alone, so you stay here." After my guru had scolded her husband, he did not come near me. I also stopped going out for singing and dancing or any outing. I spent my whole time in taking care of the house and giving service to my guru.

Then, again, my guru went back to her native place. Before she went, she went in front of the naik of our house, and with other hijras sitting there, she told them that all the vessels, clothes, and all the other items in the house will belong to Salima. Then she went to her native place and she died.

After this time, I stayed in this house. One day—it was almost 1½ years since my guru died—my guru's husband came and he had brought a bottle with him. It was a black bottle, but I don't know what was in it. He came with a naik, one he knows from the Thieves Market. He came into the house and started talking about the death of my guru. Then he started crying, talking of the guru's death. He asked me for some cold tea, and when I brought the tea, he asked for a better glass. When I brought a good glass, he told me, "You put this tea into your glass and drink it." I told him, "No, it is for you, you drink." He insisted: "We all had our share, you must drink this." He praised me in front of the naiks sitting there, but he did not turn his face to me. He was just talking to them. I didn't find anything wrong, so I just took the tea and drank. After a little while, everyone started going away, one by one; soon all those assembled there had left. I was feeling a little bit heavy, as if I'm not well. Then this man [the guru's husband] said to me, "I'm going out for some work, you lock your house," and he went away. I just put on the lock and came and slept on a plank.

Then, I don't know when he came, but he entered the house and he started behaving badly, trying to have sex with me. I never knew all this. I do not know when he came and slept with me. But before this, he had already told those naiks, "I'll be behaving badly with her." I don't know whether he did anything in front of them or not, but then, when I again met these naiks, I found them all shutting the doors against me. No one would talk with me; it was if they were slamming the doors in my face. I was so surprised, I thought, What has happened to these people?

What happened was that this man had been telling all these naiks, "See, now she's spoiled, she's no more a good person, now I can throw her out of the house." So I went to the house of each of these naiks, and I asked everyone, "Why are you doing all this, what has happened?" They answered, "Your father has spoiled you." I said, "No, this is not possible. I promise in the name of Allah, it cannot happen, he is my father." They told me, "Your father came and spoiled you, we have proof," and they showed me a photo of us together and I was shocked. I don't know how they made that photo. But I had no choice. I had to accept it. So I had to give away all the belongings of the house to them, and taking only two or three of my own belongings, I just walked out of that house. There was no one to help me. My guru's guru had gone to her native place; if she had been there, she would have beaten all those people up, but she was not there to help. So now I am homeless, as you see me.

ON THE STREET

In order to gain reentry into the community of hijras, in addition to the fine, Salima would have been required to go before the jamat and request the chief gurus of Bombay to readmit her. In 1981 this was her goal, although it seemed unreachable. By 1985 her physical health seemed to have deteriorated. I was surprised that she had lasted so long on the street. By this time I knew her better, and she talked more bitterly of how the hijras had thrown her out and the difficult life she was leading.

Yes, these people, these hijras took everything from me. They left me so completely penniless, that I have been roaming here and there aimlessly like a mendicant. My life has been this way ever since. When I didn't even have food to eat, I went and asked them for help, but they never helped me. Even when I asked for used clothes, even for old clothes, I had to listen to so much from them. They say, "Why should we give you clothes? When we give you clothes you sell them and swallow the money." So even though I told them, "See, my guru has died, I have after all been a hijra, so I ask you hijras," even then, can't they help me? They can at least help me as a poor person, if not as a hijra. If they give me food and money, won't I bless them? Or if I wear their clothes, won't I bless them? But no, they won't do anything for me. When I go and ask them to help me, they say, "Child, you collect this much money [the 500 rupees for the reentry fine] and then come back and join us." If I can collect that money I can join them, but if I don't have that kind of money, how can I join them? Where can I get that money? These days I am begging and earning these small sums of money, and when the hijras pass by and see me, they turn their face away.

Now I have come to this, and I ask Allah, have I come to this condition that I am like an insect in a dirty gutter? Nobody wants me. I don't want to live such a cruel life. If I get a little money, then I can lead a proper life. I can't go on leading this cruel life. Just last night I was sleeping out and—I don't know if you'll believe me or not—but it was 2:00, 3:00 in the morning and four urchins came. One boy came to me, the other three were standing separately. I was fast asleep, and this boy woke me up and asked, "Have you eaten your food?" I said, "Yes, I have eaten, and what right do you have to get me out of my sleep and ask me?" He said, "We have been watching you for years. There are twelve of us here, though only four have asked, my other three friends are out there. We have kept our eyes on you for a long time, but we have not been able to take you over. So we want to know what your price is—what is the price of your virtue?" So I said, "So you want to play with my virtue, do you? Well, it is not nice to play with my virtue, and while I have breath in my body, you people cannot touch my virtue. If you want to play with my virtue then you will have to kill me. So move out of my way and stop pestering me. Think of me as a helpless person, and leave me. If I'm poor, I'm poor for myself; if I'm hungry, I'm hungry within myself. I'm not dependent on anyone. If I'm without clothes, I'm in my own place, it's none of your business." Then that boy said to me, "If you don't do as we say, then we won't let you stay here." So I said, "So don't let me stay here. I have no right to stay here, I'll go and stay somewhere else. If you won't let me stay here, that's all right, but you can't play with my virtue."

I have not been feeling well and have had to go to the government hospital. Yesterday I went to the hospital, and I was saying to myself in the hospital that I have come down so much to this condition I even have to go to a government hospital. If my guru was here, or if I had a protector, I would not have had to come to this hospital; I could have gone to a private one instead.

Never mind, that is life; one minute it's like this, the next minute it's different. So I still pray only to Allah, if this is the way you want me to live, it's all right, but never put me in such a condition where I'll have to go to the hijras for help. Even if I die on the road, the municipality people will pick me up and take me away. It's all right. . . . I've run my life and it's through.

I felt very sad about Salima when I saw her in the summer of 1985. She was managing to stay alive, although barely, by earning a few pennies at odd jobs, or pawning a few rags that she had, or trying to perform with some zenanas in the outlying areas of Bombay that were not "owned" by any hijra guru. This meant long hours traveling on buses or walking, in the extreme heat and rain of the monsoon season, with little success. Salima had made friends with these zenanas; as a real hijra she was useful to them because she legitimated their performances. But now she owes them money so she avoids them too. She was at a loss as to what to do to make her life more bearable. It was in this condition that I left her when I departed from Bombay.

When I returned to India in the winter of 1986, I was in Bombay and went to see Salima. I had been to the hijra temple at Ahmedabad and had brought some amulets with the goddess's picture, which I wanted to give to her. I found her in her usual place on the street, along with a small group of people, which included one hijra and two men. She was dressed nicely, much better than when I had last seen her, in 1985, and she looked in much better health. She gave me a big smile, and I was happy to see that she seemed to be in much better circumstances. After talking with her for a while, she very shyly [and slyly] turned to the handsome young man behind her and said, "This is Ibrahim."

Salima laughed at the look of delighted surprise that came over my face. And I was delighted for her. At some point along the way of our conversations I had almost begun to think that Ibrahim was a fantasy. Well, I thought, that explains the change in her life, her health, her new clothes, and her happy face. Now I was very eager to prolong my visit and find out more about Ibrahim, and hear about their relationship from him, as well as find out what kind of life Salima was leading now that he was back. They were both happy to talk. Salima told me that she had written Ibrahim a letter calling him back to Bombay and he came. "But why," I asked Ibrahim, "hadn't you come back earlier?" Ibrahim told me that he hadn't come because Salima hadn't called him, but "once she called me, I came back immediately." This was only a few months earlier. I asked Salima why she had not written Ibrahim earlier.

I did write to him from time to time, but I did not call him to Bombay. I gave him wrong addresses, like Jogeshwar, Bandra, etc. But when my condition became very bad—it worsened even from when you saw me last year—I called him to Bombay. Now he wants to do some kind of business, maybe selling fruits, as he did before. But for the past couple of months he is not well; his leg is troubling him so he is not able to go out and do any business and he is not able to earn. He doesn't have any money to start some business.

I asked Salima how she is managing to earn for the two of them. She said she manages by borrowing a little money, "two rupees here, two rupees there."

If Ibrahim has earned a little money, he gives it to me to buy food. And now, why hide it, I comb my hair and get ready and go out for business [prostitution]. I have to go and try for something because my husband is ill and I have to look after him. I ask the customers for 12 rupees; some nights I get two or three customers, but sometimes I just stand there without any business, and in the end I have to borrow money from someone. For the place itself, I have to pay two rupees to do business, and even my clothes, I borrow from Radha [her hijra friend who has quarreled with her guru and is staying with Salima on the street]. Where do I have any clothes? I make a little money also from begging, but mostly I stay and pass my day here only. People say to me, "This guy doesn't work, he just sits and eats from your earnings. Why doesn't he work for a living?" But how can he? How can my husband go and work? His life is in trouble; do you think he likes to just sit and eat? He would earn for me himself; how could he just sit and eat but for this trouble? He has a problem, so I have to consider that too. How can I neglect his trouble? If, by the grace of Allah, he gets some money, to start some sort of a business and earns enough to support us, it will be good. For now, I earn enough to fill our stomachs.

CHAPTER NINE

❧ Hijra Lives in Context

In the previous four chapters we have heard hijras talking about their lives. Life stories like these are filtered through each individual's concept of the self. The narratives thus need to be understood not as strictly factual accounts but as subjective truths that emerge in the encounter between the author of the narrative and the audience—in this case, the anthropologist with a translator, eliciting the material. From this perspective, distortions of fact, omissions, exaggerations, and fantasies are all revealing as we seek to understand the subjectively experienced life in relation to its cultural context.[1] Although it is culture—socially established structures of meaning (Geertz, 1973:12)—that provides the framework for reflecting on and talking about one's life, it is the individual's self that acts as the interpreter of the culture. This view emphasizes the self as an active, creative, adaptive force, interpreting life events and social interactions and guiding and justifying choices within a distinctive cultural framework.

In the course of telling a life story, selection always occurs in the mind of the narrator as certain events are revealed, others omitted, some exaggerated, elaborated, or minimized. These narratives were elicited by my interest in hijras and are subject to selection in response both to my particular interest and also by each narrator's wish to present a certain picture of herself. Thus, when Meera says to the hijras that they must tell me everything so that I get the "right information," this cannot be literally accepted. In her case she neglected to tell me a number of things about herself; here, the "right information" means that information consistent with Meera's desire to present herself to me in a certain way. Similarly, when Sushila says, "Why should I lie? I was also a prostitute," she is already suggesting that people do lie about such things, as indeed hijras do. Kamladevi's admonition to her would-be chela Amudh not to lie about the fact that he left Bombay before completing the initiation also suggests that this "lack of courage" is a somewhat shameful thing in the hijra community.

Furthermore, although these narratives give the impression of a seamless web, they were not collected in that manner. Instead, they represent a double selection process: what the narrators chose to tell me and what I choose to tell the reader. Selection is involved both in what I have included and the order in which I have presented it. It is likely that other anthropologists dealing with the same material would have selected and organized it differently.

I have organized each narrative around topics that seemed to me to have the most significance for the narrator, indicated by the person's statement about their importance and also by the emotional quality of the speech and nonverbal behavior accompanying the telling of the story. Much of my conversation with the hijras was open ended, to allow them to speak about whatever they wished. Other topics were elicited by my questions, some of which are indicated in the narratives themselves. The presentation of the topics in the narratives does not follow the sequence in which the material was related to me, but rather is arranged chronologically in order to make the narratives more accessible by using a structure familiar to Western readers.

I had several aims in including these narratives in this book: One is that of increasing understanding of the processes by which individual hijras commit themselves to new gender identities and roles. Another is to show how different individuals draw on a common cultural tradition in idiosyncratic ways that are connected to each individual's sense of self and personal history. Also, I hope that these personal accounts will give the reader a stronger sense of the variety of personalities and motivations that provide the dynamic of hijra lives. In order to gain a wider perspective on these four particular individuals, I provide a more general context for the topics of major importance to these hijras in the following sections of this chapter.

HIJRA GENDER IDENTITIES AND ROLES

The hijra role is (among other things) a gender role, and for that reason it is useful to look at the hijras in terms of their gender roles and gender identities. John Money defines *gender identity/role* as constituting a unity and as two sides of the same coin (1988:201). Gender identity is the private experience of gender role, that sameness, unity, and persistence of one's individuality as male, female, or androgynous, especially as experienced in self-awareness and behavior. Gender role is everything that a person says and does to indicate to others or to the self the degree that one is either male, female, or androgynous. This includes, but is not limited to, sexual and erotic arousal and response.

Hijra narratives demonstrate that the hijra role, as a gender role (and in other aspects as well), does not mean the same thing to the different people who occupy the role. The determining of gender role among hijras is a difficult and complex undertaking. To begin with, understanding an individual's gender identity is often largely based on what people say. As such, it is subject to all of the distortions characteristic of talk about the self, as well as to the parameters imposed by cultural definitions. For example, asking an American about gender identity stacks the deck in forcing people to opt for the category of either masculine or feminine; in our culture, the answers "both" or "neither" are generally not acceptable (Kessler & McKenna, 1978:9). In Western culture, gender identity is ideally dichotomous: One is supposed to experience one's self as either a man or a woman.

Whereas for most people in most cultures, gender identity/role is also thought of as either masculine or feminine, other cultures have gender systems that have institutionalized alternative, intermediate gender roles and might therefore admit a broader range of gender identities. The hijra narratives indicate that this may well be true for India. Thus, although cross-gender behavior in childhood is a prominent theme in hijra narratives, this behavior is not necessarily connected to a clear feminine gender identity. Kamladevi says, for example, that "we are born as boys" and only afterward become hijras; in spite of her determination to dress and act like a girl in childhood, she does not speak of herself as a woman, but only as a "not man" or a hijra. Salima's description of her childhood emphasizes that she felt like a girl, for example, in cross-dressing, playing with girls, and answering only to a girl's name, but she also talks about herself as "neither a boy nor a girl" and "neither a man nor a woman." Because Western psychological studies support the view that gender identity is closely linked to sex assignment and subsequent socialization, perhaps Salima's ambivalent gender identity derives from an ambiguous socialization in regard to gender. This is likely because her ambiguous anatomy was noted at birth.

Meera most explicitly identifies herself as a woman, and her description of her childhood is constructed to confirm this, yet she was (by all accounts) a married man for many years. One can only wonder what gender identity she would have expressed and how she would have constructed her past had she been interviewed during this period of her life. Although Sushila behaves like a woman in many ways, and currently identifies herself with many feminine roles, she never says, like Meera, that she feels herself to be a woman. Her reluctance to undergo the emasculation operation suggests that her gender identity may not be completely feminine, but rather ambivalent. It seems that Sushila's feminine identity has increased as she has more completely organized her life around the feminine roles of wife and mother-in-law. It should be kept in mind that all of these accounts of childhood are subject to the distortion of reconstructing a past consistent with the present ambivalent or feminine gender identity. This partly explains the statement "I was born this way," which appears in so many hijra narratives.

A second point raised by the hijra narratives regarding gender identity/role is that it may be more subject to change than has generally been acknowledged in Western social science. Here, gender identity/role has most frequently been defined as something that is established in a critical period in early childhood (from 18 months to 3 years) and is permanent (Green & Money, 1969). The hijra stories presented here suggest that

gender identity/role may be subject to transformations later in life. Specifically, the connection of homosexual activity with the hijra role suggests
that the development of gender identity may be a more gradual process
than is generally believed, and at least in the case of some individuals,
undergoes transformations over a lifetime. Kamladevi's and Sushila's narratives, for example, indicate that the development of a strong component
of a nonman, or feminine, gender identity coalesces in early adolescence,
with increasing homosexual activity, and then becomes subject to still
further transformations as individuals begin to interact more with hijras.[2]
Indeed, Kamladevi's and Meera's narratives suggest that it may be the
recognition of the desire of others for sexual relations that is the spark
which moves the individual in a direction they were not previously aware
of as a conscious choice.

Thus, hijra narratives also confirm the importance of an interactionist
perspective on gender identity/role, supporting the arguments of those
who see sex assignment and subsequent socialization interacting with
individual biological factors, and in some cases, even overriding them.[3]
From this perspective, an intermediate or ambivalent gender identity/role
could be seen as the result of socialization, especially the effect of parents
and peers, who respond toward the intersexed person ambivalently. This
view directs our attention to what hijras say about their early lives as well
as to the possible effects of joining the hijra community on their gender
identities.

BEGINNINGS AND BECOMING

The hijra role, as I have already mentioned, is a magnet for individuals
who have different motivations, gender identities, personality con-
stellations, and cross-gender behavior. This means that one cannot assume
there is any one psychological or behavioral constellation or series of life
events which is *the* cause of becoming a hijra.

None of the hijra narratives I recorded support the widespread belief in
India that hijras recruit their membership by making successful claims on
intersexed infants.[4] Instead, it appears that most hijras join the community
in their youth, either out of a desire to more fully express their feminine
gender identity, under the pressure of poverty, because of ill treatment by
parents and peers for feminine behavior, after a period of homosexual
prostitution, or for a combination of these reasons. Sharma (1983) suggests that an important reason some hijras leave their families is to erase
the stigma that their presence casts on the family's reputation; this becomes particularly significant when it is time for their siblings to marry.
Several hijras mentioned this to me, though it was not specifically mentioned by the hijras whose narratives appear here.

All of the hijras I met who were or had been prostitutes, such as
Kamladevi, Meera, and Sushila, indicated that they had engaged in

homosexual activities during their early teen-age years and that this "spoiled" them for normal, heterosexual relationships when they got older. Hijras use the term *spoiled* here to mean two things. The first is that the pleasure they begin to take in having sexual relations in the receiver role with a man inhibits the desire to marry and raise a family "as other men do." The second, and more definitive meaning, refers to the impotence that is believed to result from frequent passive homosexual activity: As Kamladevi expressed it, "the nerve in the male organ breaks and is no longer good for sex with a woman." Although there might be a physiological basis for this belief, it cannot be taken as the actual cause of a decision to join the hijras. It is certainly not true in Meera's case as she did marry and she fathered several children. Rather, we can interpret this statement to mean that the self-acknowledgment of the pleasure an individual gets from homosexual relations in the receiving role is an important step for some individuals in the process of becoming a hijra. Because not all effeminate homosexuals become hijras, this activity by itself cannot be viewed as the sole cause in the making of a hijra.

Typically, as with Kamladevi and Sushila, hijras join the community voluntarily in the teen-age years, though some, apparently from the poorest families, join as early as 10 or 12 (Ranade, 1983). Salima's case seems typical of this pathway, because her parents, for a combination of economic and humane reasons, "gave her" to the hijras in childhood. Meera represents an atypical example of a "deviant career" as a hijra.[5] I was told by a friend of one similar case, a Muslim man with two wives and six children, who, after almost 20 years of marriage, "one fine day just up and left to join the hijras in Bombay." Meera's having been married is contrary to the norm of hijra culture that their members "should not have loved or had any sexual relations with ladies," and it is for this reason that I assume she wished to keep her marriage a secret from me.

It seems, then, that the process of becoming a hijra is a gradual one. An individual may, at a young age, exhibit a variety of cross-gender characteristics, which may be, as in Salima's case, accompanied by physical sexual ambiguity. These behavioral characteristics (passive homosexual behavior is just one possibility) elicit responses from others—the negative sanctions of parents or teachers, the teasing of peers, or the sexual advances of older boys and men. These responses combine with gradual recognition of the desires of the self—to escape the sanctions of parents by running away from home, to dress in women's clothing, to have sexual relations with men—so that the individual is pushed into informal interactions with hijras, who seem to both approve of and encourage the behavior. These informal interactions may subsequently lead to a formal joining of the hijra community. But even this formal commitment to the hijra community does not seem, at least initially, to resolve ambivalence concerning gender.

The gradual process by which many individuals eventually become hijras suggests that the initial interactions with the hijras, and even the formal joining of the community, involve more of a casting off of one's previous life, which is by now full of tension and family conflict, than any rapid and intense commitment to this new gender role. Indeed, the going back and forth to one's parents' place, as well as the movement from city to city, suggests that the decision to join the hijras, even when formalized, is fraught with ambivalence and partial, tentative choices. Although some hijras express their ambivalence by returning to their parents' home, this ultimately proves to be an unsatisfactory solution, for it does not allow them to engage in cross-gender behavior. And so they leave again.

Not all hijras have this option. Those from poorer, less educated families than Sushila's, Kamladevi's, and Meera's, have often been so badly treated by their families that they do not see returning home as an alternative. These hijras tend also to be younger (see Ranade, 1983); having left their homes with no money and no skills, they join the great crowd of the poor in India's large cities, all scrambling to find some way to earn enough money to survive. At this point, the economic opportunities and social support of the hijras may seem like a viable alternative to life on the streets.

The ambivalence of the commitment to the hijra community and identity may last for many years; it reappears most explicitly when the decision to undergo the emasculation operation is considered. Although we in the West associate the surgical removal of the male genitals with a completely feminine gender identity, this should not be assumed for India. Of the 10 hijras I met who had the emasculation operation, all but one had done so only after many years (5 to 15) in the hijra community, and the decision to have the operation was not uniformly associated with a desire to become, or the feeling that one was already, a woman. As I have noted, the operation is connected with the cultural definition of the hijra as neither man nor woman; for some individuals, the operation transforms them into hijras, not into women. Very few of the respondents in Ranade's study (1983) mentioned the conviction of being a woman in connection with their decision to get emasculated. Four-fifths of the 76 castrated hijras (out of a sample of 100) that Ranade interviewed were castrated before age 15. He concludes from the responses to his survey that there is some coercion exercised by gurus, because such young people "could hardly be aware of the consequences of that decision." Because emasculated hijras can earn more, both as prostitutes and as performers, and emasculation increases the chances that an individual will remain in the hijra community, it is clearly in a guru's interest to have her chelas emasculated. None of the gurus that Ranade interviewed, nor any that I met, would admit to coercing their chelas into having the operation. Furthermore, emasculation is a source of prestige within the community and the nirvan becomes, at that time, a center of attention and care. This is not an insignificant motivation for people, especially young people, whose lives up to this point may have been emotionally barren and who have lacked any recognition or prestige.

Even for some hijras who have the operation when they are older, like Kamladevi, it may be more of a "negative turning" from one's previous life than a whole-hearted commitment to a feminine gender identity. Kamladevi expresses her decision to have the operation as a way of changing her life and her bad luck; we can compare this to Sushila, who, having put off the operation for so many years, seems now to be thinking of it, mainly, I believe, as a logical correlation of her current immersion in so many feminine roles. But even now, Sushila never says that she feels herself to be a woman; instead, her main expressed desire appears to be to lead a respectable life, which her feminine family roles allow her to do.

The influence of husbands also appears to play some role in the decision to have the operation. In Meera's case, the ability to sexually behave like a woman, "having sex from the front" and being able to undress in front of her husband, seem critical; although Meera disparages Sushila's femininity in this area, Sushila herself never mentions her own sexual behavior in connection with her femininity. It may be that the "gendered self" is not internalized in the same way for all individuals; for some, sexuality may be the critical aspect, for others, outward role behavior, for still others, giving birth.

WORK

Occupation has a critical impact on hijra lives, both for economic reasons and for the role it plays in self-esteem. When someone joins the hijra community, she is expected to earn her keep; no guru wants a chela who does not earn for her. For those who "have some art in them" or "can earn a living with their feet," performing is one obvious choice. Performing badhai has the greatest respect within and outside the hijra community but is not necessarily very remunerative. As part of a hijra troupe, an individual performer receives only a share of a fixed sum of money, and, as Salima reports, most or all of this may be given back to the guru. There are other opportunities for hijras to dance, but these are not prestigious; in fact, as Meera indicates, a woman who dances in public for a male audience is considered immoral.

Kamladevi, as we have seen, did dance sometimes but did not limit herself to performing badhai. Bastipore has only a small North Indian community, and there are few opportunities there for hijras to perform in their traditional roles. From time to time Kamladevi will be called, as other Bastipore hijras are, to dance at college functions or stag parties. Because the crowds at these functions sometimes get drunk and rowdy, a dancer has to keep a cool head, not just to protect herself from abuse, but also so she can wheedle extra money from the audience. Kamladevi has the temperament for this; not all hijras do. Kamladevi would like to dance more than she does, but there is just not enough work to make it a secure living, so she, too, turns to prostitution, demanding and stigmatized as it is. But even working so hard as a prostitute, Kamladevi was not able to provide a comfortable life for herself. Between being in debt to the moneylenders and keeping her "boyfriends" content, she never managed to save anything. Kamladevi once told me that when she had the operation, her genitals were thrown into water instead of buried under a tree and that is why money goes through her hands like water in a sieve.

Meera has never really worked at performing. She is quite husky and ungainly, and even at our informal parties where some of the other hijras danced in either a parody of women, which is their forte, or in a more serious manner imitating classical Indian dance, Meera refrained. She strikes a dramatic dance pose, but that is all. Perhaps this has to do with the fact that she joined the hijras so late in life. At functions where hijras perform, the older hijras do not dance, unless it is in the special parody of the pregnant woman, as Tamasha does (see page 2). Meera started out in the hijra community as a "watchover" in a brothel; this was probably a function of both her size and her age. When she returned to Bastipore, she continued in this line of work, which proved profitable. As she related the incident of her performance at the college function where Ahmed saw her, she indicated a certain discomfort with that role. Peforming badhai is not a role commonly familiar to South Indian hijras; they seem more likely to go into prostitution. Now of course, married to a Muslim, Meera is not likely to think of performing at all. Nor does she need to.

When Meera became a dai ma she was able to earn much money and she also gained great prestige, more so even than by doing badhai. Furthermore, being a dai ma does not involve much hard work on a daily basis, as performing does if one is to make a living from it. This role specialization also permitted Meera to run a house of prostitution as well; indeed, performing the operation on her chelas increased their economic value to her as proprietor of a brothel. The major drawback in being a dai ma is that, if Meera were caught, she would be subject to severe punishment by the state. In my view, this was probably an important reason why she "had a dream to stop doing the operations." She has already parlayed her prestige and financial gains from this role into an advance in status in the Bastipore hijra community, and because she obviously does well financially from her chelas' prostitution, she does not need to take further risk.

Salima was a performer for most of her life; this was an important source of her self-respect, particularly because she was given special charge of the drum, a sacred object in the hijra community. Like many hijras living in respectable houses among important hijra gurus and chiefs, and who earn their living through badhai, Salima did not find prostitution either necessary or acceptable. When she was on the street, before Ibrahim returned, she did try to continue in the traditional hijra roles of begging for alms and performing, but could not earn enough. So now that she needs to take care of Ibrahim as well as herself, she is willing to make herself attractive so she can earn from prostitution. Although this occupation indicates to her how far she has sunk from her former social status and the security and comfort of her life with the hijras, she seems to find it acceptable, because it is needed to "help my man."

Sushila has never performed; she has mainly earned her living through prostitution. Despite all of her complaints about it when she worked out of Raj Dev's house, it was still apparently better than begging for alms in Bombay or in Bastipore, where the income from such an activity is inadequate because it is not a cultural tradition there as it is in North India. When Sushila moved from Raj Dev's house, she set up on her own; she lived separately from any senior person and engaged in prostitution as a "freelancer," using the facilities of the bathhouse in the neighborhood. This way she could live with her husband, keep more of what she earned, and have fewer restrictions on her freedom. But even with this independence, Sushila did not save any money, a fact that she bemoans from time to time.

Near the end of my stay in Bastipore, in the spring of 1982, Sushila told me that she was thinking of going into partnership in a bathhouse with another hijra, so that she could "stop this prostitution" and start saving for her old age. I was not surprised when I returned in 1985 to find that this had not come to pass. Sushila's temperament did not strike me as the managerial kind; she is much too irresponsible to run a business, drinking too much and getting into fights. A bathhouse is busy almost all day long, and running one necessitates effective and careful management and much hard work: The water has to be brought from outside pumps; the ovens have to be kept hot for the water; the place has to be cleaned constantly; supplies like soap have to be kept available; and the money has to be collected. Sushila's present solution as a householder seems more congenial to her temperament. I do not think she has given up prostitution entirely, as she claims, but she seems to see it now as more incongruent with the new image of respectability that she is trying to maintain—an image she did not speak of at all several years earlier.

Being a guru must certainly be considered a vocation, and as such it is for Meera, who has made a great success of her life. A guru is a route to upward mobility within the hijra community; indeed, ideally, the hijra social structure of guru and chela would seem to demand this upward mobility as people get older and become gurus by taking on chelas. But upward mobility does not depend only on the objective facts of social structure, but also on the motivations and resources of individuals who are not equally endowed to exploit the opportunities the structure offers. For example, in spite of the benefits and lack of structural barriers to becoming a guru, many middle-aged hijras I met, like Kamladevi, Sushila, and Salima, do not have any chelas. Becoming a guru requires initiative, assertiveness, careful management of one's financial resources, and a disposition to exploit the labor of others. Meera clearly has what is required to be a guru: initiative, wisdom, an interest in and intellectual capacity for learning the hijra culture and ritual, a strong sense of respectability and responsibility, a desire to live in comfort and be admired by others, plus her special skills as a dai ma.

Sushila, on the other hand, with a different personality, has chosen another career path. As a mother-in-law she has the same advantages as a guru: Others are now working for her, and she enjoys the prestige, too, that her family roles bring her. In addition, being a wife, mother, mother-in-law, and grandmother gives her a degree of personal freedom that a guru, even if she manages a fair-sized establishment, does not have.

Before I left Bastipore and Bombay, when I last saw Kamladevi, she also had spoken to me about starting to get her life together by taking on chelas "who could earn for me." As we saw, she had made a start with Amudh, but that young man failed to follow through on the process of initiation. Judging from the life style Kamladevi was living in Bombay—she told me she had a new boyfriend and was spending much money on him—I was not very confident that she would have made a very successful guru.

HUSBANDS

As we have seen in these narratives, husbands are an important, and for some hijras the most important, social relationship in their lives. Sinha (1967), in his study of hijras in Lucknow, says that "all hijras have husbands." Although I did not find this to be true, many of them certainly did, and many of those who did not either had had one in the past or looked forward to having one in the future. Because having a husband involves a sexual relationship, it is contrary to the ascetic ideal of the hijra role. Nevertheless, it has higher status than being a prostitute, as Sushila and Meera repeatedly point out.

As we saw in the cases of Meera, Sushila, and Salima, hijras who have husbands do not break their ties with the hijra community. Having a husband is not incompatible with any other hijra occupation, including prostitution. Meera is not now a working prostitute; but her narrative indicates how she uses the money from her house of prostitution to live, in many ways, a conventional life with her husband. Salima, as well, now combines prostitution with marriage. Sushila also combines prostitution with being a wife, refusing to become dependent on her husband by giving up the only secure way she could support herself.

Having a husband is an important source of hijra self-esteem. Because marriage is part of the normal expectation and main source of prestige for women in India (although it is ordinarily connected with the anticipation of motherhood), this relationship plays a particularly significant role in the self-concept of those hijras, like Meera, who view themselves as women. Indeed, it may be that the most important factor in the evolution of a feminine gender identity among hijras is connected to the marital relationship. In India, experiencing oneself as a woman is inextricably tied to the roles of wife and mother. The hope and expectation of every family is for their daughters to marry—for Hindus it is a religious obligation that they do so. Whereas in Meera's case it seems that a strong feminine identity propelled her toward marriage with Ahmed, in Sushila's case it seems that her commitment to the roles of mother and mother-in-law, and wife as well, is propelling her toward a more complete feminine identity.

As Meera's and Salima's and the later part of Sushila's narratives indicate, hijras' views of the marital relationship are highly idealistic. While it is true that the norms of Indian culture require wives to act in a deferential and submissive manner to their husbands, particularly in public, it is unusual for them to express the outpourings of love that Meera and Salima express for their husbands. In this expression of romantic love, the hijras have undoubtedly been influenced by Indian films, where romantic love and jealousy are frequent themes. These feelings and expressions of romantic love may also be connected to the fact that hijras and their husbands freely choose each other as mates, unlike most Indian marriages, which are arranged.[6]

Salima always spoke of Ibrahim with great love, even prior to his returning to her. Although Sushila does not speak much of loving her husband, as Meera and Salima do, she shares with them, at least in conversation, the view that the main role of a wife is to minister to her husband's needs and to be a respectable householder. In connection with this respectability, Salima mentioned that when she lived with Ibrahim, she wore a burka, and she was proud of the fact that many of her husband's acquaintances did not suspect she was a hijra. She kept the burka even after Ibrahim left her and put it on for me with a mixture of great pride and just a little embarrassment.

The emphasis that Meera and Sushila put on respectability in connection with their family life was, I think, exaggerated because my translators and I were seen as respectable married women with families. I also think this emphasis derived somewhat from the competition between Sushila and Meera, which showed up in many different ways in our conversations. This competition certainly existed prior to my knowing them, but when I arrived on the scene I became another resource—of attention and self-esteem—for them to compete over. But I do not think the emphasis on respectability in connection with family life was all for my benefit. It is, after all, a much emphasized Indian ideal, one that many hijras speak of in terms entirely like those used in the larger society.

I interpret the exaggerated attachment to the ideal norms of the marital relationship on the part of Salima, Sushila, and Meera as an attempt to present themselves to themselves, as well as to me (and my translators) as normal and as belonging to the mainstream rather than the margins of their society. Even their self-admitted penchant to pick fights with their husbands is consistent with this; because jealousy is the expressed motive for such squabbles, this reinforces their self-concept as extraordinarily good and loving wives.

In connection with their self-presentation as respectable people, hijras often talk about the good relations they have with the families of their husbands. Sushila's description of her first relationship with the fisherman in Madras centered on how much she was trusted by her "mother-in-law," expressed in a way I have heard from many Indian daughters-in-law, who take great pride in being allowed to hold the keys to the cupboard, where all of the family valuables are kept. Meera, too, now speaks about her good relations with Ahmed's family—how much they care for her and the care they have given to her. In other cases, of course, as with Salima, there is a more (it seems to me) realistic acknowledgment that their husbands' families will do anything they can to break up the relationship. So perhaps these parts of Meera's and Sushila's stories are fantasies, rather than realities; they are nevertheless important in telling us how people would like to see themselves in terms of cultural bases of self-evaluation.

Furthermore, Meera and Sushila have gone beyond mere fantasy to ratify their self-concepts as respectable women according to the norms of their society. They both have taken ingenious measures to implement the ideal relationships of the Indian family. They both are very sensitive about their inability to provide their husbands with children and have done something about this. They have become not only wives, but surrogate mothers as well, and they have, in different ways, given their husbands the opportunity to be fathers. The wish, and attempts, to present themselves as leading normal, even exemplary, lives may have something in common with that of other disadvantaged, marginal groups in society. I am reminded here of Robert Edgerton's poignant description of the lives of the mentally retarded living outside institutions in American society, whose greatest desire is to pass as intellectually competent—or normal—people (1971). Somewhat closer to the point is the parallel with American transsexuals, whose desire to pass as normal women is the central theme of their lives (Bolin, 1988; Garfinkel, 1984). Both of these examples highlight how those at the margins of society must consciously explicate to themselves and consciously work at what those in the mainstream take for granted. These examples also indicate that being "normal" is itself a cultural construction; it is not natural, as only those who are not "normal" become so poignantly aware.

While husbands are obviously an important source of psychological satisfaction for hijras, they do not, however, supplant the ties of the hijra community. Neither Meera, nor Sushila, nor Salima were or would be willing to give up their affiliation with the hijras for their husbands. This appears too economically risky; and they do not have to. Still, having a husband, as Sushila's story indicates, can be an important source of triangular conflict between guru and chela. Because having a husband is a source of both emotional and financial support existing outside the hijra community, many gurus (even if they have husbands themselves) appear threatened by the competition. We recall that it was Sushila's husband taking her to the doctor that was the source of the damaging argument between her and her guru—and that her husband did try to encourage her to leave her guru and save the money she earned for herself and her old age (and for him, I think, as well).

The willingness of Salima's guru to give her blessings to her relationship with Ibrahim was probably due to Salima's obvious willingness to go on earning for the guru. In Salima's case, it was the guru's husband who was the cause of her difficulties. We need not accept the details of Salima's story about her conflict with her guru's husband as fact for it to be useful in illustrating the conflicts of loyalty and the disruptive effects of sexuality that arise when hijras have husbands. In Meera's case, because her guru is in Bombay, her relationship with her husband does not interfere with her commitments to the hijra community; living separately from one's guru makes it easier to minimize conflicts while having a husband. Similarly, in contemporary India many young wives prefer to live outside the joint family with their husbands, while maintaining close family ties (Ross, 1961).

LIFE STAGES AND HIJRA LIVES

Every culture has different idealized expectations for people at different ages. In the Hindu religious tradition, individual social life is organized into four stages, so that individuals may have the opportunity to realize the instinctual, material, social, and spiritual ends of human life. These four life stages are that of the student whose duty is learning; the householder, whose duty is to procreate and raise a family; the forest dweller, who gradually withdraws from society; and finally the sannyasi, the ascetic who has renounced society and material attachments. From a philosophical standpoint these stages apply to women as well as men; in actuality there are limitations on women in both the religious and social fields, and the most important obligation for a woman is marriage and procreation. For both men and women this Hindu ideal of a life organized into four stages has an important influence on action, even when, as is the case for most people, it is not followed in practice to the letter.[7] In spite of their ambiguous gender, and their position at the margins of society, hijra lives also show the influence of this ideal pattern of life stages.

The hijra hierarchy of guru and chela provides a useful structure in which the norms of the Hindu life stages can at least partly be realized, particularly in the householder stage. The process of becoming a guru involves "procreation": One only becomes a guru by social recruitment of chelas, that is, assimilating new members from the larger community, an activity that can be seen as analogous to having children. Gurus also take care of their chela "children," and as we have seen, are conceptualized as parents. As individuals get older they are expected to move from a role in which they are being taken care of to a role in which they care for others; and the obligations and norms of the guru-chela relationship are explicitly modeled on the Indian family. Not all hijras do become gurus and thus fulfill the requirements of the Hindu life stages, but the structure that motivates individuals to move in this direction is there, just as is the institution of the family in the larger society.

The ideal concept of the hijra as a sannyasi, or religious ascetic, is also connected to this cultural norm of life stages and has its effect on hijra lives. It might seem that the sexual desires and activities of hijras would rob that cultural ideal of all of its meaning for them, but this is not the case.

In this conflict between the ideal and the real, hijras are not different from other Indians, who must also deal with the seemingly conflicting value that Hinduism places on eroticism and procreation on the one hand and nonattachment and asceticism on the other. The concept of the four life stages is a way of attempting to resolve these conflicting values. Each stage of life has its appropriate sexual behavior: The student should be chaste, whereas the householder must engage in sexual relations as a married person with an obligation to procreate. In the third stage, sexual activity has already dwindled as the forest dweller prepares for the renunciation of sex in the final stage of sannyasi. Thus, the Hindu ideal is a fully integrated life in which each aspect of human nature, including sexuality, has its time. Hijra lives indicate the influence of these cultural ideals.

Although Kamladevi ridicules the idea that any hijras were ever chaste, she does acknowledge that "as these hijras, like Gopi and Bellama, get older, they do not engage in sex and all and become very religious." This change parallels that among Indian women generally. In the Hindu cultural ideal, women whose sons are married are expected to give up sexual activity. In truth, not all women do, despite the social pressure to conform. People ridicule and gossip about middle-aged women who act in ways that suggest an active sexual interest (Vatuk, 1985). This presentation of self as a nonsexual person with advancing age also appears among hijras. The middle-aged hijras wear more conservative clothing, often donning white rather than boldly colored saris. They act in a less sexually suggestive manner and do not "roam about" in public, preferring domestic roles that keep them at home.

Meera is a good example of this development, although there are contradictions. She likes to costume herself flamboyantly and strike sexually suggestive poses for photographs, but in ordinary circumstances she dresses conservatively and is always conscious of the respect associated with her status of guru and middle-class housewife. This is contradicted somewhat by her public declarations—in word and deed—of her extreme love for and jealousy of her husband, behavior considered most inappropriate for someone of her age and stage of life. She is thus sometimes referred to disparagingly by other hijras as having "husband fever."

Nevertheless, in other ways Meera is making strenuous attempts to model her behavior so that it is congruent with her age and her life stage. She has done this both in her role as guru and as householder, particularly in reference to the latter, by adopting a child.

The influence of the Hindu cultural ideal of life stages is most spectacularly seen in Sushila's life. More than any other hijra I met, Sushila has attempted, and succeeded, in fulfilling Hindu cultural ideals in this respect. By making her husband her adopted son and by arranging his marriage, Sushila became a mother-in-law and then a grandmother, through which she has gained enormous self-esteem. Sushila's satisfaction with her life parallels that of many Indian women. She has managed to achieve fulfillment of the cultural ideal of a woman in India—no mean achievement for someone born a man!

Seemingly, Kamladevi was the least influenced by Hindu cultural ideals of respectability and generativity associated with middle age or, for that matter, the chastity associated with youth. Yet even she showed signs of changing her behavior as she got older. Though nothing apparently came of it, she was talking about the importance for her of taking some chelas. Salima's life stages in the hijra community were interrupted by her expulsion; but now that Ibrahim has returned she shows signs of moving into a new role, not only as his wife, but also as an elder of sorts. She has begun to gather around her a small group of hijras who have quarreled with their own gurus and is beginning to take care of them, as a guru does. Whether as gurus or as wives (and sometimes even mothers), hijra lives are oriented to the life stages constructed by the tenets of Indian culture.

In this chapter I have tried to put the four hijra narratives into a wider context, showing how, like all individuals, they draw on common cultural meanings and values to interpret their lives in ways that are consistent with their sense of self. Given the obstacles that hijras have had to overcome to do this, their narratives and, more to the point, their lives, are a poignant testimony to the strength of the human personality as it seeks not merely to adjust to culture, but to actively interpret it and, to some extent, create it anew.

CHAPTER TEN

🦋 The Hijras in Cross-Cultural Perspective

And God said unto Noah . . .
[W]ith thee will I establish my covenant;
And of every living thing of all flesh,
two of every sort shalt thou bring into the ark
to keep them alive with thee;
they shall be male and female.

GENESIS 6:13–19

Nothing seems more natural, unchangeable, or desirable than that "human beings are divided without remainder into two biological sexes," male and female (Geertz, 1975:10). For all social purposes, this division of people into two sexes takes place at birth, when sex ascription is made; and such assignment is assumed to be permanent. The concept of sex as a system of binary oppositions which are ascribed and invariant is so strong that it is taken for granted not only by common sense, but also in both the biological and the social sciences (Kessler & McKenna, 1978). Until recently, with few exceptions (for example, Mead, 1963) *gender*—the psychological, social, and behavioral aspects of being male and female, which we call masculine and feminine—was also treated as largely biologically determined and, like sex, assumed to be dichotomous and permanent. With the rise of feminist scholarship in anthropology, the concept of gender has been intellectually extricated to a large extent from biological determinism. Cross-cultural studies have shown such a wide variety of attributes of masculine and feminine roles and characteristics in different societies that we now accept almost as a truism that gender is a cultural construction,[1] the content of which varies from society to society, and that the psychological and behavioral aspects of gender are more likely to be caused by socialization than by biology.

The view of gender as a cultural construction has been enormously liberating: It has opened up the whole subject of gender systems to disciplined inquiries about cultural influences and has made gender systems and gender relations a legitimate and important subject for anthropological study. But even as cross-cultural research has begun to raise questions about the content of gender categories and the mutual exclusivity of masculine and feminine, the view of *sex* (the biological categories of male and female) as dichotomous and unchanging over the individual's lifetime has been so authoritative that this view is still extended to many aspects of gender. In the everyday thinking of ordinary people, this is not only how it is, but how it should be.[2] Placed firmly within a popular biological framework, the dichotomous and presumably permanent nature of gender continues to resist attempts at cultural analysis. Reinforced by the assumptions of many scientists, it is extraordinarily difficult for most of us to even think about any alternative to our cultural construction of reality, which tells us that there are only two genders, masculine and feminine; that they cannot change in a person's lifetime; and that they are identical with our biological sex.

So committed is our Western view of sex and gender as dichotomous, ascribed, and unchanging, that its logic and rightness exclude exceptions. Every society, including our own, is at some time or other faced with people who do not fit into its sex and gender categories—persons born intersexed (hermaphrodites) or those who exhibit behavior deemed appropriate for the opposite sex (homosexuals or transsexuals). Various cultures deal with these challenges differently (Edgerton, 1964). As we have seen in India, the hijras are evidence that the Indian—or at least Hindu—cultural system not only conceives of more than two genders, but also incorporates the idea, both in myth and reality, that both sex and gender can be changed within an individual's lifetime.

In the following sections, I examine some other cultural systems that, like India, have institutionalized alternative sex and gender roles. It is in this larger context of a cross-cultural comparison of alternative gender roles that a study of the hijras takes on a significance beyond its own distinctive features. The hijra role is not merely a unique cultural aberration in a world in which gender is otherwise seen as exclusively dichotomous. On the contrary, the hijras illustrate but one example of the many gender systems that include alternatives to the Western dualism of masculine and feminine. A look at alternative gender roles in other cultures provokes us to reexamine the nature and assumptions of our own gender system: the cultural basis of its categories, the relations within the system, and the relation of aspects of the system to other parts of our culture. As we look at other cultures, we alter our interpretation of our own. This strategy lies at the heart of the cross-cultural perspective and the value of anthropological data.

THE XANITH: AN INTERMEDIATE GENDER IN OMAN

Unni Wikan (1977) describes one such alternative gender role, the *xanith* (han · eeth), in Oman, an Islamic society located on the Saudi Arabian peninsula. Xanith means "impotent, effeminate, and soft." Individuals so labeled are regarded by Omanis as neither man nor woman, but with characteristics of both. Xanith are born as males; they have male genitals and do not, like the hijras, practice emasculation. Xanith have masculine names and are referred to in the masculine grammatical gender form. Under Islamic law they have all the rights of a man, for example, the right to testify in court, a right that is denied to women. They also worship in the mosque with men. Like men but unlike women, xanith also support themselves economically.

In other ways, however, xanith are like women. They do women's work in their households and are complimented and feel flattered by attention to their cooking and housekeeping abilities. Their appearance is judged by standards of female beauty: white skin, shiny black hair, large eyes, and full cheeks. In Omani society, where women are in *purdah* (seclusion) and men and women are strictly segregated in social interaction, xanith are classed with the women for many social purposes. On festive occasions they join the women in singing and dancing; they visit and gossip with women where other men would not be allowed to do so; they may walk down the street arm in arm with a woman; and in this society, where eating is considered an extremely intimate act, they eat with women. Most significantly, only they, and never other men, are allowed to view the face of a bride on her marriage night. This clearly indicates that, although the xanith have some characteristics of men, "they are not men."

The most important reason xanith are considered "not men" has to do with the fact that in Oman, the definition of a man centers on sexual potency, demonstrated through marriage. On the morning after a wedding there must be public verification of the consummation of a marriage, either by showing a bloody handkerchief or by the groom claiming that his bride was not a virgin. It is only by this public demonstration of his ability to perform sexual intercourse in the male role (as penetrator) that a person is validated as a man.

The xanith act as male homosexual prostitutes; and any male homosexual prostitute will be classed as xanith because he takes the receptive, passive role in sex associated with being a woman. Indeed, in Oman one of the important distinctions between a man and a woman is that men take an active, penetrating role in sexual intercourse, whereas women are viewed as passive receivers. Because it is the active and potent role in sexual intercourse that is the essential characteristic of a man, a xanith is not a man. This definition of manhood, however, makes it possible for a xanith to *become* a man. If he chooses to marry, and if he can demonstrate publicly in the approved ways that he is indeed potent in the male sexual role, a xanith moves into the category of man. From that point on he is subject to the same constraints on his behavior with regard to interacting with women as are other men. Thus, upon questioning the gender role of a particular individual, Wikan occasionally was told "X was once a xanith, but now he is a man."

Xanith, then, are definitely not men by Omani standards; they say, when asked, that they are women, and yet they are also not women. Xanith are prohibited by law from wearing women's clothing, including the mask and veil that all adult women must wear. Unlike women, xanith freely move around outside their houses, though only during the day. Most importantly, xanith are prostitutes, an activity not acknowledged for any Omani woman. In truth, female prostitutes do exist in Oman, but they are few and not officially—or even unofficially—recognized. Women in Oman are regarded as pure; xanith, as prostitutes, cannot be pure and are therefore not women in this most important sociological sense.

Much xanith behavior falls in-between that of men and women. Although the facial expressions, voice, laugh, movements, and swaying walk of the xanith imitate those of women, they wear clothing that is a mixture of men's and women's styles. A xanith wears the ankle-length tunic of the men, but belted tightly at the waist as a woman would do. Men generally wear white clothing, women wear bright-colored patterned clothes; xanith wear unpatterned colored clothes. Men wear their hair cut short and women wear it long; xanith wear their hair at middle length. Men comb their hair backward from their face, whereas women comb it diagonally from a center part; xanith comb theirs forward from a side part and oil it in the manner of women. In Oman both men and women cover their heads; xanith go bareheaded. Both men and women in Oman use perfume; xanith use it more heavily than either. Thus, the xanith demonstrate their intermediate gender role in many aspects of their public presentation of self.

THE ALYHA: AN ALTERNATIVE GENDER ROLE AMONG THE MOHAVE

Alternative gender roles have been reported for many societies in native North America. These roles are generally referred to as *berdache,* a word that comes from the Persian/Arabic via Italian and French into English. In French and English, its meaning, as it was applied to native North America in the 17th and 18th centuries by European observers, meant "kept boy," or "male prostitute," or slave. The phenomenon has most often been referred to by European observers and anthropologists as a form of "institutionalized homosexuality."[3] Whereas in some societies, such as the Navaho, the berdache were said to be intersexed persons (Hill, 1935), in most cases (including, apparently, the Mohave) the role appeared to be taken on by anatomically normal men. In many societies, berdache took ordinary men as their husbands; these men were not classified as berdache or as homosexuals. The early European accounts of the berdache emphasized the cross-dressing and homosexual activity associated with the role; these appeared to be common elements in what was—and is—otherwise a very diverse phenomenon.

Many anthropologists today hold that this early emphasis on sexual activity as central and definitive in the various alternative gender roles collectively referred to as the berdache is a result of an ethnocentric perspective that projects our own Western criterion of gender—that is, choice of sexual partner—inappropriately onto other cultures. Contemporary writings on the berdache call attention to other aspects of the berdache role, for example, cross-gender occupations, and its sacred status as neither man nor woman.[4]

A major difficulty in discussing the alternative gender roles in native North America is that most are so poorly documented. Contact with the West substantially altered the indigenous functioning of these roles, and the ethnographic data are generally unreliable and biased. One of the better documented ethnographic accounts of an alternative gender role in native North America is given by George Devereux for the Mohave Indians from California (1937). It should be kept in mind, however, that even Devereux's ethnography contains many inconsistencies and difficulties with documentation, as Devereux himself acknowledges. The transvestite ceremonies, which were the public acknowledgment of these roles, had disappeared by the time of Devereux's study and only a few, very old, informants remembered having seen them and were familiar with the role on a first-hand basis. The Mohave had two such alternative gender roles: male transvestite homosexuals, known as *alyha,* and female homosexuals, known as *hwame.* Here I shall describe only the alyha.

Among the Mohave, pregnant women had dreams forecasting the anatomic sex of their children. Mothers of a future alyha dreamt of male characteristics, such as arrow feathers, indicating the birth of a boy, but it was said that their dreams also included hints of their child's future alternative gender status. A boy indicated he might become an alyha by "acting strangely" around the age of 10 or 11, before he had participated in the boys' puberty ceremonies. It was at this age that young people began to seriously engage in the activities that would characterize their adult lives as men and women: For example, boys learned to hunt and ride horses, make bows and arrows, and to develop sexual feelings for girls. The future alyha avoided these masculine activities; instead, he played with dolls, imitated the domestic work of women, tried to participate in the women's gambling games, and demanded to wear the female bark skirt rather than the male breech clout.

The alyha's parents and relatives were ambivalent about this behavior; at first his parents would try to dissuade him, but if the behavior persisted his relatives would resign themselves and begin preparations for the transvestite ceremony. The ceremony was meant to take the boy by surprise: It was considered both a test of his inclination and an initiation. Word was sent out to various settlements so that people could watch the ceremony and get accustomed to the boy in female clothing.

At the ceremony the boy was led into a circle of onlookers by two women. At this point the singing of the transvestite songs was begun in the crowd. If the boy began to dance as women do, he was confirmed as an alyha. He was then taken to the river to bathe and given a girl's skirt to wear. This initiation ceremony confirmed his changed gender status, which was considered permanent.

After this point the alyha assumed a female name (though he did not take on the lineage name that all females assumed) and would resent being called by his former, male name. In the frequent and bawdy sexual joking characteristic of Mohave culture, an alyha resented male nomenclature being applied to his genitals. He insisted that his penis be called a clitoris, his testes, labia majora, and anus a vagina. Alyha were also particularly sensitive to sexual joking, and if they were teased in the same way as others they responded with assaults on those who teased them. Because they were very strong, people usually avoided angering them.

Alyha often had husbands and were considered highly industrious and much better housewives than were young girls. It is partly for this reason that they had no difficulty finding spouses. Alyha were not courted like ordinary girls, however (where the prospective husband would sleep chastely beside the girl for several nights and then lead her out of her parents' house), but rather like widows, divorcees, or "wanton" women. Intercourse with an alyha was surrounded by special etiquette. Like Mohave heterosexual couples, the alyha and her husband practiced both anal and oral intercourse, with the alyha taking the female role. Alyha were reported to be embarrassed by an erection and would not allow their sexual partners to touch or even comment on their erect penis.

When an alyha found a husband, he would begin to imitate menstruation by scratching himself between the legs with a stick until blood appeared. The alyha then submitted to puberty observations as a girl would, and her husband also observed the requirements of the husband of a girl who menstruated for the first time. Alyha also imitated pregnancy, particularly if their husbands threatened them with divorce on the grounds of barrenness. At this time they would cease faking menstruation and follow the pregnancy taboos, with even more punctiliousness than ordinary women, except that they publicly proclaimed their pregnancy, which ordinary Mohave women never did. In imitating pregnancy, an alyha would stuff rags in his skirts, and near the time of the birth, would drink a decoction to cause constipation. After a day or two of stomach pains, he would go into the bushes and sit over a hole, defecating in the position of childbirth. The feces would be treated as a stillbirth and buried, and the alyha would weep and wail as a woman does for a stillborn child. The alyha and her husband would then clip their hair as in mourning.

Alyha were said to be generally peaceful persons (except when teased) and were also considered cowards. They did not have to participate in the frequent and harsh military raids of Mohave men. Alyha would participate, as women do, in the welcoming home feast for the warriors, where, like old women, they might make a bark penis and go through the crowd poking the men who had stayed home, saying, "You are not a man, but an alyha."

In general, alyha were not teased or ridiculed for being alyha (though their husbands were teased for marrying them), because it was believed that they could not help it and that a child's inclinations in this direction could not be resisted. It was believed that a future alyha's desire for a gender change was such that he could not resist dancing the women's dance at the initiation ceremony. Once his desires were demonstrated in this manner, people would not thwart him. It was partly the belief that becoming an alyha was a result of a "temperamental compulsion" or predestined (as forecast in his mother's pregnancy dream) that inhibited ordinary Mojave from ridiculing alyha. In addition, alyha were considered powerful shamans, particularly effective in curing sexually transmitted diseases (called alyha) like syphilis.

Keeping in mind the uneven and unreliable nature of the data on the many diverse alternative gender roles among native North American societies, it does appear that these roles might accurately be called intermediate gender roles. Alyha, as we see, imitated many aspects of the women's role: dress, sexual behavior, menstruation, pregnancy, childbirth, and domestic occupations. And yet in other ways, alyha were different from women; they did not take on women's lineage names; they were not courted like ordinary women; they publicly claimed their pregnancies; and they were considered more industrious at women's domestic tasks than were ordinary women. Among ordinary Mohave, if a person dreamed of having homosexual relationships, the person would be expected to die soon, but this was not true of the alyha. The most persuasive evidence that alyha were indeed conceptualized as an alternative gender was that, like many other alternative gender roles in native North America, they were considered to have special supernatural powers which they used in curing illness.

Devereux notes that the Mohave believe that at creation and during the early periods of the mythical era there existed sexually undifferentiated people, so that it was not too difficult for the Mohave to believe in the reality of the gender shift which characterized the alyha.

THE MAHU OF TAHITI

Another culture that institutionalized a third gender role is that of traditional Tahiti. This role is called *mahu.* Eighteenth-century accounts suggest some of the features of this role:

> [The mahu] are like the Eunichs [sic] in India but they are not castrated. They never cohabit with women but live as they do. They pick their beards out and dress as women, dance and sing with them and are as

effeminate in their voice. They . . . do women's employment and excell in some crafts. It is said that they converse with men as familiar as women do (Morrison, in Levy, 1973:130).

Captain Bligh, commander of the *Bounty,* also noted the behavior of the mahu, observing that the mahu participated in the same ceremonies as women and ate as women did. Their effeminate speech led him to think they were castrated, but he later found out that they were not, noting however, that "things equally disgusting were committed" (referring to homosexual relations). Bligh was told that the mahu were selected when they were boys and kept with the women solely for the caresses of the men. In order to learn more about such people, he had one mahu remove his loin cloth, which led to the following description:

> He had the appearance of a woman, his yard [penis] and testicles being so drawn in under him, having the art from custom of keeping them in this position.

Upon further examination of the mahu's genitals, Bligh found them

> both very small and the testicles remarkably so, being not larger than a boy's five or six years old, and very soft as if in a state of decay or a total incapacity of being larger, so that . . . he appeared . . . a Eunuch [as much as if] his stones were away. The women treat him as one of their sex and he observed every restriction that they do, and is equally respected and esteemed" (Bligh, in Levy, 1973:130–131).

Bligh's account goes on to report that the men who had sexual relations with a mahu "have their beastly pleasures gratified between his thighs" but that they denied practicing sodomy. A nineteenth-century account declared that the mahu fellated the man he had relations with, swallowing the semen, which is believed to give them strength (Levy, 1973:135). Contemporary accounts verify this behavior, and some Tahitian men talk of the exceptional strength of the mahu. The mahu's partner never fellates the mahu; and mahu are described as passive participants in the sexual relationship. Today, intercourse between the thighs is not practiced in Tahiti.

Although, as was often the case with Western observers of third gender roles in non-Western cultures, the sexual behavior of the men occupying the mahu role drew both immediate and disapproving attention, it is clear from both early and contemporary accounts that the mahu was not merely a homosexual and that the role involved much more than institutionalized homosexuality. Indeed, although Western observers saw homosexuality as central to the mahu's function, contemporary Tahitian men say that it is not, and some of the older men in the more traditional districts of the Society Islands claim that the mahu did not engage in homosexual relations, though the younger men dispute this.

In any case, it is clearly not sexual object choice alone that defines the mahu role, as the men who have sexual relations with the mahu are never called mahu just as the male partners of the berdache are not called berdache. Nor are the sexual partners of the xanith and the hijras labeled homosexual. Generally, in non-Western cultures, male partners of "not man, not woman" are in no way considered to be different from other men, nor set apart linguistically because of this sexual activity. No stigma or shame is attached to the mahu's partner, and the mahu, as fellator, is seen as a substitute for a woman.

Additional evidence that the mahu is a third gender role incorporating more than homosexual activity is the fact that homosexuality in the modern context, which the Tahitians believe to be a European importation, is called by a different name, *raerae*. This word, used to refer to sodomy, means "sex-role reversal" and would apply also to a reversed role in sexual relations between a man and a woman (Levy, 1973:140). While effeminate men may be described as mahuish, such an individual is assumed to be an ordinary man, involved in standard male activity, and engaged in normal heterosexual practices, or in any case *not* to be engaged in the mahu's practices of fellatio.

Each district in Tahiti has only one mahu and every district has one. The role is culturally available and filled by someone voluntarily. The defining criterion for the mahu is that he *publicly* takes on the activities and dress of a woman. Speaking of the mahu in one district, the ethnographer Robert Levy says: "His feminine role taking is demonstrated for the villagers because he performs women's household activities, cleans the house, takes care of babies, braids coconut palm leaves into thatching plaits" (1973:140). The mahu in another district associates with the adolescent girls of the village and walks with his arm interlocked with theirs, "a behavior otherwise seen only among people of the same sex."

Whether a physical anomaly is involved in recruitment to the mahu role is unclear. One of Levy's mahu informants, for example, said that the mahu are not supercised (a traditional coming of age ceremony for boys that involves incisions made on the shaft of the penis) because a mahu's penis is too small. On the other hand, based on one observation, Levy seemed to feel that diminuitive size is not necessarily a physical correlate for the mahu role and that a boy might be "coached" into the role of mahu by his elders, perhaps just for their amusement, by dressing a boy child in girl's clothes. Furthermore, if a male child seems determined to wear girl's clothes, adults will not stand in his way, and a child's insistence in some cases is felt to be "irresistible" (Levy, 1973:140).

Although Tahitians generally claim that "changing their sex" is not possible, and seem also to have few fantasies regarding this, it is possible to stop being a mahu, "as one can discontinue being a chief." Levy reports of one man in the village he studied who in his early adolescence, dressed from time to time in girl's clothes and was thus considered a mahu, but in his early twenties "cast off" the role. It was assumed in the village that this was the end of it and that the person was now leading an ordinary masculine life (Levy, 1973:133).

DICHOTOMOUS GENDER ROLES AND TRANSSEXUALISM IN THE WEST

Unlike the alternative gender roles found in other cultures, the *transsexual* in American culture is definitely not viewed as a third, or alternative, gender. Rather, transsexualism is defined in such a way as to reinforce our cultural construction of both sex and gender as invariably dichotomous. Robert Stoller, a leading authority on transsexualism, defines it as "the conviction of a biologically normal person of being a member of the *opposite* sex" (in Kessler & McKenna, 1978:115), a definition that admits no possibility of a third, alternative gender.

Given the unyielding Western commitment to a dichotomous gender system, the dilemma for American culture is how to deal with the person who desires to be of a sex and gender class he or she was not born into, when our "incorrigible proposition" tells us that sex and gender are ascribed and permanent. We resolve this dilemma by defining the transsexual as a *transitional* status, a view promoted most strongly by transsexuals themselves.

In this view, a person is a transsexual when he or she is in a *temporary,* transitional, in-between sex status. Indeed, we view an intermediate sex or gender category as nothing other than transitional; it cannot be, in our culture, a permanent possibility. The reconstructive genital surgery that transsexuals desire aims at moving them from just such an in-between state—"a woman trapped in the body of a man" (in the case of male transsexuals)—to the status of a real woman, with female sex organs. In a provocative analysis of the cultural construction of sex and gender, Kessler and McKenna (1978:120) in fact suggest that the category of transsexual was created to "relieve ambiguity," that is, to avoid the kinds of sex/gender combinations and alternatives that make us uncomfortable because they violate our basic cultural rules that gender is ascribed, invariant, and dichotomous.

One of the ways we reconcile our standard view of gender with the "cultural challenge" presented by people born as males who want to live as women, is through the use of the term *gender identity*. Gender identity (see p. 114) refers to the inner psychological conviction of an individual that he or she is either a man or a woman. The concept of gender identity allows transsexuals to maintain that, in spite of a male body, they are and always have been women. Their situation can then be seen as discordance between their anatomy and their subjectively experienced gender identity: The male organs are viewed as "merely" a mistake that must be corrected.

The term *gender identity,* which was invented in America and is not found indigenously in other cultures, is thus useful in maintaining the Western cultural notion that gender is ascribed and invariant. It allows the transsexual to maintain that he really is not changing genders, but only altering or correcting the wrong anatomy. This view permits society, and the transsexual himself, to be assured that gender will continue to be viewed as dichotomous and permanent, not amenable to transformation.

All data on transsexuals in the United States emphasize that, in their own view, they are only in a transitional state—one that the transsexual wants to and will eventually alter. The aim of male transsexuals is, invariably, to merge into the general population of females. Sometimes transsexuals join a support group, such as the national Berdache Society, to help them through the preoperative "liminal" period. But once preoperative transsexuals have begun living full-time as women, they find such support groups no longer relevant and, indeed, even a hindrance to their being accepted as women by men and other women (Bolin, 1988).

The central theme of transsexualism as a transitional stage is "passing," that is, learning how to conceal the fact that one is a transsexual. As transsexuals become more adept at acting like women, and spend more time doing it, they come to feel more and more like "natural women." At this point they reject the transsexual identity and the term *passing,* insisting that they are not transsexuals, but women: No longer are they aberrations concealing a defect; now they are being what they really are—women. When surgery removes the male genitals and constructs the genitals of a female, the transitional stage is over. The new female gender status is then strengthened by the construction of a revised life story and by making certain legal changes, such as revising one's sex on the birth certificate. In this way our society provides a process for transforming disorder—an in-between gender status—into order, allowing a male to adopt the legal, social, and personal status of a woman.

Medical and mental-health professionals in the United States have played a critical role in constructing this new cultural definition of the transsexual as a woman (or man) trapped in the body of a man (or woman). In order to qualify for genital surgery, a transsexual must obtain the approval of a mental-health professional, most often a psychiatrist or psychologist. For this approval, male transsexuals must claim that they have *always* believed themselves to be women; any expressed ambivalence or confusion about their gender identity will most likely disqualify them for surgery. Transsexuals must also convince the mental-health professionals that they can live full-time as women and be accepted as women. Both of these abilities are taken as evidence that the person is indeed a transsexual. Because most medical and mental-health specialists are committed to a conventional view of the Western gender dichotomy and its associated gender roles, this process undoubtedly contributes to the stereotypically defined femininity that research indicates most transsexuals exhibit.[5] Thus, far from being an alternative gender role, as found in India, Oman, Tahiti, or among native Americans, transsexualism in the United States reinforces our standard cultural beliefs about the dichotomy of gender categories and inhibits any alternative gender category from developing.

RETHINKING GENDER CATEGORIES

Earlier in this chapter I raised the question of whether our own view of sex and gender as dichotomous, ascribed, and permanent is as universal as we assume it to be. The examination of alternative gender roles as they exist in a wide variety of cultures requires us to rethink these powerfully persuasive, but nevertheless culturally constructed, assumptions. Going beyond our own gender system to a comparative study of intermediate gender roles in other cultures highlights the culturally variable nature of gender systems and the variable criteria that define masculinity, femininity, and alternative gender roles in different societies.[6] This comparative perspective also raises questions as to whether there are any universal criteria for gender categories and the degree to which gender is considered a permanent status. Still other questions arise about how the cultural concepts underlying gender categories are related to other, broader themes in a culture.

In the concluding sections I suggest some possibilities, more provocative than final, in response to such questions, as these are indicated by the alternative gender roles described here.

The roles of the hijra, xanith, berdache, and mahu, as well as the Western definition of the transsexual, suggest that defining criteria of gender are dissimilar in different cultures. In our own culture, for example, the notion of the transsexual as a person who does not change gender, but merely changes genitals, suggests that anatomy is, for ourselves, the minimum criterion of our *culturally* constructed categories of masculine and feminine (see Kessler & McKenna, 1978). When this cultural construction becomes problematical, as it is in the personal and social experiences of those who claim to be other than what they are identified as anatomically, our determination to retain our traditional dual gender system leads to a redefinition of what gender is. The two minimum prerequisites now include genitals (a transsexual does not become a female till he has had the penis removed and a vagina constructed) and gender identity.

In India, too, the definition of the hijra indicates that male genitals are an essential defining criterion of a man. A man who dresses and acts like a woman is still a man; unless he has had his genitals removed he is "only" a man impersonating a woman. But sexual and reproductive capacity is also important in defining who is man and who is woman: for example, in India an impotent man is often identified as a eunuch. Because hijras do not have sexual or reproductive capacities as either men or women, they are neither men nor women. In Oman the basic criterion for the masculine gender is not male genitals—which xanith have and retain—but the position taken in sexual intercourse and demonstrated sexual potency. If they do prove their sexual potency, they will be regarded as men. In native American cultures, it does not appear to be genitals or sexual potency that defines masculine and feminine. Persons born as male who publicly engage in women's work and wear women's dress and, in some cases, as with the alyha, assume the women's role in sexual intercourse, are conceptualized as having adopted a new gender status: They are no longer considered men, but something else. For the Tahitians, too, women's work and dress appear to be more important criteria for defining gender than are genitals: A man with imperfect genitals, even with other feminine characteristics, including having sexual intercourse with other men, is not considered a mahu unless he publicly takes on the clothing and work of women.

As we look at the hijras, the xanith, the berdache, and the mahu, we see that our Western view of gender as permanent within an individual's lifetime is also not universal. Gender transformations are not only part of Indian cultural beliefs, but also are permitted and occur, in society, as the hijra case illustrates. Salima, a hermaphrodite and a true hijra, referred to other hijras as "converts," a term that nicely illustrates the Indian view that people can either remain the gender they were born into or they can change their gender, just as one converts to a different religion. In Oman the xanith can become men if they marry and can prove their sexual potency. Then they are reclassified as men for all social purposes, no matter how effeminate they remain.

Among the Mohave, too, men can change their gender, an event anticipated in their mothers' dreams and confirmed when these men undergo an initiation ceremony. Here again, it requires a public transformation for the gender change to be legitimated. The mahu also represent a changeable gender status, even in a cultural system where gender is otherwise seen as permanent. By abandoning the wearing of women's clothing and women's occupations, a man ceases to be a mahu in the eyes of the community.

ALTERNATIVE GENDER ROLES AND GENDER DIFFERENTIATION

So far there have been few systematic attempts to correlate alternative gender roles with other aspects of culture. One such study examined the possible correlation between the presence of alternative gender roles and gender differentiation. Gender differentiation refers to the extent to which gender roles are well defined, specialized, and hierarchical. This study indicated that alternative sex/gender categories and roles appear in cultures with different levels of gender differentiation (Munroe & Munroe, 1977; Munroe, Whiting, & Hally, 1969). The hijra role appears in a culture where gender roles for ordinary purposes are sharply hierarchical and quite well defined and differentiated, yet admits gender overlap, gender transformations, and alternative genders in both myth and ritual.

In Oman the role of the xanith also appears in distinct contradiction to the otherwise well-defined distinctions, separation, and hierarchy of masculine and feminine roles. Indeed, in Wikan's analysis, she is at pains to show that the role of the xanith serves to uphold this otherwise dichotomous gender system. The different alternative gender roles grouped under the collective term *berdache* also appear in cultures with very different levels of gender differentiation. Native American societies are very diverse: In some of these societies, men and women do similar work and are regarded as relatively equal in status, whereas native American societies that contain alternative gender roles are highly differentiated with men and women engaging in different and specialized activities and having different amounts of power and prestige.

In further contrast, the mahu role in Tahiti occurs where the sexes and gender roles are not highly differentiated. Observers have consistently commented on the physical androgyny of the Society Islanders, on the general lack of specialization in gender roles, and on the general egalitarianism between men and women. The lack of gender-role differentiation is attested to by an ethnographer's comment that when he was told about several births which occurred during his fieldwork in Tahiti, the person who told him did not know the sex of the infants (Levy, 1973:439). Robert Levy, who has most completely analyzed the mahu role, holds that it is this lack of gender differentiation which gives the role its special meaning in Tahitian society. In a gender system with so little masculine/feminine differentiation, the mahu provides a way for males to internalize a strong masculine identity: By seeing the mahu—of which there is only one in each village—a man has a local model of a nonmasculine gender role and can say, "I am not he, therefore I am masculine" (Levy, 1971).

ALTERNATIVE GENDER ROLES AND THE CULTURAL CONCEPT OF THE PERSON

Culturally patterned constructs or beliefs other than those specifically connected to gender may also be helpful in understanding why some cultures permit intermediate gender roles and others do not. One of these is the cultural concept of the person.

In the Hindu philosophical and religious tradition, one of the most important concepts is that of *dharm,* meaning moral duty or rightful action. Rightful action is seen as unique to each individual, depending on the historical era and group into which he or she is born, the particular life stage he or she is in, and the innate traits in the individual carried over from previous lives. The concept of dharm leads to a tolerance, in India, of an enormous diversity of occupations, behaviors, and personal styles as long as these are seen as the working out of a life path; this is particularly so when the behavior is sanctified by tradition, formalized in ritual, and practiced within a group. This tolerance extends to behavior that we in the West would label pathological or criminal and would seek to cure or punish.

In addition, Hinduism explicitly recognizes that humans achieve their ultimate goals—salvation, bliss, knowledge, and pleasure—by following many different paths, because it is recognized that humans differ in their special abilities and competencies. Thus, Hinduism affords the individual temperament the widest latitude in behavior, including compulsive extremes (Lannoy, 1975:119): This results in a greater tolerance for individual diversity, especially in matters of sexuality, than does our own culture. It is within this framework of the Indian concept of the person that hijras can find meaning in their ambiguous gender identity.

Wikan suggests that the Omani concept of the person is directly related to the tolerance of the xanith role. Homosexuality is considered shameful behavior in Oman because males take the passive role in sex associated with being a woman. However, Omanis acknowledge that the sexual deviant cannot be suppressed, and they let him practice his deviance in peace. In the Omani view of life the world is imperfect. People are created with dissimilar natures and are likewise imperfect. Thus, the passive, effeminate homosexual is acknowledged and reclassified as a xanith.

It is difficult to generalize with regard to the alternative gender roles in native North American societies. In a reexamination of these roles, Whitehead (1981) suggests that native American cosmologies give wide scope to individual differences, institutionalizing them in social roles, rather than driving them underground. Such societies, she says, seem less concerned in general with why individuals become the way they are or why they change from one role to another. Devereux noted, in his study of the Mohave, that there is believed to be an element of predestination or fate involved in becoming an alyha, and the Mohave belief that a person cannot resist an inclination to become an alyha inhibits negative moral evaluations or sanctions. Instead, as in Oman, the sexually different person is given a publicly acknowledged social status and participates in the full life of the society in his specialized role.

In Tahiti, too, concepts of the person appear to be relevant in understanding the creation of, and community response to, the mahu role. The people in the most traditional district studied by Levy also had little interest in why a person becomes a mahu; the mahu is considered natural, and the cause of becoming a mahu is not an issue of concern. Nor is the mahu subject to any negative moral evaluations or sanctions. People say that the mahu "is born like that," and he is simply accepted. In Tahiti generally, Levy reports, people are reluctant to generalize about the quality of an individual's character based on his or her membership in a gender category; such reluctance inhibits generalizations about ordinary men and women and mahus as well. In Tahiti, the self is seen as a natural state of being and not easily changeable, which inhibits not only a curiosity about the cause of becoming a mahu, but any desire to correct or cure him. All of this contrasts vividly with the Western idea of the person who is ofen characterized in terms of essential qualities. Homoerotic choice in our culture, for example, is not seen as just an aspect of a personality, but as integral to identity: One becomes a homosexual and other qualities are presumed to follow (Boswell, 1982–1983).

Western culture is characterized generally by its propensity for dichotomies—body/mind, male/female, homosexual/heterosexual, and so forth. It would appear that in cultures where the world is not divided so rigidly into binary oppositions, but which are more open to overlapping and contradictory categories, the view of gender will also be more flexible. Under such conditions, alternative gender roles will be more likely to exist.

This brings us back to the hijras, a gender category that cannot be understood with reference only to our own gender system, with its dichotomous and permanent gender categories. The hijra role has meaning only with reference to the particular culture and history of India, just as the role highlights many Indian cultural themes. Much of hijra behavior, which we in the West would be likely to label as pathological and bizarre, becomes understandable when studied from the point of view of the cultural system in which the hijras operate. The significance and persistence of the hijra role in India—and similar alternative gender roles in other cultures—are a strong and vivid testimony to the fact that our Western views of sex and gender are culturally constructed and are not universal. As we become increasingly aware of this cultural diversity in gender systems, we can begin looking at our own culture in new ways and perhaps become more flexible in accommodating those individuals who do not fit into our traditionally prescribed categories.

Notes

INTRODUCTION

1. A key defining criterion of a hijra is that he is sexually impotent with women. This does not necessarily say anything about whether he is or is not able to have an erection in homosexual relations. When I use the term *impotence* without any qualifier, I am always referring to heterosexual relations.

2. The most important religious division in India is between the Hindus, who make up about 83% of the population, and the Muslims, who are about 11%. Hinduism is therefore the religion with the major cultural impact in India, and it provides the major context in which hijras view themselves as *religious* figures. Islam, introduced into India in the eighth century, has also, therefore, had an important impact on Indian culture. Over the past 1,200 years some syncretism has taken place between Hinduism and Islam, although in terms of theology the religions are quite different.

   A major difference between Hinduism and Islam involves their connection to the caste system, the principle that organizes Indian society. The Indian caste system may be defined as a system of ranked, culturally distinct, interdependent endogamous groups. An individual belongs to the caste of his or her parents and cannot move from one caste to another. Castes are usually associated with traditional occupations, and there are definite social boundaries between castes involving, for example, prohibitions on intermarriage, interdining, and other spatial and social contacts. In India, caste is related to the Hindu ideas of spiritual purity and pollution, and the castes are ranked on the basis of these criteria. While the Indian constitution specifically outlaws the demeaning and oppressive aspects of the caste system, particularly those that limit the full participation of the lowest castes and untouchables (now called scheduled castes), caste consciousness, and hierarchical relations between persons and groups based on caste distinctions, has by no means disappeared from the modern political and social scene.

   Islam, as a religion, does not recognize caste, although in many Indian local communities, Muslim populations are treated as if they were a caste and are subject to (unofficial) social restrictions. A major tenet of Islam is that all believers are equal in social, political, and legal status, and the major distinction is made between believers and nonbelievers. It is this egalitarian aspect of Islam that has great appeal for the hijras.

CHAPTER ONE

1. As has often been noted, rituals of reversal have a cathartic function in highly organized communities and hierarchical relationships. See, for example, McKim Marriott's description of Holi, the spring festival, in an Indian village, in which the experience of communitas involves persons in lower castes and statuses ridiculing those in higher positions (1966). For an extended discussion of

communitas and the role of lower-status, marginal persons, such as court jesters, who operate as "privileged arbiters of morals, given license to gibe at king and courtiers, or lord of the manor," and "third sons," "little tailors," and "simpletons," who strip off the pretensions of those of high rank and office and reduce them to the level of common humanity and morality, see Turner (1969:95–130, 131–165). The hijras seem to play this role in marriage celebrations.

2. For an excellent, provocative discussion of the relationship between ambiguous, in-between social categories and sacred status, see Douglas (1966).

CHAPTER TWO

1. The theme of attempted seduction of ascetics by prostitutes, in order to test (and strengthen) their commitment to chastity, occurs frequently in Hindu mythology (see O'Flaherty, 1973:43).

2. Anderson (1977) had several interviews with a hijra who was brought up as a girl. She did menstruate, but at puberty a gynecological examination indicated that she had a rudimentary penis. As a result of this discovery, she joined the hijras. In a study of 18 hijras in North India, Pimpley and Sharma (1985:44) found 7 who claimed to have been brought up as females from birth.

3. In South India there is a role similar to the hijra, which is called *jogappa*. The jogappas are male temple servants of the goddess Yellamma. Hijras in South India, who are familiar with Yellamma, say that she is the sister of their own goddess, Bahucharaji. Nicholas Bradford does not describe the jogappas as "neither men nor women," but rather as "men who have become women; or . . . more precisely, ordinary men who have become sacred female men" (1983:311). Jogappas are similar in some ways to hijras: They wear female dress, take female names, wear their hair long in a woman's style, engage in bawdy bantering and flirting with men in public "on pretext of demanding alms," and perform at auspicious life-cycle ceremonies such as marriage and after the birth of a male child. While impotence is one of the symptoms by which a man knows he has been "caught" by Yellamma, sexual identity problems are not normally mentioned by jogappas as part of their recruitment to the cult. Unlike hijras, jogappas do not get emasculated and are never called eunuchs or referred to as such. Though Bradford says that jogappas are "invariably homosexuals," he believes that they do not become involved with ordinary men as male prostitutes. Like hijras, jogappas are viewed as vehicles of the power of their goddess, and attitudes toward them include both fear and respect.

4. According to Bradford, jogappas never shave, but rather use a special instrument for plucking out their facial hair. Jogappas say that if they were to shave, they would break out in skin diseases with which the goddess Yellamma afflicts people who displease her (1983:311).

5. There is some inconsistency in historical sources on this point. Ibbetson, MacLagen, and Rose (1911:331) say that hijras "affect the names of men," but most sources—for example, Faridi (1899), Bhimbhai (1901), and Preston (1987)—say that hijras take women's names. Most hijras I met had female

names, but some did keep male names, for example, Raj Dev, an important hijra elder in Bastipore.

6. But Wendy O'Flaherty cites the following from an unidentified newspaper headline: "In California, recently, a man who underwent a sex-change operation was able to become pregnant and then took hormone injections so that he could breast-feed the baby" (1980:298). I'm not sure if Meera was referring to this incident or not.

7. The Hindu Triad, or Trinity, is made up of Brahma, the creator; Vishnu, the preserver (protector and sustainer of the world); and Shiva, the destroyer. Brahma is the Supreme Being and the creator of all creatures. Vishnu is believed to descend into the world in many different forms (*avataras,* or incarnations) and is worshiped throughout India. One of Vishnu's incarnations is Ram. Krishna is sometimes considered an aspect or incarnation of Vishnu, but more commonly is worshiped as a god in his own right. Shiva is the god of destruction or absorption, but he also creates and sustains life. In addition to the Triad, Hinduism includes a large number of deities, both male and female, all of whom are aspects of the Absolute. This concept of the Absolute Reality also includes matter and finite spirits as its integral parts; the divine spirit is embodied in the self and the world, as well as in more specifically religious figures. The religious concepts of Hinduism are expressed in the two great Hindu epics, the Mahabharata and the Ramayana, both of which are familiar to every Hindu and many nonHindus as well. These epics, along with other chronicles of the gods and goddesses, are frequently enacted in all forms of popular and elite culture. Thus, for the hijras, particularly the Hindu hijras, the incorporation of these divine models of behavior into their own world view and community image is in no way unusual.

8. In an editor's note, Burton (1962:124) suggests that this practice is no longer common in India and has been replaced by sodomy, which was introduced after the Muslim period began in the 10th century. In a later chapter we will see that Meera, a hijra elder, specifically says that oral sex is "not a good thing and goes against the wishes of the hijra goddess" and that it brings all kinds of problems for those who practice it.

CHAPTER THREE

1. Recently, a case of hijra emasculation made national headlines (Bobb and Patel, 1982; Mitra, 1983). An adolescent boy who had run away from home claimed he was forceably emasculated by the hijras and subsequently kept prisoner by them. He managed to escape, returned to his home, and, with his father, made a case against the hijras with the police. The hijras involved were arrested and are currently awaiting trial. They claim that the boy volunteered to undergo emasculation and asserted that they never force anyone to join their community.

2. Many of these elements are used in Hindu pujas. Symbolic analyses (see Spratt, 1966, and O'Flaherty, 1980) of some of the puja elements note their sexual significance, for example, the equation of milk with semen, the coconut with the female genitals, and the oil lamp with the male genitals. *Prasad* (literally, "free

gift" or graciousness) is the remnants of the food offered to the deity at a puja by the worshipers. The food is then distributed to those assembled. Prasad symbolizes the deity's benevolence in sharing food with the devotees.

3. The aim of yogic practices is to lose all consciousness of external and material objects, including the body. The yogin is thus prohibited from looking in a mirror (Lannoy, 1975:371).

4. Brief descriptive accounts of the emasculation operation are given in Preston (1987), Salunkhe (1976), Rao (1955), and Faridi (1899). Some variation is reported though the main details are similar.

5. Because the emasculation operation is illegal and is always done in secret, there is no way to know how many hijras die as a result. Hijra conversations indicate that some do die; obviously, many do not. One of the most serious medical difficulties that seems to arise as a result of the operation is urinary tract infection. This was told to me by several doctors who have treated hijras and by hijras themselves.

6. An important concept in Hinduism is the balance of cold and hot elements in the body. Turmeric, a plant that is made into powder or paste, is frequently and variously used in India. When applied to the skin, it is said to be able to redress the balance in those whose bodies are too cool or too hot. For example, turmeric is rubbed on the overheated bodies of women just after they have given birth. Turmeric is also believed to make the skin smooth and is applied routinely by women in India on their faces and bodies, especially at the time of festivals and weddings.

7. I never met any hijras who had emasculated themselves, but Ranade (1983) and Lynton and Rajan (1974) mention that one of their informants did so. Both of these sources note that a hijra who emasculates himself has very high prestige within the community.

8. See, for example, Carstairs (1957), Spratt (1966), Babb (1970), O'Flaherty (1980), Kakar (1981), Obeyesekere (1984), and Marglin (1985) for discussions of the dual aspects of the Indian Mother Goddess. For a psychoanalytical perspective on Mother Goddess cults in ancient Greece and the Near East, which also involved castration of the devotees, see Weigert-Vowinkel (1938). Many of the details described here for the cult of the Magna Mata are similar to those described for the hijras.

9. Kakar reflects the tendency for many writers to equate Indian and Hindu. In Hindu India, the ideal family structure is patrilocal (a woman moves into her husband's home upon marriage), extended (includes several generations of males and their wives and children), joint (the males own property in common), and hierarchical (seniority distinctions operate between generations and between elder and younger members of the family, as well as between the sexes). Some of the norms that govern family life emphasize the unity of the males related by blood (fathers and sons, and brothers), at the expense of the conjugal tie between husbands and their wives. Other norms also emphasize maintaining social distance between a woman and her elder brothers-in-law and her father-in-law. The implementation of this ideal of family structure is affected

by the degree of religious orthodoxy and social class, among other factors, including ones of individual temperament.

10. See Person and Ovesy (1976) for the view that the unconscious desire for fusion with the mother grows out of a pathological problem with the self, specifically, an attempt to allay unsolved problems of separation and individuation. Other studies associate such unconscious desires with problems of aggression, castration anxiety, gender envy, and warding off decompensation.

CHAPTER FOUR

1. Ranade (1983) gives a figure of 2,000–2,500 hijras in Delhi; Mitra (1983) gives figures of 20,000 in Gujarat and 50,000 in India. Several of my hijra informants told me that they were counted as women in the latest census.

2. Hijra houses (not households) appear to be similar to the *gharanas* (literally, houses) or lineages among classical musicians, each of which is identified with its own particular musical style. A similar division existed among the courtesans in North India (Veena Oldenburg, personal communication). The term *jati* is frequently translated as caste, in English, but in fact is used in a variety of more inclusive ways to refer to a primary social identification. This identification changes with the social situation. The flexibility of the term *jati* explains its use by hijras in making the analogy with their houses.

3. In Ranade's study (1983) of 100 hijras in Delhi, he found that 7 of the 67 Hindu respondents had converted to Islam.

4. Strictly speaking, a guru is a man or woman who gives initiation into a sect of renouncers. Lannoy (1975:347) sees the complete submission and surrender of the disciple's will to that of the guru as implicit in the inequality of the relationship.

5. Pan is a preparation of betel leaf and areca nut. It is distributed and eaten on many social occasions, and the betel leaves are used in all hijra gatherings.

6. The economic and psychological adaptiveness of a mode of living that permits individuals a high degree of geographic mobility has been demonstrated for such diverse groups as hunters and gatherers (Lee, 1984; Turnbull, 1961), black lower-class urban families (Stack, 1974), American tramps (Spradley, 1970), and Samoan adolescents (Mead, 1961).

7. I am grateful to Miriam Lee Kaprow for calling my attention to this phenomenon among the gypsies in Spain (see Kaprow, 1982). The fear of hijras as shameless creatures parallels to some extent the fear of renouncers by established Indian society: Renouncers also transcend networks of social obligations and thereby threaten the social order on which established society depends (Lannoy, 1975:211–212; van der Veer, 1987:689).

CHAPTER FIVE

1. Many lower-class and working-class houses in India do not have running water, and thus public bathhouses are found in many cities. These are for men only and are used primarily for bathing. In Bastipore, however, the bathhouses are

also used as a point of contact for prostitution. I am not sure why the bathhouses in Bastipore are all owned and/or run by hijras. This is not the case in other cities, nor are bathhouses generally associated with prostitution.

CHAPTER SIX

1. Meera was taking an over-the-counter preparation that is used by women to lessen menstrual cramps.

2. This statement is not true. A recent newspaper article (Pal, 1989) cites two VD specialist doctors in Bombay who report that hijras do come to them with venereal lesions contracted through homosexual activity.

CHAPTER NINE

1. The view that social science data are not facts, but rather interpretations of stories that people tell, is becoming increasingly acknowledged in anthropology and psychology. See, for example, Geertz (1973), Crapanzano (1980), Crapanzano, Ergas, and Modell (1986), Kaufman (1986), Langness and Frank (1981), and Spence (1982). For a moving account of a hermaphrodite's story that contained a secret, see Herdt and Stoller (1985). For an excellent early account of the personal dimensions of fieldwork, particularly the role of the research assistant in ethnographic research in India, see Berreman (1962).

2. Although much of the data on transsexualism in the United States suggests that it is a condition that begins early in life, prior to any interaction with other transsexuals, some research has indicated the importance of interaction with other transsexuals as an important factor in developing and maintaining a transsexual identity (see, for example, Driscoll, 1977; Levine, Shaiova, & Mihailovic, 1975; Siegel & Zitrin, 1978; and Lothstein, 1982).

3. The work of John Money and his associates (1955, 1986) indicating the importance of sex assignment at birth and subsequent early gender-role socialization in the formation of gender identity in hermaphrodites has been confirmed by other studies (see, for example, Lev-Ran, 1974). Because Money's view with regard to the connection between sex assignment, subsequent socialization, and gender identity has been so influential, I quote a summary of it here:

The very effort to argue a genetic, hormonal or morphologic origin for gender identity, as compared with a social-interactional one, is . . . anachronistic. Every informed person in genetics knows that the genotype cannot express itself in a vacuum, but only in interaction with the environment. Interactionism is the key concept. . . . It is not a case of constitutional versus acquired [which is] a fake dichotomy. . . . A more productive schema is to see gender identity as the end product of a *sequence* of events that begins with sex chromosomes and ends with social learning. In the matter of gender identity, the period of social exposure in the early years of life is an essential and profoundly important step in the sequence of events whereby a gender identity is differentiated. It is so important, that it can override antecedent events in the sequence, including chromosomal sex, in certain circumstances (Money, 1970).

For critiques and an opposing point of view, see Zuger (1970) and Imperato-McGinley et al. (1979). For ethnographic data from New Guinea, see Herdt & Davidson, n.d.; see also Money, Devore, & Norman (1986); for a similar perspective on transsexuals, see Risman (1982).

4. There may be important social class differences here. Persons from the upper-middle, educated classes would seem to be unlikely candidates to allow such claims to be made on their children. I heard of three cases of intersexed persons in this class: All were born with ambiguous genitals but were assigned to the male sex at birth and raised as boys. In two of these cases, the men are adults. One was sent abroad to study for a career in science with the expectation that he would never marry, but at least would have the satisfaction of a prestigious career. The other was married to a girl who, it was known, could not have children. The third case is still a toddler.

   I have been assured many times, however, even by highly educated people, that such claims are indeed successfully made by hijras, with regard to both infants and adults, and that even members from their own class are not immune. Sharma (1983) cites one example of an adult claimed by hijras who, with his family, tried to resist by calling the police, but the police refused to interfere, validating the right of the hijras to claim intersexed persons for their community. In Ranade's study in Delhi (1983), which is both more extensive and more reliable than most, none of the 100 respondents were claimed by the hijras; all joined the community voluntarily.

5. For a useful distinction between respectable and deviant careers, see Luckenbill and Best (1981); for application of this concept as it applies to the hijras, see Nanda (1990, in press).

6. An important account of the ideals of romantic love and the realities of arranged marriages among upper-middle–class women occurs in Roy (1975). For an interesting exception to a literature that generally attaches little importance to the ideal of love in the conjugal relationship in India, see Jacobson (1978).

7. For a useful, concise description of Hindu life stages, see Morgan (1953).

CHAPTER TEN

1. The wealth of material now available on this subject makes it impossible to cite here. For an early and important contribution in this field, see Ortner and Whitehead (1981).

2. Garfinkel (1984:122–123) lists what he calls the "commonsense view" of "natural, normally sexed persons" in our culture, a view that he notes is not limited to nonprofessional opinion, but is widely shared in the social and psychological sciences. Kessler and McKenna (1978:113–114) summarize these "incorrigible propositions" as follows:

   (1) There are two, and only two, sexes and genders (male and female; masculine and feminine).

   (2) One's gender is invariant. (If you are female/male, you always were female/male and you always will be female/male.)

(3) Genitals are the essential sign of sex and gender. (A female is a person with a vagina; a male is a person with a penis).

(4) Any exceptions to two sexes are not to be taken seriously (they must be jokes, pathology, etc.).

(5) There are no transfers from one gender to another except ceremonial ones (masquerades).

(6) Everone must be classified as a member of one sex and gender or another. (There are no cases where sex or gender is not attributed.)

(7) The male/female dichotomy is a "natural" one. (Males and females exist independently of scientists' [or anyone else's] criteria for being male or female.)

(8) Membership in one sex and gender or another is "natural." (Being female or male is not dependent on anyone's deciding what you are.)

3. For recent reinterpretations of the berdache as institutionalized homosexuality, see Whitehead (1981), Callender and Kochems (1983), and Williams (1986). In contrast to most other scholars, who take the position that berdache roles largely disappeared in native North America under the onslaught of enforced Westernization, Williams maintains that berdache still exist in many tribes and that there is a continuous line between the indigenous berdache and contemporary gay native Americans.

4. Callender and Kochems (1983) and Williams (1986) cite evidence from various native American societies which supports the view that berdache roles were alternative gender roles and that berdache were viewed as "mixed creatures." For example, in some groups a berdache was seen as uniting male and female within himself and this is why he fulfilled a go-between role in marriage (Williams, 1986:41); the berdache were often considered more productive economically than ordinary women (Callender & Kochems, 1983:447); in some societies, berdache did not wear women's clothing but rather a mixture of men's and women's clothing (Williams, 1986:73–76); in the Cheyenne Scalp Dance, the half-man/half-woman status of the berdache was symbolized by their circulating between the men and the women and by their having both male and female names (p. 84); and among the Lakota, *winkte* were said to act and talk like women, but "[were] different, neither man nor woman" (p. 77). Greenberg (1985) and Thayer (1980) also emphasize that it was because the berdache had a position in-between the genders that they received special recognition as healers and shamans.

5. For a critique of the cultural construction of transsexualism by the medical and mental-health professions, see Bolin (1987), Raymond (1979), Billings and Urban (1982), and Kessler and McKenna (1978).

6. I have limited myself here to describing the most complete and reliable published ethnographic data in English on alternative gender roles. Other such roles described in the anthropological literature are the *shaman* among the Inuit (d'Anglure, 1986); the *quetho* among the Tewa (Jacobs, 1983); the *serrer* among the Pokot (Edgerton, 1964); and the *turnim-man* among the Sambia

(Herdt & Davidson, n.d.). Three important general perspectives on the berdache using data from a number of different Native American societies are Whitehead (1981), Callender and Kochems (1983), and Williams (1986). The gender role *guevedoche* ("balls at 12") in the Dominican Republic suggests that in some cultures, not only are alternative gender roles and gender transformations possible, but anticipated.

Glossary

alyha An intermediate gender role among the Mohave whereby a man adopts the dress and behavior of a woman.

Ardhanarisvana (Ardha · nari · svana) Literally, half-man/half-woman. One of the most popular forms of the Hindu deity Shiva.

Arjun Hero of a Hindu epic, the Mahabharata, who disguises himself as a eunuch.

ascetic A person who practices extreme self-denial, including renunciation of sex, for religious purposes.

avatar An incarnation of a god, usually Vishnu.

badhai The donations given to hijras when they perform for the birth of a male child.

Bahuchara (Bahucharaji) The goddess worshiped by the hijras; one of the many forms of the Indian Mother Goddess.

berdache The name collectively applied to cross-gender and intermediate gender roles among native American societies.

bindi The colored dot applied to the forehead of all Hindu women who are not widows, which Hindu hijras also apply when in female attire.

Brahma A deity of the Hindu Triad; considered creator of the universe.

burka A long black cloak that married Muslim women wear; covers them from head to toe, including face.

chapati Flat wheat bread, which is an important part of the Indian diet.

chela Literally, disciple. Refers here to the junior members of the hijra community.

dadi Paternal grandmother.

dai ma Literally, midwife. Refers here to the hijra who performs the emasculation surgery.

dand (dund) Literally, a "fine." Refers here to the money paid as an entry fee into the hijra community.

deen The Urdu word for religious duty; uttered by the elders at hijra initiation ceremonies.

dharm Religious duty, righteousness; one of the most important concepts in Hindu philosophical and religious tradition.

dholak The two-sided drum that accompanies all hijra performances.

dimorphism The characteristic of a species having male and female forms.

gender The social, psychological, and behavioral aspects of being male or female.

gender identity/role Gender identity is the private experience of gender role, and gender role is the public manifestation of gender identity. Together they constitute the unity of gender identity/role. Gender identity is the sameness, unity, and persistence of one's individuality as male, female, or androgynous, especially as experienced in self-awareness and behavior. Gender role is everything that a person says and does to indicate to others or to the self the degree to which one is either male, female, or androgynous.

gotra Lineage, which is renounced when one joins a Hindu religious sect or the hijra community.

guru Literally, teacher or spiritual guide. Refers here to the senior members of the hijra community.

hamam (hamaam) Bathhouse. Used for prostitution by some hijras.

hermaphrodite A person who has the genital attributes of both sexes.

hijra In India, the name given to a full-time female impersonator who is a member of a traditional social organization, part cult and part caste, of hijras, who worship the goddess Bahuchara Mata. Hijras may be eunuchs with partial surgical sex reassignment; their sexuoerotic role is as women with men.

jamat The council of hijra elders, which gathers to make important decisions for the hijras.

jati An inclusive, self-classificatory grouping of people. Literally meaning species or "kind," it roughly denotes what Westerners refer to as a caste.

kama Sexual desire.

kazi A Muslim religious functionary who draws up marriage contracts.

kismet Fate.

Krishna Sometimes viewed as an aspect or incarnation of the Hindu deity Vishnu, but more often worshiped as a deity in his own right.

linga Phallus; phallic representation of Shiva.

lungi Sarong worn by Indian men.

Mahabharata (ma · ha · bha · ra · ta) The great Hindu epic poem written in its final form around 200 A.D. whose story revolves around martial struggles and heroic exploits.

mahu An intermediate gender role in Tahiti, referring to a man who adopts women's clothing, work, and sexual role.

Mata Literally, mother. Refers here to the Indian Mother Goddess.

mehndi A red vegetable dye. Used to decorate the hair parting, hands, and feet of a newly initiated hijra.

naik Chief. Each hijra house has a naik, and the naiks decide on policy for the hijras in their house.

nani Maternal grandmother; a female kinship term often used for an elder hijra who is not one's guru.

nirvan A state of extreme calm and passivity, the "extinction" of desire. The name of the hijra emasculation ritual that precedes the "rebirth" of an individual as a hijra.

paisa Penny; money.

pan (paan) A preparation of betel leaves and areca nuts, used in hijra rituals.

panchayat Village council, to which a hijra jamat can be compared.

pandit Hindu wise man or priest.

pottai A Tamil word meaning woman, or effeminate man, which Tamil-speaking hijras use to refer to themselves.

prasad Sanctified food, retrieved from the altar and distributed to worshipers in a puja.

puja Ritual worship of a sacred object.

pukka Literally, cooked, pure. A pukka hijra is one who has had the emasculation operation.

purdah Seclusion of women in some Hindu and Muslim societies, introduced by the Muslims into India.

Ram (Rama) Hero of a Hindu epic, the Ramayana; an incarnation of the Hindu god Vishnu.

Ramadan The ninth month of the Muslim year, observed as a sacred month, during which Muslims fast from sunup to sundown.

sannyasi A wandering, homeless ascetic.

sari Female dress in India; 7–9 yards of cloth wrapped around the body.

sex The biological categories of male and female; one's personal and reproductive status as male, female, or uncertain, as declared on the basis of the external genitalia.

salwar-kameez The loose pants and long shirt worn by women and hijras in North India.

shakti The active energy of a deity; usually conceived of as female.

Shiva A deity of the Hindu Triad; god of destruction and creation. Sometimes represented in a half-man/half-woman form.

suttee The former Hindu custom of a widow throwing herself on the funeral pyre of her husband's body.

syana Aware of sex; the age of 10 or 11, when one becomes aware of sex.

tapas Heat; the power generated by ascetic practices.

tapasya The practices of asceticism, including emasculation.

transsexual A person who identifies with the sex other than that assigned to him or her at birth. Involves the condition of crossing over to live full-time in the role of the other sex, with hormonal and surgical sex reassignment. Term is also used in anthropology to refer to a person with a cross-sex identity regardless of his or her pre- or postsurgical status.

transvestite Clinically, a form of fetishism typified by periodic cross-dressing. Here, the term refers to a person who dresses in clothing appropriate to the opposite sex, without any psychological or sexual orientation implied.

turmeric A plant whose powder or paste is used as a condiment. In India it is also applied to the face and body for smoothing the skin and balancing hot and cold elements.

Vishnu A deity of the Hindu Triad, regarded as the preserver of the world order.

xanith (han · eeth) An intermediate gender role in Oman, an Islamic society located on the Saudi Arabian peninsula, that refers to men who act like women.

yoni Symbol of the female genitals.

zenana Literally, woman. Commonly used in North India to refer to effeminate homosexual males who act as prostitutes.

References

ANDERSON, CHRISTOPHER

1977   *Gay men in India.* Unpublished manuscript. University of Wisconsin, Madison.

D'ANGLURE, BERNARD SALADIN

1986   Du foetus au chamane: La construction d'un "troisieme sexe" inuit (The foetus of the shaman: Construction of a third sex among the Inuit). *Etudes/ Inuit/Studies, 10*(1/2), 25–113.

BABB, LAWRENCE

1970   Marriage and malevolence: The uses of sexual opposition in a Hindu pantheon. *Ethnology, 9*(2), 137–148.

BASHAM, A. L.

1954   *The wonder that was India.* New York: Grove Press.

BERREMAN, GERALD D.

1962   *Behind many masks: Ethnography and impression management in a Himalayan village* (Society for Applied Anthropology Monograph No. 4). Ithaca, NY: Cornell University.

BHIMBHAI, K.

1901   *Pavayas* in Gujarat population, Hindus. In J. M. Campbell (Compiler), *Gazetteer of the Bombay presidency* (vol. 9, pt. 1, pp. 586–588). Bombay: Government Central Press.

BILLINGS, DWIGHT, & URBAN, THOMAS

1982   The socio-medical construction of transsexualism: An interpretation and critique. *Social Problems, 29*(3), 266–282.

BOBB, DILIP, & PATEL, C. J.

1982   Fear is the key. *India Today,* September 15, pp. 84–85.

BOLIN, ANNE

1987   Transsexuals and caretakers: Power and deceit in intergroup relations. *City and Society, 1*(1), 64–79.

1988   *In search of Eve: Transsexual rites of passage.* South Hadley, MA: Bergin and Garvey.

BOSWELL, JOHN

1982–83 Towards the long view: Revolutions, universals and sexual categories. *Salmagundi,* nos. 58/59, 89–113.

BRADFORD, NICHOLAS J.

1983   Transgenderism and the cult of Yellamma: Heat, sex, and sickness in South Indian ritual. *Journal of Anthropological Research, 39*(3), 307–322.

BULLOUGH, V.

1976   *Sexual variance in society and history.* Chicago: University of Chicago Press.

BURTON, R. F. (Trans.)

1964   *The Kama Sutra of Vatsyayana.* New York: E. P. Dutton.

CALLENDER, CHARLES, & KOCHEMS, LEE M.

1983   The North American berdache. *Current Anthropology, 24*(4), 443–456. (See also comments and reply that follow, pp. 456–470.)

CARRIER, JOSEPH

1980   The Omani *xanith* controversy. *Man: The Journal of the Royal Anthropological Institute, 15*(3), 541–542.

CARSTAIRS, G. MORRIS

1956   Hinjra and jiryan: Two derivatives of Hindu attitudes to sexuality. *British Journal of Medical Psychology, 29,* 128–138.

1957   *The twice born.* London: Hogarth Press.

CRAPANZANO, VINCENT

1980   *Tuhami: Portrait of a Moroccan.* Chicago: University of Chicago Press.

CRAPANZANO, VINCENT, ERGAS, YASMINE, & MODELL, JUDITH

1986   Personal testimony: Narratives of the self in the social sciences and the humanities. *Items. New York Social Science Research Council, 40*(2), 25–30.

DEVEREUX, GEORGE

1937   Institutionalized homosexuality of the Mohave Indians. *Human Biology, 9,* 498–527.

DOUGLAS, MARY

1966   *Purity and danger.* Middlesex, England: Penguin.

DRISCOLL, JAMES P.

1977   Transsexuals. In James M. Henslin (Ed.), *Deviant life styles* (pp. 167–198). New Brunswick, NJ: Transaction Books.

EDGERTON, ROBERT

1964   Pokot intersexuality: An East African example of the resolution of sexual incongruity. *American Anthropologist, 66,* 1288–1299.

1971   *The cloak of competence: Stigma in the lives of the mentally retarded.* Berkeley: University of California Press.

FARIDI, F. L.

1899   Hijdas. In J. M. Campbell (Compiler), *Gazetteer of the Bombay presidency:* Vol. 9, pt. 2. *Gujarat population, Musalmans* (pp. 21–22). Bombay: Government Central Press.

FREEMAN, JAMES M.

1979   *Untouchable: An Indian life history.* Stanford, CA: Stanford University Press.

GARFINKEL, HAROLD

1984   *Studies in ethnomethodology.* Cambridge, England: Polity Press. (Originally published in 1967 by Prentice-Hall.)

GEERTZ, CLIFFORD

1973   *The interpretation of culture.* New York: Basic Books.
1975   Common sense as a cultural system. *Antioch Review, 33*(1), 5–26.

GREEN, RICHARD, & MONEY, JOHN (Eds.)

1969   *Transsexualism and sex reassignment.* Baltimore: Johns Hopkins Press.

GREENBERG, DAVID F.

1985   Why was the berdache ridiculed? *Journal of Homosexuality, 11,* 179–190.

HERDT, GILBERT

1988   *The new configuration of anthropology and gender studies.* Paper presented at the Conference on the New Gender Scholarship: Women's and Men's Studies, University of Southern California.

HERDT, GILBERT H., & DAVIDSON, JULIAN

n.d.   The Sambia "turnim-man": Sociocultural and clinical aspects of gender formation in male pseudo-hermaphrodites with 5-alpha-reductase deficiency in Papua New Guinea. Printed manuscript.

HERDT, GILBERT, H., & STOLLER, ROBERT J.

1985   Sakulambei—A hermaphrodite's secret: An example of clinical ethnography. *Archives of Sexual Behavior, 11,* 115–156.

HILL, W. W.

1935   The status of the hermaphrodite and transvestite in Navaho culture. *American Anthropologist, 37,* 273–279.

HILTELBEITEL, A.

1980   Siva, the goddess, and the disguises of the Pandavas and Draupadi. *History of Religions, 20*(1/2), 147–174.

IBBETSON, D. C. J., MacLAGEN, M. E., & ROSE, H. A.

1911   *A glossary of the tribes and castes of the Panjab and North-West Frontier Province.* (vol. II, pp. 331–333). Lahore, Pakistan: Civil and Military Gazette Press.

IMPERATO-McGINLEY, J., GUERRERO, L., GAUTIER, T., & PETERSON, R. E.

1979   Androgens and the evolution of male-gender identity among male pseudohermaphrodites with 5-alpha-reductase deficiency. *New England Journal of Medicine, 300,* 233–237.

JACOBS, SUE-ELLEN

1983   Response to the North American berdache. *Current Anthropology, 24*(4), 459–460.

JACOBSON, DORANNE

1978   The chaste wife: Cultural norm and individual experience. In Sylvia Vatuk (Ed.), *American studies in the anthropology of India* (pp. 95–138). New Delhi: American Institute of Indian Studies and Manohar Publications.

KAKAR, SUDHIR

1981   *The inner world: A psychoanalytic study of childhood and society in India.* Delhi: Oxford University Press.

KAPROW, MIRIAM LEE

1982   Resisting respectability: Gypsies in Saragossa. *Urban Anthropology, 11*(3/4), 399–431.

KAUFMAN, SHARON

1986   *The ageless self: Sources of meaning in late life.* New York: New American Library.

KESSLER, SUZANNE J., & McKENNA, WENDY

1978   *Gender: An ethnomethodological approach.* New York: John Wiley and Sons.

LANGNESS, L. L., & FRANK, GELYA

1981   *Lives: An anthropological approach to biography.* Novato, CA: Chandler and Sharp.

LANNOY, RICHARD

1975   *The speaking tree.* New York: Oxford University Press.

LEE, RICHARD B.

1984   *The Dobe! Kung.* New York: Holt, Rinehart and Winston.

LEVINE, EDWARD, SHAIOVA, CHARLES H., & MIHAILOVIC, MIODRAG

1975   Male to female: The role transformation of transsexuals. *Archives of Sexual Behavior, 4*(2), 173–185.

LEV-RAN, ARYE

1974   Gender role differentiation in hermaphrodites. *Archives of Sexual Behavior, 3*(5), 391–424.

LEVY, ROBERT

1971   The community function of Tahitian male transvestism: A hypothesis. *Anthropological Quarterly, 44,* 12–21.

1973   *Tahitians: Mind and experience in the Society Islands.* Chicago: University of Chicago Press.

LOTHSTEIN, L. M.

1982   Sex reassignment surgery: Historical, practical and theoretical issues. *American Journal of Psychiatry, 139*(4), 417–426.

LUCKENBILL, DAVID F., & BEST, JOEL

1981   Careers in deviance and respectability: The analogy's limitations? *Social Problems, 29*(2), 197–206.

LYNTON, H., & RAJAN, M.

1974   *Days of the beloved.* Berkeley: University of California Press.

MARGLIN, FREDERIQUE APFFEL

1985   Female sexuality in the Hindu world. In Clarissa Atkinson, Constance H. Buchanan, & Margaret R. Miles (Eds.), *The immaculate and the powerful* (pp. 39–59). Boston: Beacon Press.

MARRIOTT, McKIM

1966   The feast of love. In Milton Singer (Eds), *Krishna: Myths, rites and atitudes* (pp. 200–212). Chicago: University of Chicago Press.

MEAD, MARGARET

1961   *Coming of age in Samoa.* New York: Dell. (Originally published 1928.)
1963   *Sex and temperament in three primitive societies.* New York: Dell. (Originally published 1935.)

MEHTA, S.

1947   Eunuchs, *pavaiyas* and *hijadas.* In *Gujarat ahitya Sabha, Amdavad, Karyavahi* 1945–46 (pt. 2, pp. 3–75). Ahmedabad, India.

MITRA, NIRMAL

1983   The making of a hijra. *Onlooker,* February 18, pp. 18–25.

MONEY, JOHN

1970   Critique of Dr. Zuger's manuscript. *Psychosomatic Medicine, 32,* 463–465.
1988   *Gay, straight, and in-between: The sexology of erotic orientation.* New York: Oxford University Press.

MONEY, JOHN, DEVORE, HOWARD, & NORMAN, BERNARD

1986   Gender identity and gender transposition: Longitudinal outcome study of 32 male hermaphrodites assigned as girls. *Journal of Sex and Marital Therapy, 12*(3), 165–181.

MONEY, JOHN, HAMPSON, J. G., & HAMPSON, J. L.

1955   An examination of some basic sexual concepts: The evidence of human hermaphroditism. *Bulletin of Johns Hopkins Hospital, 97,* 284–300.

MORGAN, KENNETH W. (Ed.)

1953   *The religion of the Hindus.* New York: Ronald Press.

MUNROE, ROBERT L., & MUNROE, RUTH H.

1977   Male transvestism and subsistence economy. *Journal of Social Psychology, 103,* 307–308.

MUNROE, ROBERT L., WHITING, JOHN W. M., & HALLY, DAVID J.

1969   Institutionalized male transvestism and sex distinction. *American Anthropologist, 71,* 87–91.

NANDA, SERENA

1990   *The hijras of India.* In Morris Freilich, Douglas Raybeck, and Joel Sha-vishinsky (Eds.), *Deviance: Cross-cultural perspectives.* South Hadley, MA: Bergin and Garvey. In press.

OBEYESEKERE, GANANATH

1984   *The cult of goddess Pattini.* Chicago: University of Chicago Press.

O'FLAHERTY, WENDY DONIGER

1973   *Siva: The erotic ascetic.* New York: Oxford University Press.

1980   *Women, androgynes, and other mythical beasts.* Chicago: University of Chicago Press.

OPLER, M.

1960   The hijara (hermaphrodites) of India and Indian national character: A rejoinder. *American Anthropologist, 62,* 505–511.

ORTNER, SHERRY B., & WHITEHEAD, HARRIET (Eds.)

1981   *Sexual meanings: The cultural construction of gender and sexuality.* New York: Cambridge University Press.

OVESEY, LIONEL, & PERSON, ETHEL

1976   Transvestism: A disorder of the sense of self. *International Journal of Psychoanalytic Psychotherapy, 5,* 219–236.

PAL, BULBUL

1989   Man, woman and eunuch. *Sunday Magazine.* Bombay: Times of India.

PIMPLEY, P. N., & SHARMA, S. K.

1985   Hijaras: A study of an atypical role. *Avadh Journal of Social Sciences (India), 2,* 42–50.

PRESTON, LAURENCE W.

1987   A right to exist: Eunuchs and the state in nineteenth-century India. *Modern Asian Studies, 21*(2), 371–387.

RAGHUVANSHI, MANJOJ, & NAVALKAR, PRAMOD

1980   The third sex. *Probe,* November, pp. 10–19.

RANADE, S. N.

1983   *A study of eunuchs in Delhi.* Unpublished manuscript. Government of India, Delhi.

RAO, BHOOSHANA I.

1955   Male homosexual transvestism—A social menace. *Antiseptic, 52,* 519–524.

RAYMOND, JANICE

1979   *The transsexual empire: The making of the she-male.* Boston: Beacon Press.

RISMAN, B.

1982   The (mis)acquisition of gender identity among transsexuals. *Qualitative Sociology, 5*(4), 312–325.

ROLAND, ALAN

1982   Toward a psychoanalytical psychology of hierarchical relationships in Hindu India. *Ethos, 10*(3), 232–253.

ROSS, AILEEN

1961   *The Hindu family in its urban setting.* Toronto: University of Toronto Press.

ROY, MANISHA

1975   *Bengali women.* Chicago: University of Chicago Press.

SALUNKHE, G.

1976   The cult of the hijaras. *Illustrated Weekly of India,* August 8, pp. 16–21. Bombay: Times of India.

SETHI, P.

1970   The hijras. *Illustrated Weekly of India.* December 13, pp. 40–45. Bombay: Times of India.

SHAH, A. M.

1961   A note on the hijadas of Gujarat. *American Anthropologist, 61,* 1325–1330.

SHARMA, SATISH

1983   Eunuchs: Past and present. *Eastern Anthropologist, 37*(4), 381–389.

SIEGEL, LLOYD, & ZITRIN, ARTHUR

1978   Transsexuals in the New York City welfare population: The function of illusion in transsexuality. *Archives of Sexual Behavior, 7*(4), 285–290.

SINGH, JASPAL (Compiler)

1981   *Indian penal code.* Vol. 2, sec. 320, pp. 1068–1069. Delhi: Pioneer Publications.

SINHA, A. P.

1967   Procreation among the eunuchs. *Eastern Anthropologist, 20,* 168–176.

SPENCE, DONALD

1982   *Narrative truth and historical truth: meaning and interpretation in psychoanalysis.* New York: Norton.

SPRADLEY, JAMES P.

1970   *You owe yourself a drunk: An ethnography of urban nomads.* Boston: Little, Brown.

SPRATT, PHILIP

1966   *Hindu culture and personality: A psychoanalytic study.* Bombay: Manaktalas.

STACK, CAROL

1974   *All our kin.* New York: Harper and Row.

THAYER, JAMES S.

1980   The berdache of the northern plains: A socioreligious perspective. *Journal of Anthropological Research, 36,* 287–293.

TURNBULL, COLIN

1961   *The forest people.* New York: Simon and Schuster.

TURNER, VICTOR

1969   *The ritual process: Structure and anti-structure.* Ithaca, NY: Cornell University Press.

VAN GENNEP, ARNOLD

1960   *Rites of passage.* Chicago: University of Chicago Press.

VAN DER VEER, PETER

1987   Taming the ascetic: Devotionalism in a Hindu monastic order. *Man,* (NS) *22*(4), 680–695.

VATUK, SYLVIA

1985   Sexuality and the middle-aged woman: South Asian cultural conceptions. In J. K. Brown & V. Kerns (Eds.), *In her prime: A new view of middle-aged women* (pp. 137–152). South Hadley, MA: J. F. Bergin.

WALTERS, WILLIAM A. W., & ROSS, MICHAEL W.

1986   *Transsexualism and sex reassignment.* Melbourne, Australia: Oxford University Press.

WEIGERT-VOWINKEL, EDITH

1938   The cult and mythology of the Magna Mater from the standpoint of psychoanalysis (Frances M. von Wimmersperg, Trans.). *Psychiatry, 1,* 347–348.

WERNER, DENNIS

1979   A cross-cultural perspective of theory and research on male homosexuality. *Journal of Homosexuality, 4*(4), 345–362.

WHITEHEAD, HARRIET

1981   The bow and the burden strap: A new look at institutionalized homosexuality in native North America. In S. B. Ortner & H. Whitehead (Eds.), *Sexual meanings: The cultural construction of gender and sexuality* (pp. 80–115). New York: Cambridge University Press.

WIKAN, UNNI

1977   Man becomes woman: Transsexualism in Oman as a key to gender roles. *Man,* (NS) *12,* 304–319.

WILLIAMS, WALTER

1986   *The spirit and the flesh.* Boston: Beacon Press.

ZUGER, B.

1970   Gender role differentiation: A critical review of the evidence from hermaphroditism. *Psychosomatic Medicine, 32,* 449–463.

References for Foreword

ALLEN, L. S., HINES, M., SHRYNE, J. E., AND GORSKI, R.

1989   Two sexually dimorphic cell groups in the human brain. *Journal of Neuroscience* 9:497–506.

HERZER, M.

1985   Kertbeny and the nameless love. *Journal of Homosexuality* 12:1–26.

KENNEDY, H.

1988   *Ulrichs: The life and works of Karl Heinrich Ulrichs, pioneer of the modern gay movement.* Boston: Alyson Publications.

MONEY, J.

1988   *Gay, straight, and in-between.* New York: Oxford University Press.

MONEY, J.

1989   *Genes, genitals, hormones and gender.* Amsterdam: Global Academic Press (In press).

MONEY, J.

1955   Hermaphroditism, gender and precocity in hyperadrenocorticism: Psychologic findings. *Bulletin of the Johns Hopkins Hospital* 96:253–264.

MONEY, J.

1986   *Venuses penuses.* Buffalo: Prometheus Books.

MONEY, J., & EHRHARDT, A.

1972   *Man and woman, boy and girl: The differentiation and dimorphism of gender identity from conception to maturity.* Baltimore: Johns Hopkins Press.

MONEY, J., & LAMACZ, M.

1984   Gynemimesis and gynemimetophilia: Individual and cross-cultural manifestations of a gender-coping strategy hitherto unnamed. *Comprehensive Psychiatry* 25:392–403.

SWAAB, D. F., & HOFMAN, M.A.

1988   Sexual differentiation of the human hypothalamus: Ontogeny of the sexually dimorphic nucleus of the preoptic area. *Developmental Brain Research* 44:314–318.

ULRICHS, K. H.

1864   (Numa Numantius) *Forschungen über das Räthsel der* mannmännlichen Liebe (Inquiry into the enigma of man-to-man love). Vol. 2, *"Inclusa": Anthropologische Studien über mannmännliche Geschlechtsliebe, Natur-*

*References are for the foreword, pages xi–xiv.

wissen schaftlicher Theil: Nachweis das einer Classe von männlich gebauten Individuen Geschlechtsliebe zu Männern geschlechtlich angeboren ist ("Inclusa": Anthropological studies of man-to-man sexual love, natural science section: Proof of a class of male-bodied individuals for whom sexual love for men is sexually inborn). Leipzig: Selbstverlag der Verfassers. In Commission bei Heinrich Metthes.

WILLIAMS, W. L.

1986   *The spirit and the flesh.* Boston: Beacon Press.

Index